Living Values Education

Living Values Education Activities for Young Adults, Book 1

DEVELOPED AND WRITTEN BY
Diane G. Tillman

WITH ADDITIOANL ACTIVITIES AND STORIES FROM
Paulo Barros
Sabine Levy
Ruth Liddle
Marcia Maria Lins de Medeiros
Natalie Ncube
Pilar Quera Colomina
Trish Summerfield
Eleanor Viegas
and other educators around the world

www.livingvalues.net

Tillman, Diane G.

   Living Values Education Activities for Young Adults, Book 1 / developed and written by Diane G. Tillman with additional stories and activities from Paulo Barros . . . [et al].

   Includes bibliographical references
   ISBN: 9781731097590

This is an update and expansion of the 2000 original book, *Living Values Activities for Young Adults,* published by Health Communications, Inc. The expanded version has two volumes, Book 1 and Book 2, and is published independently by the Association for Living Values Education International (ALIVE), a non-profit Swiss Association, through Kindle Direct Publishing.

ALIVE Address: Rue Adrien-Lachenal 20, 1207 Genève, Switzerland
For information about professional development workshops and LVE generally, please visit ALIVE's website at www.livingvalues.net.

The development and advancement of Living Values Education is overseen by the **Association for Living Values Education International** (ALIVE), a non-profit-making association of organizations around the world concerned with values education. ALIVE groups together national bodies promoting the use of the Living Values Education Approach and is an independent organization that does not have any particular or exclusive religious, political or national affiliation or interest. The development and implementation of Living Values Education has been supported over the years by a number of organizations, including UNESCO, governmental bodies, foundations, community groups and individuals. LVE continues to be part of the global movement for a culture of peace following the United Nations International Decade for a Culture of Peace and Non-violence for the Children of the World.

Graphic design of cover by David Warrick Jones
Cover image of globe with children purchased from Shutterstock
Values pictures given to LVE many years ago by a wonderful young man; still searching for his name!
Former editors: Carol Gill and Allison Janse

CONTENTS

Values Units . . .

Peace I . Respect I . Love and Caring . Tolerance
Simplicity and Caring for our Earth and Her Oceans . Honesty . Happiness
Optional Unit on Substance Abuse . Responsibility

Unit One: Peace I   47

Unit Two: Respect I 86

Unit Three: Love and Caring

Unit Four: Tolerance

Unit Five: Simplicity and Caring for the Earth and Her Oceans

Unit Six: Honesty — 246

Unit Seven: Happiness

Optional Substance Abuse Lessons

A note from the author

I have had the privilege of being involved with Living Values Education (LVE) for 23 years, writing educational resource books and traveling around the world to conduct workshops and seminars — at UNESCO, schools, universities, retreat centers and refugee camps. When I initially became involved with LVE, I focused on developing a program that would help all young people explore and develop values. I wanted to develop something that would involve and inspire marginalized youth and also act to challenge privileged youth to look beyond their usual circles. I was yet to deeply understand the importance of values or values education. Twenty-two years later, I now see the world through a values lens. I am honored to be part of the global LVE family as we continue to co-create LVE.

I've often felt devastated, as I'm sure you have, when reading of violence and atrocities toward children and adults, the continuing plight of women and children in many parts of our world, the misery of refugees, and the horrors of violence in so many countries around the globe. I believe nurturing hearts and educating minds is an essential component in creating a sensible peaceful world of wellbeing for all.

A lack of basic education leaves young people incredibly vulnerable, apt to be taken advantage of and usually condemned to a life of poverty. They are susceptible to believing whatever those in authority tell them. For example, if you were a young person without an education and a powerful soldier handed you a rifle and offered wellbeing for you and your family if you killed.... Yet, in developed countries where there are functional education systems, thousands of young people have traveled to join radical groups. Many of these young people are marginalized and want to belong to a larger "family", to be in a place where their courage and qualities are admired. The first instance decries the lack of basic education, the second the lack of providing safe nurturing, supportive environments and educating hearts. The importance of Education for All and the development of a values-based learning environment as an integral part of values education cannot be overstated.

If we were to expand this view outward, we could ask how humanity became embroiled in a state of seemingly continuous violence. What are the anti-values that create violence and war? What are the values, attitudes and communication skills that create peace, equality, dignity, belonging and wellbeing for all? What do we want in our world?

What young people learn is later woven into the fabric of society. When education has positive values at its heart, and the resulting expression of them as its aim, we will create a better world for all. Values such as peace, love, respect, honesty, cooperation and freedom are the sustaining force of human society and progress.

Thank you for joining the Living Values Education family to help make a positive difference for children, educators, families, communities, and the world.

Diane G. Tillman

SETTING THE CONTEXT

Living Values Education is a global endeavor dedicated to nurturing hearts and educating minds. LVE provides an approach, and tools, to help people connect with their own values and live them. During professional development workshops, educators are engaged in a process to empower them to create a caring values-based atmosphere in which young people are loved, valued, respected, understood and safe. Educators are asked to facilitate values activities about peace, respect, love and caring, tolerance, honesty, happiness, responsibility, simplicity, caring for the Earth and Her Oceans, cooperation, humility, compassion, freedom and unity to engage students in exploring and choosing their own personal values while developing intrapersonal and interpersonal skills to "live" those values. The sixteen values units in the updated Living Values Education Activities books include other related universal values such as kindness, fairness, determination, integrity, appreciation, diversity, gratitude, inclusion and social justice. Students soon become co-creators of a culture of peace and respect. A values-based learning community fosters positive relationships and quality education.

The Need for Values and Values Education

The values of peace, love, respect, honesty, cooperation and freedom create a social fabric of harmony and wellbeing. What would you like schools to be like? What would you like the world to be like? Reflect for a moment on the school or world you would like....

Children and youth grow toward their potential in quality learning environments with a culture of peace and respect. Relatively few young people have such a values-based learning atmosphere. A culture of judging, blaming and disrespect is often closer to the norm and is frequently mixed with varying levels of bullying, discrimination, social problems and violence.

The challenge of helping children and youth acquire values is no longer as simple as it was decades ago when being a good role model and relating moral stories was usually sufficient. Violent movies and video games glorify violence, and desensitize youth to the effect of such actions. Youth see people who display greed, arrogance and negative behavior rewarded with admiration and status. Young people are increasingly affected by bullying, social problems, violence and a lack of respect for each other and the world around them. Social media often negatively impacts teens who are already emotionally vulnerable. Cyberbullying and sexting have been linked to the increase in the suicide rate of pre-teens and teens. Marginalized and troubled young people rarely achieve their potential without quality education. Feelings of inadequacy, hurt and anger often spiral downward and meanness, bullying, drug use, drop-out rates, crime and suicide increase.

As educators, facilitators and parents, there are many things we can do to reserve this downward trend and create wellbeing … for young people and our world. As Aristotle said, "Educating the mind without educating the heart is no education at all."

LVE's Purpose and Aims

The purpose and aims of Living Values Education were created by twenty educators from around the world when they gathered at UNICEF's headquarters in New York in August of 1996. The purpose remains unchanged. The aims have been slightly augmented as has our experience and understanding since that time.

LVE's purpose is to provide guiding principles and tools for the development of the whole person, recognizing that the individual is comprised of physical, intellectual, emotional, and spiritual dimensions.

The aims are:
♦ To help individuals think about and reflect on different values and the practical implications of expressing them in relation to themselves, others, the community, and the world at large;
♦ To deepen knowledge, understanding, motivation, and responsibility with regard to making positive personal and social choices;
♦ To invite and inspire individuals to explore, experience, express and choose their own personal, social, moral, and spiritual values and be aware of practical methods for developing and deepening them; and
♦ To encourage and support educators and caregivers to look at education as providing students with a philosophy of living, thereby facilitating their overall growth, development, and choices so they may integrate themselves into the community with respect, confidence, and purpose.

The Living Values Education Approach

After ten years of implementing Living Values Education, a team of LVE leaders around the world gathered together to describe what they felt LVE was … and had become.

Vision Statement

Living Values Education is a way of conceptualizing education that promotes the development of values-based learning communities and places the search for meaning and purpose at the heart of education. LVE emphasizes the worth and integrity of each person involved in the provision of education, in the home, school and community. In fostering quality education, LVE supports the overall development of the individual and a culture of positive values in each society and throughout the world, believing that education is a purposeful activity designed to help humanity flourish.

Core Principles

Living Values Education is based on the following core principles:

On the learning and teaching environment

1. When positive values and the search for meaning and purpose are placed at the heart of learning and teaching, education itself is valued.

2. Learning is especially enhanced when occurring within a values-based learning community, where values are imparted through quality teaching, and learners discern the consequences, for themselves, others and the world at large, of actions that are and are not based on values.

3. In making a values-based learning environment possible, educators not only require appropriate quality teacher education and ongoing professional development, they also need to be valued, nurtured and cared for within the learning community.

4. Within the values-based learning community, positive relationships develop out of the care that all involved have for each other.

On the teaching of values

5. The development of a values-based learning environment is an integral part of values education, not an optional extra.

6. Values education is not only a subject on the curriculum. Primarily it is pedagogy; an educational philosophy and practice that inspires and develops

positive values in the classroom. Values-based teaching and guided reflection support the process of learning as a meaning-making process, contributing to the development of critical thinking, imagination, understanding, self-awareness, intrapersonal and interpersonal skills and consideration of others.

7. Effective values educators are aware of their own thoughts, feelings, attitudes and behavior and sensitive to the impact these have on others.

8. A first step in values education is for teachers to develop a clear and accurate perception of their own attitudes, behavior and emotional literacy as an aid to living their own values. They may then help themselves and encourage others to draw on the best of their own personal, cultural and social qualities, heritage and traditions.

On the nature of persons within the world and the discourse of education

9. Central to the Living Values Education concept of education is a view of persons as thinking, feeling, valuing whole human beings, culturally diverse and yet belonging to one world family. Education must therefore concern itself with the intellectual, emotional, spiritual and physical wellbeing of the individual.

10. The discourse of education, of thinking, feeling and valuing, is both analytic and poetic. Establishing a dialogue about values within the context of a values-based learning community facilitates an interpersonal, cross-cultural exchange on the importance and means of imparting values in education.

Structure

The development and advancement of Living Values Education is overseen by the **Association for Living Values Education International** (ALIVE), a non-profit-making association of organizations around the world concerned with values education. ALIVE groups together national bodies promoting the use of the Living Values Education Approach and is an independent organization that does not have any particular or exclusive religious, political or national affiliation or interest. The development and implementation of Living Values Education has been supported over the years by a number of organizations, including UNESCO, governmental bodies, foundations, community groups and individuals. LVE continues to be part of the global movement for a culture of peace following the United Nations International Decade for a Culture of Peace and Non-violence for the Children of the World.

ALIVE is registered as an association in Switzerland. In some countries national Living Values Education associations have been formed, usually comprised of educators, education officials, and representatives of organizations and agencies involved with student or parent education.

Activities

In pursuing its mission and implementing its core principles, the Association for Living Values Education International and its Associates and Focal Points for LVE provide:

1. *Professional development courses, seminars and workshops* for teachers and others involved in the provision of education.

2. *Classroom teaching material and other educational resources*, in particular the original award-winning series of five resource books containing practical values activities and a range of methods for use by educators, facilitators, parents and caregivers to help children and young adults explore and develop widely-shared human values. This series of books, now updated and expanded, plus Living Green Values and an additional 11 values-education resources for young people at risk, are specified in the following LVE Resource Materials section. The approach and lesson content are experiential, participatory and flexible, allowing — and encouraging — the materials to be adapted and supplemented according to varying cultural, social and other circumstances.

3. *Consultation to government bodies, organizations, schools, teachers and parents* on the creation of values-based learning environments and the teaching of values.

4. *An extensive website*, www.livingvalues.net, with materials available for downloading free of charge, including songs, posters and a distance program for adults, families and study groups.

LVE Resource Materials

Designed to address the whole child/person, Living Values Education Activities engage young people in exploring, experiencing and expressing values so they can find those that resonant in their heart, and build the social and emotional skills which enable them to live those values. The approach is child-centered, flexible and interactive; adults are asked to act as facilitators. The approach is non-prescriptive and allows materials and strategies to be introduced according to the circumstances and interests of the users and the needs of students.

The Living Values Education Series

The Living Values Education series, a set of five books first published in April of 2001 by Health Communications, Inc. (HCI), was awarded the 2002 Teachers' Choice Award, an award sponsored by *Learning* magazine, a national publication for teachers and educators in the USA. Materials from the books, and in some cases up to all five of the books, were published in a dozen languages.

The original Living Values Education Series
♦ *Living Values Activities for Children Ages 3–7*
♦ *Living Values Activities for Children Ages 8–14*
♦ *Living Values Activities for Young Adults*
♦ *Living Values Parent Groups: A Facilitator Guide*
♦ *LVEP Educator Training Guide*

In 2018, the Association for Living Values Education International began updating this initial set of five books. Building on the original material, updated information, an expansion of activities and additional values units were added. Because of the amount of added content, the Living Values Education Activities books are published by ALIVE as two volumes, Book 1 and Book 2. ALIVE's intent in separating from HCI, our esteemed publisher, was to make these educational resources more accessible to educators in all continents by offering the series not only as regular books but as eBooks and small free downloadable units.

The updated and expanded Living Values Education Series
♦ *Living Values Education Activities for Children Ages 3–7, Book 1*
♦ *Living Values Education Activities for Children Ages 3–7, Book 2*
♦ *Living Values Education Activities for Children Ages 8–14, Book 1*
♦ *Living Values Education Activities for Children Ages 8–14, Book 2*
♦ *Living Values Education Activities for Young Adults, Book 1*
♦ *Living Values Education Activities for Young Adults, Book 2*
♦ *Living Values Education Parent Groups: A Facilitator Guide*
♦ *Living Values Education Training Guide*

Living Values Education Activities for Children Ages 3–7, 8–14, and *Young Adults* — LVE utilizes a wide range of modalities and activities, with the hope that each young person will be inspired to love values and experience their strength and beauty. Reflection points teach the importance of valuing all people, discussions help students grow in empathy, role playing builds conflict resolution skills and a myriad of facilitated cognitive, artistic, and experiential activities increase positive intrapersonal and interpersonal social and emotional skills. Reflective, imagining and artistic activities encourage students to explore their own ideas, creativity and inner gifts. Mind mapping values and anti-values builds cognitive understanding of the practical effect of values and encourages a values-based perspective for analyzing events and creating solutions. Other activities stimulate awareness of personal and social responsibility and, for older students, awareness of social justice. The development of self-esteem and respect, acceptance and inclusion of others continues throughout the exercises. Educators are encouraged to utilize their own rich heritage while integrating values into everyday activities and the curriculum.

Sixteen Values Units — and Related Values

The updated Living Values Education Activities books have sixteen values units, eight in Book 1 and eight in Book 2. This allows schools to easily plan to implement one value a month during the school year, rotating through eight values a year. The universal values explored in all three books are peace, respect, love and caring, tolerance, honesty, happiness, responsibility, simplicity and caring for the Earth and Her Oceans, cooperation, humility, compassion, freedom and unity. The value unit exploring freedom for children ages three to seven is titled "Brave and Gentle".

There are two values units on both peace and respect as these values are so important to young people and present the opportunity to help them build important intrapersonal and interpersonal social and emotional skills. It is recommended that educators in schools begin with the Peace I and Respect I values units in Book 1 during the first year of implementation and Peace II and Respect II values units in Book 2 during the second year, rotating through eight values each year.

The sixteenth values unit is titled "Another Value We Love". This offers activities on a few values and an invitation to educators to explore a value they feel is needed locally or nationally.

The values units in the updated Living Values Education Activities books also include many related values such as kindness, fairness, determination, integrity, appreciation, diversity, human rights, valuing education, trust, gratitude, inclusion, equality and social justice.

Living Values Education Parent Groups: A Facilitator Guide — This book offers both process and content for facilitators interested in conducting LVE Parent Groups with parents and caregivers to further understanding and skills important in encouraging and positively developing values in children. The first section describes content for an introductory session, and a six-step process for the exploration of each value. The second section offers suggestions regarding values activities the parents can do in the group, and ideas for parents to explore at home. In the third section, common parenting concerns are addressed, and parenting skills to deal with those concerns. Parent group facilitators are encouraged to use *Nurturing with Love and Wisdom, Disciplining with Peace and Respect: A mindful guide to parenting* in conjunction with the parent group facilitator guide.

LVE Educator Training Guide — Formerly known as *LVEP Educator Training Guide*, this updated guide contains the content of sessions within regular LVE educator workshops as well as staff building activities. It contains the content of sessions within regular LVE educator workshops. This includes introductory activities, an LVE overview, values awareness reflections, the LVE Approach and skills for creating a values-based atmosphere. LVE's Theoretical Model, Developing Values Schematic, and sample training agendas are included.

Materials for Young People At Risk

There are special LVE programs for young people at risk. These materials are restricted, made available only to educators who undergo LVE training for these particular modules. The ability to create a values-based atmosphere, and use active listening and validation skills, are an important part of the process. These educational resources are:

- *Living Values Education Activities for At-Risk Youth*
- *Living Values Education Activities for Children Affected by Earthquakes Ages 3–7*
- *Living Values Education Activities for Children Affected by Earthquakes Ages 8–14*
- *Living Values Education Activities for Drug Rehabilitation*
- *Living Values Education Activities for Refugees and Children Affected by War Ages 3–7*
- *Living Values Education Activities for Refugees and Children Affected by War Ages 8–14*
- *Living Values Education Activities for Street Children Ages 3–6*
- *Living Values Education Activities for Street Children Ages 7–10*
- *Living Values Education Activities for Street Children Ages 11–14*
- *Living Values Education Activities for Young Offenders*
- *Living Values Education Supplement, Helping Young People Process Difficult Events*

Living Values Education Activities for At-Risk Youth (LVAARY) **and** *Living Values Education Activities for Young Offenders (LYAYO)* — These resources for youth 14-years and older weave in values activities on peace, respect, love, cooperation, honesty, humility and happiness, with lessons related to crime, violence, drug use, gang involvement, negative influences and concomitant emotional issues, along with the building of social and relapse-prevention skills. Based on LVE methodology, educators are asked to create a values-based atmosphere. Participants are encouraged to explore and develop values in a group-facilitated process by first exploring their own dreams for a better world. Lessons on peace and respect build self-confidence and a supportive values-based atmosphere in the group, prior to beginning choice-related lessons in which participants are asked to explore and share their journey and the consequences in their lives. The 90 lessons in LVAARY and the 103 lessons in LVAYO include experiences to help young adults deal with their pain and anger, learn to self-regulate more effectively, and learn life-lessons. Positive intrapersonal and interpersonal social skills are taught, encouraged and practiced in the facilitated activities. In LVAARY, a series of stories is related to engage the young adults in a process of healing and to learn about a culture of peace and respect. Through discussion, art, role-playing and dramas, participants explore many aspects of their experiences and build relapse-prevention skills.

Living Values Education Activities for Children Affected by Earthquakes — These resources were developed at the request of educators in El Salvador after the earthquake. It was developed specifically for that situation and culture, hence, the materials would need to be adapted for use by other cultures and for other sets of circumstances.

Living Values Education Activities for Drug Rehabilitation — The 102 lessons in this curriculum weave in values activities on peace, respect, love, cooperation, honesty, humility and happiness from *Living Values Activities for Young Adults*, with lessons related to drug use, emotional issues that arise with addiction and concomitant behaviors, and the building of social and relapse-prevention skills. It is designed for use with young people 14- through 26-years old but has been used in rehabilitation clinics with adults in their 40s.

Living Values Education Activities for Refugees and Children Affected by War — These supplements contain activities that give children an opportunity to begin the healing process while learning about peace, respect and love. Designed to be implemented by refugee teachers of the same culture as the children, there are 49 lessons for children three to seven years old and 60 lessons for students eight to fourteen years old. The lessons provide tools to begin to deal with grief while developing positive adaptive social and emotional skills. A section on camp-wide strategies offers suggestions for creating a culture of peace, conducting values-education groups for parents/caregivers, cooperative games, and supporting conflict resolution monitors. Teachers are to continue with the regular Living Values Education activities after these lessons are completed.

Living Values Education Activities for Street Children (LVASC) Ages 3–6, 7–10 and 11–14 — These three resources contain adapted Living Values Education Activities on peace, respect, love and cooperation and a series of stories about a street-children family. The stories serve as a medium to educate about and discuss issues related to domestic violence, death, AIDS, drug sellers, drugs, sexual abuse and physical abuse. The issues of begging, being scared when adults argue, safety, being safe from unsafe adults, sex, being scared at night and wanting to learn are also addressed. The 70 lessons in the LVASC 3–6 book include discussions, activities, and the development of positive adaptive social and emotional skills and protective social skills. In addition to the issues just mentioned, the 77 activities in the LVASC 7–10 book also address caring for younger siblings, eating in a healthy way, cleanliness, lack of food, stealing, the effects of drugs and the right to education. The 80 LVASC 11–14 activities, in addition to the above, addresses female and male maturation, prostitution, sex trafficking, labor trafficking, corruption, eating in a healthy way and hygiene. The issues of the risk of dying quickly from diarrhea, cycles of violence versus non-violence, child rights and making a difference are also addressed. The materials also include suggestions for greater community involvement in the area of vocational training as well as educating the community about AIDS and other relevant issues through dramas/skits.

LVE Supplement, Helping Young People Process Difficult Events — Originally developed in response to a request from educators in Afghanistan, this special supplement contains 12 lessons to help young people express and process their reactions to violence and death. Designed to be used with *Living Values Education Activities for Children Ages 8–14*, it also contains guidelines to help children begin to process their reactions to other circumstances which may be emotionally traumatic. The lessons can be done in a classroom setting by educators that have undergone an LVE Workshop and learned the skills of active listening and validating and how to create a values-based atmosphere.

Living Green Values

Living Green Values Activities for Children and Young Adults — A special Rio+20 edition, this supplement is dedicated to the Earth in honor of the United Nations Conference on Sustainable Development convened in Rio de Janeiro, Brazil, in June 2012. Living Green Values activities help build awareness of the importance of taking care of the Earth and her resources. Stories and lessons for children 3 to 7, 8 to 14 and young adults infuse love for nature and her creatures along with learning specific ways to be a friend to the Earth. This is downloadable free of charge from the LVE international website.

LVE Distance for Adults, Families and Study Groups

Living Values Education Distance for Adults, Families and Study Groups — Several activities have been selected from each of the 12 value units featured in *Living Values Activities for Young Adults*, along with additional material from *LVEP Educator Training Guide*, to provide a *Living Values Education Home Study Course for Adults* who wish to explore their values in a personal, family or community environment. Using both enjoyable practical values activities and awareness building techniques for which LVE is known, these attractive downloadable booklets make LVE accessible to adults, families and groups. The LVE Distance webpage also includes supporting audio files, a guide to *Running an Effective Group*, together with the *LVE 12-Week Self Reflection for Adults*. All are available free of charge on the LVE international website.

Extent and Variety of Use
. . . and some of LVE's partners in different countries

The Living Values Education approach and materials are producing positive results in more than 40 countries at thousands of sites. While most implementation settings are schools, others are day-care centers, boarding schools, community centers, centers and informal settings for children in difficult circumstances, drug rehab facilities, centers, camps, homes, and prisons. The number of people doing LVE at each site varies considerably; some involve a few people with one teacher or facilitator while other sites have involved 3,000 students.

In some countries LVE is implemented by a small number of dedicated educators who feel values education is important for the wellbeing of students, the community and the world. In other countries, ALIVE Associates have expanded into several areas while other ALIVE Associates have found partners to implement LVE widely, serving local and country-wide needs. There are many
examples of collaborative partnerships. A few examples are below:

Vietnam — LVE has been disseminated widely, to more than 18,000 educators, through partnerships with the Hanoi Psychological Association, PLAN International, World Vision International, the Ministry of Labor, Invalids and Social Affairs, Drug Rehabilitation Department and VTV2 Education Channel, a television station in Vietnam.

Israel — the ALIVE Associate works with the Informal Education Department within the Ministry of Education, AMEN — Youth Volunteering City, and JOINT Israel. They have jointly developed a project to implement values in schools and in the communities and reinforce the values base of volunteering as a way of life.

Brazil — The Brazilian ALIVE Associate has provided training to thousands of teachers, including street educators and youth detention authorities. Many large networks of regular schools or NGOs that work with children in difficult circumstances have received LVE training through these collective programs: São Sebastião, São José dos Campos, Itápolis, São Bernardo do Campo, Campinas, Valinhos, Guarujá, Araraquara, Limeira in the state of São Paulo, Três Corações, in the state of Minas Gerais, Recife, in the state of Pernambuco, and the social networks: Nossas Crianças, Rede Fiandeiras, Rede Oeste, Bompar — Centro Social Nossa Senhora do Bom Parto in the city of São Paulo. Trainings have also been held in São Paulo for the Young Offenders agency and the CASA Foundation. These educators from numerous outside agencies and private and public schools have facilitated the exploration and development of values with more than 500,000 young people in normal schools and 75,000 street children. The Itau Foundation, Santos Martires Society and the public regular schools Boa Esperança, Peccioli and Josefina have given tremendous assistance to children, young adults and the community through an LVE project in an especially vulnerable neighborhood in Sao Paulo.

Indonesia — The ALIVE Associate, Karuna Bali Foundation, works with a number of organizations in line with the LVE vision, one of which is The Asia Foundation with its implementing partners in Jakarta, Paramadina Foundation, Paramadina University, PPIM UIN Jakarta and LSAF, in Yogyakarta, LKiS, Mata Pena and Puskadiabuma UIN Yogyakarta, and in Ambon, ARMC IAIN Ambon and the Parakletos Foundation. Another cooperating organization is Jesuit Refugee Service which works with internally displaced people, refugees and asylum seekers in several nodes of Indonesia.

From 2009, The Asia Foundation and its partners have actively supported LVE development through its Pendidikan Menghidupkan Nilai program, with LVE workshops for teachers and lecturers of madrasah, Islamic boarding schools, schools, and universities. Now in 50 Islamic boarding schools, one of the program's goals is mainstreaming high quality values-based education where values can be implemented directly in daily life. Great attention is given to character-based education by integrating the approach in all subjects.

During the program, at least 10,119 teachers and 1,423 lecturers from schools and universities all over Indonesia were involved. The evaluation of this program was published in a book format titled *Success Stories* by TAF in the Indonesian language. Parallel to TAF programs, JRS since 2009 also intensively used LVE methods in its work with post disaster and post conflict communities in Aceh province. From 2012, the Peace Education program in Ambon, a collaboration of The Asia Foundation, State's Islamic Institute of Ambon, and Parakletos Foundation, has been working hard to sow the seeds of peace in the land broken up with strife. More than 300 facilitators of LVE and Peace Education have been trained, and more than 10,000 students, teachers, and members of communities have been involved in peace education activities.

Karuna Bali Foundation also implements LVE in its program, especially with Campuhan College, a one-year program for high school graduates who wish higher education, and EduCare, doing workshops for schools in rural areas. A lot of lessons have been learned, especially the need for educators to live their values before facilitating values awareness in students. There are many requests for training from schools and institutions from all over Indonesia. In 2015, there were 48 LVE workshops, from the eastern most point of Palembang to the western most point of Ambon. In 2016, there were 41 workshops involving 1055 people. This only counts three-day LVE Educator Workshop. There are many more one-day seminars and professional development courses. Since the 20th Anniversary of LVE Conference hosted by ALIVE Indonesia in November of 2016, the requests for workshops have grown even more.

History of Living Values Education

LVE was initially developed by educators for educators in consultation with the Education Cluster of UNICEF, New York, and the Brahma Kumaris. This came to pass as Cyril Dalais, a Senior Advisor with the Early Childhood Development Program Division at UNICEF, read the "Sharing Values for a Better World: Classroom Curriculum" chapter written by Diane Tillman in *Living Values: A Guidebook*, a Brahma Kumaris publication. In June of 1996, he called the Brahma Kumaris to say, "The world needs more of this." Feeling that children would benefit by values education and safe, nurturing quality learning environments, UNICEF and the Brahma Kumaris invited 20 educators from five continents to meet at UNICEF Headquarters in New York in August of 1996.

The group discussed the needs of children around the world, their experiences of working with values, and how educators can integrate values to better prepare students for lifelong learning. Using the values concepts and reflective processes within *Living Values: A Guidebook* as a source of inspiration, and the *Convention on the Rights of the Child* as a framework, the global educators identified and agreed upon the purpose and aims of values-based education worldwide — in both developed and developing countries.

Diane Tillman, a Licensed Educational Psychologist who became the primary author of the LVE Resource Materials, had worked for 23 years as a School Psychologist in public schools in a multi-cultural area of southern California. Having traveled widely internationally, she appreciated many cultures and religious traditions. She was well versed in keeping the educational process separate from religion as that is required by the public education system in the U.S.A. The team of 20 professional educators from around the world agreed that they wanted the approach to be global, infused with respect for each person and culture. They worked cooperatively together to make sure the books had a variety of values activities from diverse cultures, religions and traditions. Several educators contributed substantially, including Marcia Maria Lins de Medeiros from Brazil, Diana Hsu from Germany and Pilar Quera Colomina from Spain. As LVE spread to different countries and the books were translated into different languages, LVE educators in different countries added in their own cultural stories and activities.

Twenty-two years later, the directors and advisors of the Association for Living Values Education International (ALIVE) wish to offer their deep appreciation to the numerous organizations and individuals who have contributed to the development of LVE, and who have implemented LVE in countries around the world. Many dedicated LVE coordinators, trainers, artists and even film makers around the world have served as volunteers. The approach, materials, training programs and projects continue to be developed as new requests for special needs populations are received, and as different countries well versed in the LVE methodology create new materials for their context.

In the early stages of development of LVE, the Brahma Kumaris contributed extensively. They helped edit the initial pilot materials and disseminated LVE through their global network of centers and their relationships with educators. A peace organization deeply interested in values, the Brahma Kumaris continue to provide support or partnership when such is desired by a national LVE group.

Other organizations which also supported LVE in its beginning stages were the Educational Cluster of UNICEF (New York), UNESCO, the Planet Society, the Spanish Committee of UNICEF, the Mauritius Institute of Education and the regional UNESCO Office in Lebanon.

An Independent Organization

In 2004, LVE created its own independent non-profit organization, the Association for Living Values Education International (ALIVE). ALIVE was formed with the aim to benefit more educators, children, young adults and communities through the involvement of a host of other organizations, agencies, governmental bodies, foundations, community groups and individuals. LVE educators in some countries formed their own non-profit LVE associations in order to become an ALIVE Associate while other NGOs became ALIVE Associates. ALIVE Associates and Focal Points for LVE act as the lead for LVE in their country and train educators in schools and agencies to implement LVE. Examples of NGOs who became ALIVE Associates are: Club Avenir des Enfants de Guinée in Guinea Conakry, Yayasan Karuna Bali in Indonesia, Hand in Hand in the Maldives, and the National Children's Council in the Seychelles.

None of the above cooperation would have been possible without the dedication, work and love of the educators who believe in Values Education, the LVE national teams around the world, the ALIVE Associates and Focal Points for LVE, the LVE trainers and volunteers, and those who serve on the ALIVE board and International Advisory Committee. We would like to thank each one of you for your work towards safe, healthy, caring, quality learning environments for children and a better world for all.

Results — Reports, Evaluations and Research

Educator evaluations collected from teachers implementing LVE in countries around the world frequently note positive changes in teacher-student relationships and in student-student relationships both inside and outside the classroom. Educators note an increase in respect, caring, cooperation, motivation, concentration, and the ability to solve peer conflicts on the part of the students. Within a matter of months, educators note that students spontaneously begin to discuss challenges in the language of values, become aware of the effects of values on the self, others and the community, and strive to live their values by making positive socially-conscious choices. Bullying and violence decline as positive social and emotional skills increase. Research also notes academic gains. LVE helps educators co-create with students safe, caring, values-based atmospheres for quality learning.

A Few Observations and Stories

From Kenya: Catherine Kanyi noted, "With LVE the children changed so quickly you could notice which value worked well. Parents also notice the difference in schools implementing LVE. There is no fighting at school. The teacher-pupil relationship is good; there is polite language at school. The parent-teacher relationship is good. Children miss being at school all the time for there is love, peace, freedom and unity."

From Malaysia: Shahida Abdul-Samad, the Focal Point for LVE in Malaysia, wrote about an educator's reaction to an LVE workshop she and Diane Tillman facilitated in 2002. Shahida wrote: "I remember vividly Rahimah's comments after the LVE training ended. She said, 'Shahida, I promise you I will try and implement what I have learnt from you and Diane and see if it works. I will do that. If I see results, I will let you know. That's my commitment to you.'

Every school Rahimah Sura headed she implemented LVE school wide. From inner city schools with major disciplinary problems, to rural schools with drug addiction problems, to the best boarding schools with teachers challenging her positive teaching strategies, she was able in every instance to turnaround each and every school to become the best schools in Malaysia attaining national awards. Children who were drug abusers became actively involved in drama and dance and won competitions locally and nationwide. Teenagers who used to destroy toilets and common facilities changed over a new leaf and took responsibility for the cleanliness of their toilets. They took pride in what they did. Destruction and vandalism dwindled down to zero.

Today these schools are the Exemplary schools. They are rated highest amongst school rankings. From being in the worst band, they moved to the highest band, i.e., from D to A. Not only did this positive environment impact the school and its inhabitants, the positive energy overflowed to their homes and communities, bringing parents, community leaders together — all lending their support to further Rahimah's effort in the 'magic' she created. It wasn't easy for her in the beginning. As usual there was resistance to change. She persisted in the belief that this was the way forward — to bring about change using LVE's Theoretical Model as her compass.

The use of canes was thrown out; students were given the freedom to move from classroom to classroom without being monitored; teachers who refused to follow the LVE approach were counseled and encouraged to use the techniques and activities from the LVE activity books.

With Rahimah's skill set and experience in implementing LVE through PBB, values activities and setting clear guidelines that everyone adhered to, the teachers' hearts and minds began to change. Rahimah once again proved that LVE wasn't just magic or something that happened by chance, it was actually a systematic and well-designed program that brings out the best that is in all of us — our innate values. Rahimah went on to be honored and recognized by the Ministry of Education and was awarded the highest award a civil servant can achieve due to her untiring efforts to bring about positive change through LVE."

From Egypt: A teacher reported that a girl in her class who used to have the highest record of absences in previous years, recorded the highest rate of attendance after using LVE activities with the children. Another student who was on the verge of leaving the school due to his poor educational performance, became attentive in class and scored better academic results after implementing the LVE program.

From Indonesia: An observation team wanted to know why corporal punishment was not used in an Islamic boarding school at which LVE was being used. The reply: "If you want change for two days use physical punishment; if you want long-term transformation use LVE.

From China: Peter Williams worked with students for several months in a middle school in Beijing. When he asked his Chinese colleague, Ms. Ao Wen Ya, why she thought a peace visualization was successful, she said: "It helped the children to find peace by themselves. It helped the children to feel happy and relaxed. It made them really want to be happy and motivated to build a better world and be kind to each other." She additionally noted, "Sometimes the children can be naughty in class; they don't concentrate. Now they are more engaged in their subjects because they are interested. They are motivated to learn because they are valued as people ... they are now calmer and not as naughty. The quality and standards of work are higher. They are willing to take risks to express themselves well with more confidence." Mr. Williams added, "The lessons REALLY DID something. Their attitude is more positive, and they are better organized both individually and as a group." An observer from the Chinese Academy of Sciences commented that the motivation of the children had been greatly enhanced, and it transferred to other lessons.

From Canada: Lisa Jenkins, a grade 6 teacher from Canada wrote. "I went to my first LVE workshop a few days before the most challenging school year I have ever faced, began. I knew the history of the class I was to have. There were eight students who were very challenging. The behaviour of this group had been a concern since grade one. They were routinely in the hall, or office, and many of the class members had been suspended on a regular basis. The many and varied discipline initiatives were done to them and had become a meaningless joke to the students. The other children in the school were unsafe and staff, parents and the members of the community were frustrated.

Every day, I see evidence all around our school and community that the anti-bullying programs are not effective. The kids realize it is the next bandwagon and go through the motions but don't put it into practice. After the workshop I felt hope. I began the year with the unit on respect and it took us almost five months to explore it fully. The changes were dramatic but came slowly. The language the children used to speak to each other was the biggest change I witnessed. Instead of 'put downs,' foul language and words of hate, they progressed to passionate debate. 'I'm not attacking you, but I don't agree with you...' became regular conversation. The discussions we had were awe-inspiring. By naming violence, exclusion, etc. and talking about these kinds of behaviors in reference to respecting self and others, I think we are having more success with students.

Walking the Talk: They see us living what we speak and seeing that peace can be attained, and that there are alternatives to aggressive behavior. When we treat children with respect, listen to them and ensure they have a loving and safe environment and actively name these things they may not be familiar with, we have more chance of reaching them and seeing them explore their own values and asking the difficult questions of themselves and others.

A lot of time was spent on discussing how our playground/school/ community was unsafe. Eventually the realization hit that many of them were the cause of this. They began to explore their behaviour choices in a whole new light and they initiated a peer helper program that spring. Our administration team noticed a significant drop in the number of visits these children were making to the office. There was only one suspension all year. Other staff members commented that 'something big' had changed the atmosphere of the school. The hallways, bathrooms, playground, bus stops and community hangouts were not seeing the violence and aggression they once had. These were the gauges I used to measure success.

The journey was a long one but well worth the effort. Every child had increased self-worth and self-respect when the year ended. They were not perfect. They were more aware of how they affected the world around them and wanted that to be more positive than it had been. I wish that we could have stayed together another year. The LVE workshop I attended changed my attitude toward how the year was going to go and the LVE activities we did together changed all of us for the better.

The personal changes are major for me. They are a huge part of why I continue using the program. I know the difference it has made in my own life and the lives of my family. I am much more peaceful, and calm. I use the language of values and talk about them in daily life with my children and students. Through working with the LVE program I am more in tune with my own weaknesses and am practicing simplicity to balance things."

Evaluations and Research Results

From Paraguay: Educators rated 3243 students from 4- to 22-years of age who were engaged in LVE. Despite being from many different schools with a variance in adherence to the LVE Model, the educators found that 86% of the students improved in the conflict resolution skills and the ability to concentrate, 87% improved in responsibility, 89% improved in respect shown to peers and honesty, 92% improved in their ability to relate socially in a positive way, 94% showed an improvement in motivation and more interest in school, 95% showed more respect for adults, and 100% had more self-confidence and cooperated more with others.

From Vietnam: Axis Research Company conducted an evaluation on the effects of implementing LVE on teachers and students three months and one year after an LVE training. The summary showed:
- 100% students have more self-confidence, respect toward teachers/ adults, honesty, interest in school, and a safe feeling physically/emotionally.
- Considerable improvement in respect toward peers, ability to resolve conflict, ability to cooperate, responsibility, ability to concentrate in class, and ability to share/give opinion. Students are more united and care for each other.
- 90% of teachers see positive improvement in themselves, from better to much better. They can control emotions, feel more peaceful, lighter, and happier.

From Kuwait — A school which implemented LVE for 18 years: Peter Williams, the Head Teacher of Kuwait American School (KAS) and a former President of the Association for Living Values Education International submitted the following report.

"The K-12 Kuwait American School was founded on the Living Values Education Program in 1999 with the fundamental aim of helping to heal the trauma in the hearts and minds of children after the Gulf War. After 18 continuous years of implementing Living Values Education, the school's vision and mission to 'Build Minds, Characters and Futures' within an international context of 'Learning without Borders' has gone from strength to strength.

In addition to delivering a fully accredited and rigorous academic curriculum, the Living Values Education Program with its vision, creativity, clarity, guidance and practicalities has enabled the school to identify and nurture three key principles.

1. The Loving Presence of the Educator in a Values-Based Atmosphere who models and lives their values with Kindness.
2. The Importance of Enabling a Community of Trust and a Family of Learners especially with parents in the promotion of wellbeing, care and high-quality education for their children.
3. The nurturing and education of the Healing Strength of Living Values Education for all through the education of the heart.

As the years progressed and as the school went deeper into the benefits of Living Values Education, we all began to wonder if Living Values Education could truly deliver what it set out to achieve. According to our Family of Learners, the answer was 'Yes'.

Some of the evidence indicating the benefits of Living Values Education include:

❖ The school has grown to be a family — a community of learners.
❖ There is a strong feeling of welcome, joy and acceptance.
❖ There is a powerful and peaceful values-based learning atmosphere.
❖ The students express their values using their own moral compass
❖ The students became ambassadors of how to live their values.
❖ There are virtually no referrals for any form of physical violence.
❖ Peace Time and Mindfulness are widely practiced.
❖ The level of achievement and the academic standards are higher.
❖ Living Values Education lessons are supported by unique Etiquette, Public Speaking and Life Skills programs that are "taught" each week.
❖ The school's student and teacher assemblies provide an essential focus for the Living Value of the Month.
❖ Values-based learning is incorporated into the Middle and High School years.

❖ For everyone, the school is a happy and hard-working place to be.

Living Values Education has helped the school to grow to a population of 600+ representing 33 nationalities who speak with one language — the language of values.

A recent visitor from the Ministry of Youth commented: 'Why are these students so happy and learning so well? We responded: "It's a Living Values Education School."

The school is very grateful to the Living Values Education program for its vision, clarity, guidance and practicalities. It's a great invitational model to explore, experience and express. Living Values Education invites in learning without borders and learning from the heart."

From Brazil: Hundreds of organizations in Brazil have implemented LVE over a 14-year period. Paulo Sérgio Barros, one of the leaders of the ALIVE Associate in Brazil, shares some of the results in the article *Atmosfera de Valores: O Princípio do Programa Vivendo Valores na Educação* (Values Atmosphere: The Principle of Living Values Education). A few excerpts from his article follow; further excerpts are on the Research page of the LVE international website. The full article in Portuguese is available on the Brazil Country Report page, as are other research articles.

"The educational institutions that have effectively inserted LVE methodology into their classes have been surprised at the positive effect on the personal and academic life of students. There are many successful experiences in schools developed from the partnership with LVE recorded in surveys and reports, in reports submitted to the coordinators of the program, or in educator reports during our LVE events in various parts of the country.

After activities with values at the Center for International Education (CEICOC) in Sao Luis, students/boosted their solidarity, cooperation, respect and love and started volunteer activities in the school's project of Action and Social Responsibility. They organized exhibitions on values, produced peace manifestos, etc., and became involved with other activities such as values classes, round-tables on ethics, collective meditation and art events. Motivated by these activities and by the much more humane awareness of their children, many parents were attracted to the school and stressed the importance of an education based on values for the formation of children and youth.

The PH3 Educational Parnamirim Center in RN inserted into its pedagogical program for employees, teachers, students and the community in general the implementation of LVE activities, training courses and seminars. The constant and effective practice of values in the school environment, the subject of academic research (ALVES, 2005;

HENRY & ALVES, 2008), has provided clear changes in the ethos of PH3. Deeper experiences and higher-level sharing of values has enabled a dynamic school atmosphere that is more positive and involves everyone who participates in the school. In addition, there has been an increase in concentration, interest, and consequently the students' academic performance and more involvement of parents, etc.

Also noteworthy are the examples of Maria José Medeiros and John Germano schools, both in Fortaleza. The latter is a good example of holistic education that met in LVE a partner to strengthen current projects, inspire others, and systematize the school's educational policy on values that relied on: teacher training, the implementation of LVE activities in the classroom, daily collective moments to strengthen the atmosphere, mediation of everyday conflicts between children, ethos meetings to keep the link alive between the teachers, and the school and community, and various projects within the school and community. Among these projects are: A Values Fair, a human values bank, a loving school honesty bar and a child disarmament campaign. This group of experiments and the support of LVE have proven effective in the development of values for students, and vital for maintaining the direction of the educational policy of the Institution, established in a region with high social exclusion and marked by great violence.

At the School Maria José Medeiros, a group of educators has been devoted to the implementation of LVE activities with some classes. Pereira (2006) and Barros (2008) reported the positive effect of activities on behavioral change for many students. They noted progress in students' cognitive skills. They developed a better aesthetic sense in their assignments when they were able to express their ideas and feelings, their creativity in individual and collective activities their skills in intrapersonal and interpersonal relationships, and interest in issues like human rights and sustainability associated with collective projects at school. The authors concluded that students care about their values and develop them when they have opportunities. Their way of living, their experiences, their individual transformation, their work/products and the student evaluations at the end of academic year, led us to infer that students have developed many skills such as: deeper concentration, greater self-esteem, more harmonious living, an understanding and practice of greater peace, tolerance and respect, and knowing how to contribute to a better world.

A researcher from the Department of Foundations of Education, Federal University of Ceará, Dr. Kelma Matos, in a recent publication (MATOS, BIRTH, JR NONATO, 2008) recorded some experiments and inferences about the LVE proposal in some schools in Fortaleza, citing it as: "a new way to tune the school into a more welcoming and humanizing environment, where the aspect of emotion is the mediator in knowledge construction and the building of human relationships (BIRTH & Matos, 2008, p. 75), and as a way to recover the meaning of life," which is "the challenge for any education in values, and the act of driving students to regain their confidence and hope and sense of sacredness of life" (Mendoca, 2008, p.199). Scholars of educational practices weave the web of "peace culture" in schools, and a significant number of the articles that make up the book, point out that LVE is an effective program for the process of both individual and social transformation."

"The experiments reported here illustrate a little of what has happened in hundreds of institutions where LVE is, or has been implemented in its 14 years in Brazil. … The program is a live and effective magic for those who have worked with it.

LVE weaves a network of a 'culture of peace' for those who believe that sowing these seeds in education is essential if we are to harvest the changes that will create a better world. LVE has inspired schools and educators to continue to open doors and hearts of students with a humanizing education which focuses on an atmosphere of peace, cooperation, understanding, dialogue and sharing. It is an invitation to the macro-structure of the education system to continue revising the curricula for the training of our children and youth; it is not focused exclusively on the rational, the "analytical thinking", but is in balance with emotion, intuition, spirituality — with all dimensions of our limitless human capacity."

Results in a Refugee Camp and with Street Children

There are also wonderful stories from educators in special circumstances. In Thailand, one year after implementing LVE in a Karen Tribe refugee camp, nine out of 24 refugee-camp teachers working with children and youth, reported 100-percent improvement in violent behavior; the others cited an 80-percent reduction in aggressiveness. Within two years of initiating the program, the high frequency fights between young people from different sections of the camp had completely ceased. In its place was spontaneous play, creative play, caring, happiness and cooperation.

The LVE program for street children is bringing in very positive reports. In Brazil, incarcerated youth that had been so violent that they were housed separately were able to return to the regular setting after three months of the *Living Values Activities for Street Children* materials. They were much more peaceful and compliant with authority. Other street children who were attending a government educational facility were able to obtain a regular job; others were able to learn to care for their children in a nurturing way.

In Vietnam, educators reported considerable decreases in aggression and at-risk behaviors. They noted about the young people: "Now they are confident and friendly with adults and their peers. There is almost no conflict in the classes and they now do not get into trouble after school either. The students have also developed many skits on how to keep safe from dangerous adults and really enjoy performing them. Now when they are on the streets and see children that are new to the streets, they give support and advice to the new children and invite them to meet their teacher and join their classes."

Results with LVE's Drug Rehabilitation Program

Living Values Activities for Drug Rehabilitation are used in many government drug rehab centers in Vietnam. The Ministry of Labor reported in March of 2008 that LVE's program for drug rehabilitation was the most successful program in government drug rehabilitation clinics. They had been using it for three years.

A story from Vietnam: "Visitors to Binh Minh Village Drug Rehab Center in HCMC are amazed to see patients reading in a relaxed manner and walking around with smiles on their faces. They feel the secret lies in the Living Values Education program which has been applied at PLV since 2006. This year (written in 2015) Binh Minh Village's English name is Peace and Light Village, or as they also call it, People and Living Values (PLV).

PLV is a private rehab center established in May 15, 2002. Using education as the key approach, the management here considers 80% of the success of the treatment process to be due to 'mental therapy'. Based on the results achieved since its inception, PLV now applies two education programs simultaneously to change the behavior of drug addicts: the 12-step program and the Living Values Education's program for drug rehabilitation. They have observed that these two programs together produce the best rehabilitation effect for even long-time drug users, especially during the two final stages of the rehab process: building a new life style, new behaviors, and helping peers. The LVE program has very practical skills which can be applied in reality.

The founders of PLV had attended LVE workshops conducted by Trish Summerfield since 2000. At that time, they found LVE a simple but scientific, highly educative method, which could fit quite well with Vietnamese culture, especially for drug addicts. *Living Values Activities for Drug Rehabilitation* was created in 2005. They began implementing it in 2006. By the end of 2008, the positive results had won their hearts and infused them with inspiration. They then assigned a board member to focus on LVE to become PLV's trainer of LVE."

For More Research Results and Success Stories

For research studies on LVE, and more success stories, kindly refer to those pages on the LVE international website: www.livingvalues.net.

EXPLORING
AND DEVELOPING VALUES

Teaching Values

The choices of young people are critically important, not only for their own happiness and wellbeing at this vulnerable time in their lives, but also for their future. If they are to resist the powerful messages of negativity ubiquitous in our society and on social media, and move toward a love for values and positive socially-conscious choices, they need positive role models and the opportunity to cognitively discern the difference between the impact of values and anti-values on their lives, the community and the world.

LVE values activities are designed to motivate students, and to involve them in thinking about themselves, others, the world in relevant ways. The activities are designed to evoke the experience of values within, and build inner resources. They are designed to empower, and to elicit their potential, creativity and inner gifts. Students are asked to reflect, imagine, dialogue, communicate, create, write about, artistically express and play with values. In the process, personal social and emotional skills develop as well as positive, constructive social skills. This is done most effectively when there is a values-based atmosphere and when teachers are passionate about values.

The Living Values Education Activities resource books are arranged to present a series of skills that build sequentially. However, it is important for educators to integrate values throughout the curriculum; each subject opens a window to view the self and values in relation to the world.

Three Core Assumptions

LVE resource materials are built on three assumptions. The first assumption is drawn from a tenet in the Preamble of the United Nations' Charter, *"To reaffirm faith in fundamental human rights, in the dignity and worth of the human person . . . ."*

- ◆ Universal values teach respect and dignity for each and every person. Learning to enjoy those values promotes wellbeing for individuals and the larger society.

- Each student does care about values and has the capacity to positively create and learn when provided with opportunities.
- Students thrive in a values-based atmosphere in a positive, safe environment of mutual respect and care — where students are regarded as capable of learning to make socially conscious choices.

Developing Values Schematic — the LVE Method

How are values "taught?" How do we encourage young people to explore and develop values and the complementary social skills and attitudes that empower them to reach their potential? We would all like our own children as well as our students to be peaceful, respectful and honest. How can we let them know they can make a difference in this world and feel empowered to create and contribute?

Students need many different skills if they are to be able to love values, commit to them, and have the social skills, cognitive discernment and understanding to carry those values with them into their life. It is with this intention that the LVE Theoretical Model and the Living Values Education Activities were constructed. LVE provides methods and activities for educators to actively engage and allow students the opportunity to explore, experience and express 12 universal values.

After a few months of implementing LVE, dedicated educators find school cultures are infused with more communication, respect and caring. Often even students with very negative behaviors change dramatically. In an effort to understand why this approach works, some educators have asked to know more about LVE's theoretical basis. What methods are used within LVE? The schematic below describes the values exploration and development process. There are two complementary processes. The first is the creation of a values-based atmosphere; the second is the process within the facilitation of the activities.

Developing Values Schematic — the LVE Method

Explore … Experience … Express

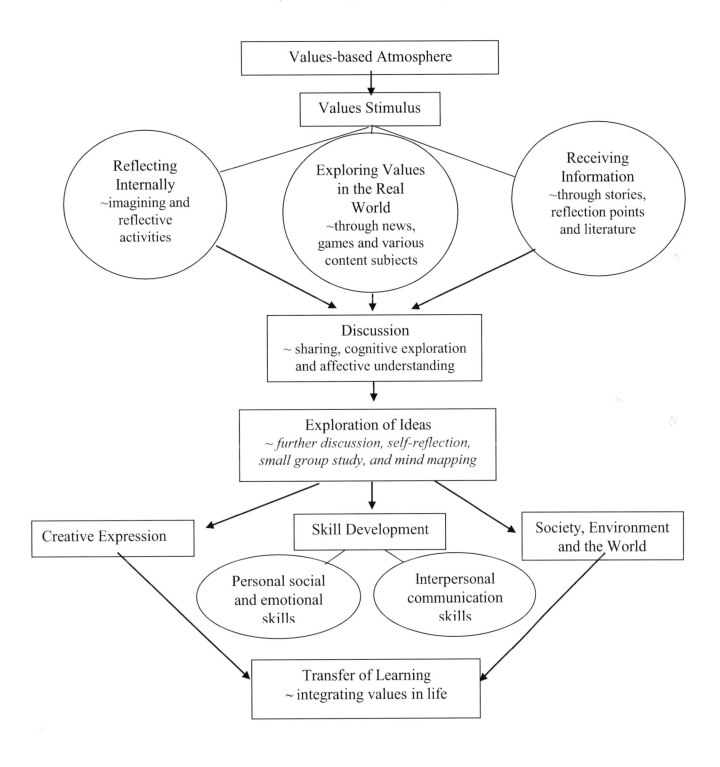

Values-based Atmosphere
Feeling Loved, Valued, Respected, Understood and Safe

As values must be caught as well as taught, the adults involved are integral to the success of the program, for young people learn best by example and are most receptive when what is shared is experienced. The establishment of a values-based atmosphere is essential for optimal exploration and development. Such a student-centered environment naturally enhances learning, as relationships based on trust, caring, and respect have a positive effect on motivation, creativity, and affective and cognitive development.

Creating a "values-based atmosphere" is the first step in LVE's Developing Values Schematic. During LVE Educator Workshops, educators are asked to discuss quality teaching methods that allow students to feel loved, respected, valued, understood and safe.

LVE Theoretical Model
The LVE Theoretical Model postulates that students move toward their potential in nurturing, caring, creative learning environments. When motivation and control are attempted through fear, shame and punishment, youth feel more inadequate, fearful, hurt, shamed and unsafe. In addition, evidence suggests that repeated interactions loaded with these emotions marginalize students, decreasing real interest in attending school and/or learning. Students with a series of negative school relationships are likely to "turn off"; some become depressed while others enter a cycle of blame, anger, revenge — and possible violence.

Why were these five feelings — loved, valued, respected, understood and safe — chosen for the LVE Theoretical Model? Love is rarely spoken about in educational seminars. Yet, isn't it love and respect that we all want as human beings? Who doesn't want to be valued, understood and safe? Many studies on resiliency have reinforced the importance of the quality of relationships between young people and significant adults in their lives, often teachers.

What happens to the learning process when we feel loved, valued and respected? What happens in our relationships with educators who create a supportive, safe environment in the classroom? Many people have had the experience as a child of an educator who they found positive, encouraging and motivating. In contrast, how do we feel when an educator, at school or home, is critical, punitive and stressed or when the peers are derogatory or bully? While an interesting stimulus can heighten the creative process, high anxiety, criticism, pressure and punitive methods slow down the learning process. Simply the thought that others may be critical or have dislike can distract one from a task. Neurophysiologists have found positive effects on brain development when a child is nurtured, and deleterious effects when there are traumatic experiences. Lumsden notes that a caring, nurturing school environment boosts students' motivation, that is, students' interest in participating in the learning process; their academic self-efficacy increases as well (Lumsden, 1994). A caring, nurturing school environment has also been found to reduce violent behavior and create positive attitudes toward learning (Riley, quoted in Cooper, 2000).

Currently in education, in many countries there is considerable pressure on teachers to raise student achievement levels. Constant pressure and an emphasis on memorization and test scores often reduce "real" teaching as well as distract teachers from focusing on nurturing relationships with students. Much of the pleasure inherent in teaching well is lost. It is also harmful to levels of motivation and the classroom atmosphere. Alfie Kohn writes of "… fatal flaws of the steamroller movement toward tougher standards that overemphasize achievement at the cost of learning. Kohn argues that most of what the pundits are arguing for just gets the whole idea of learning and motivation wrong, and that the harder people push to force others to learn, the more they limit that possibility" (Janis, quoted in Senge, 2000).

Real Learning Comes Alive in a Values-Based Atmosphere

Achievement automatically increases as real learning increases. Real learning and motivation come alive in values-based atmospheres where educators are free to be in tune with their own values, model their love of learning and nurture students and the development of cognitive skills along with values. This is not to say that excellent teaching will always occur when there is a values-based atmosphere; a values educator must also be a good teacher.

As Terry Lovat and Ron Toomey concluded from their research: "Values Education is being seen increasingly as having a power quite beyond a narrowly defined moral or citizenship agenda. It is being seen to be at the centre of all that a committed teacher and school could hope to achieve through teaching. It is in this respect that it can fairly be described as the 'missing link' in the quality teacher . . . and quality teaching (2006)."

Modeling the Values from the Inside

In LVE Workshops, educators are asked to reflect on the values in their own lives and identify which are most important to them. In another session, they are asked to share quality teaching methods they can use to create their desired class climate.

Modeling of values by adults is an essential element in values education. Students are interested in educators who have a passion to do something positive in the world and who embody the values they espouse, and are likely to reject values education if they feel teachers are not walking their talk. LVE educators have shared amazing stories of change with angry and cynical pre-teens and teens, when they were able to stick to their values in challenging circumstances.

Teaching values requires from educators a willingness to be a role model, and a belief in dignity and respect for all. This does not mean we need to be perfect to teach LVE; however, it does require a personal commitment to "living" the values we would like to see in others, and a willingness to be caring, respectful and non-violent.

Skills for Creating a Values-based Atmosphere

The Theoretical Model and LVE's workshop session on "Acknowledgement, Encouragement and Building Positive Behaviors" combine the teachings of contingency management with a humanizing approach, that is, understanding that it is love and respect that we want as human beings. Showing interest in and giving respect to students while pointing out well-done relevant characteristics over time can be used to build the ability of students to analyze their own behavior and academic skills, and develop positive self-assessment and intrinsic motivation. In this approach, there is a focus on human relationships as well as sensitivity to the level of receptivity and needs of the students.

Skills for creating a values-based atmosphere also include: active listening; collaborative rule making; quiet signals that create silence, focus, feelings of peace or respect; conflict resolution; and values-based discipline. Active listening is useful as a method of acknowledgement with resistant, cynical and/or "negative" students. A key tool of counselors and therapists, active listening is an invaluable tool for teachers. Thomas Gordon's understanding of anger as a secondary emotion is a concept that is useful to educators in dealing with resistant students.

Collaborative rule making is a method to increase student participation and ownership in the rule-making process. Many educators have found that when students are involved in the process of creating, they are more observant, involved and willing to be more responsible in monitoring their own behavior and encouraging positive behaviors in their peers.

LVE training in values-based discipline also combines the theories of contingency management with a humanistic understanding of students and the belief in the importance of healthy relationships and wellbeing. Some people use the methods of contingency management as though the young person is a machine; the need for feeling accepted and valued as a person — by teachers and/or peers — is not factored into the behavioral plan. When social and relationship needs are considered as part of the intervention plan, outcomes are far more successful.

Educators can use the LVE Theoretical Model to assess the positive and negative factors affecting one student, a classroom, a school or an organization, and adjust the factors to optimize young people experiencing being loved, valued, respected, understood and safe rather than shamed, inadequate, hurt, afraid and unsafe. In conflict resolution or disciplinary settings, the emphasis is on creating a plan which supports building positive student behavior. Educators focus on treating the student in such a way that she or he feels motivated to be responsible in regulating their own behavior. There are occasions when students hold onto a negative attitude and logical consequences are needed; during the time period in which that consequence is paid it is recommended that the student not be treated as a "bad person." While at times an educator may find it best to be firm, serious or even stern, opportunities are looked for to build the young adult's ability to self-monitor and build relationship while the consequences are being carried out. This reflects back to Virginia Satir's work; people feeling full of love and wellbeing are more positive in their interactions and behaviors.

LVE Workshops

The creation of a values-based atmosphere facilitates success with young people, making the process of education more enjoyable, beneficial, and effective for both students and teachers. LVE Educator/Facilitator Training for all members of the school or an organization's staff is highly recommended whenever possible, however workshops are often given to educators from many different schools and educational organizations. Depending on the student population, consideration of additional training for the use of the LVE at-risk materials may be appropriate.

Components of Living Values Education Activities Units

The sixteen values units in *Living Values Education Activities for Young Adults*, Book 1 and Book 2, allow schools to easily plan to implement one value a month, that is, eight values a year. Peace and respect are important to young people and provide a wonderful opportunity to build intrapersonal and interpersonal emotional and social skills as well as a solid basis for understanding and loving values. As the values of peace and respect provide such a rich perspective from which to view the self, others and the world, and develop the social and emotional skills to live those values, there are Peace I and Respect I units for the first year of implementation and Peace II and Respect II units for the second year. If you are in an organization that invites people to explore and develop values for twelve months a year, simply facilitate a value a month.

Each values unit is designed for all students with the wellbeing of marginalized and resistant students in mind. The sequence of activities is aimed to maximize the fullest engagement/path of least resistance — by making the value relevant and beneficial to the student and his or her life. For example, lecturing to students about not fighting in school is an ineffective method to create peace and respect and can serve to further the apathy or resentment of already disenfranchised students. In contrast, beginning a lesson on peace with an imagination exercise elicits the natural creativity of all students. Once students develop a voice for peace they are more empowered to discuss the effects of peace — and violence. Each value unit is designed to begin with a values stimulus to create relevance/meaning.

Far too often, values are only taught at the awareness level, without building the cognitive understanding and social and emotional skills important in being able to "live" those values. For this reason, it is recommended that educators use all or almost all the lessons found in each value unit that they wish the students to explore. They are more likely to develop a love for values and be committed to implementing them if they explore values at many levels and develop the personal and social skills that allow them to experience the benefits of living those values. As students' backgrounds and needs vary, please feel free to adapt the activities to their needs and your style.

A lesson on values can be launched in many learning settings. Educators are encouraged to relate values to the subject matter they are teaching or relevant events. For example, a lesson on values can be launched in relation to literature, history, etc., or in response to current local or world news about which students are concerned.

Values Stimulus

Each LVE Activity begins with a values stimulus. The three types of values stimuli noted in the schematic are receiving information, reflecting internally, and exploring values in the real world.

Receiving Information — This is the most traditional way of teaching values. Literature, stories and cultural information provide rich sources for exploration about values. Care is taken in the LVE Activities to provide stories about the use of holding or developing a positive value. Stories about failures because of holding an anti-value can be instructive at this age level, if they are perceived as socially relevant by the students. However, it is important to also create motivation through positive examples of people succeeding with values. Educators are asked to find relevant literature or media that they feel the students will relate to, and will help them see the effect and importance of values and their own actions.

Within each value unit there are reflection points which provide information about the meaning of the value being explored. The reflection points are at the beginning of every unit, and are incorporated in the lessons. "Understanding core values is essential to teaching values if students are to develop lifelong adherence to high principles" (Thomas Lickona, 1993). The reflection points are intended to be universal in nature, while holding an interdependent perspective of the importance of dignity and respect for each and every one. For example, a point in the unit on Respect is: *Everyone in the world has the right to live with respect and dignity, including myself.* A Tolerance Reflection Point is: *Tolerance is being open and receptive to the beauty of differences.* This universal perspective is important if we wish to create a better world for all.

The teacher may wish to add a few of his or her own reflection points, or use favorite sayings from the culture of the community and historical figures. Students can make up reflection points or research favorite sayings of their own.

Reflecting Internally — Imagining and reflective activities ask students to create their own ideas. For example, students are asked to imagine a peaceful world. Visualizing values in action makes them more relevant to students, as they find a place within where they can create that experience and think of ideas they know are their own. The process of creation, ownership, and a sense of hope are essential if students are to be motivated about living their values.

Reflective exercises ask students to think about their experiences in relation to the value. Students are also asked to reflect about different aspects at a later step within the lessons. It is important for students to be able to work as reflective learners if they are going to be able to discern and apply values most appropriately to a particular situation.

Exploring Values in the Real World — Some LVE Activities use games, real situations, news or subject matter content to launch the lesson. Too often in today's world, local and national events can be of concern to students. Please look for areas in which they have concern or interest, be it bullying, poverty, violence, drugs or the illness or death of a classmate or neighbor. Providing a space to air their concerns is helpful and allows meaningful discussion about the effect of values and anti-values and how our actions do make a difference.

Discussion — Meaningful and validating sharing

Creating an open, respectful space for discussion is an important part of this process. Sharing can then be more meaningful and validating. Talking about feelings in relation to values questions can clarify viewpoints and develop empathy. Discussions in a supportive environment can be healing; students who are often quiet can experience that others hold the same viewpoint. Shame can be released and/or diminished when students discover that others feel the same way. Children who think that everyone holds the same viewpoint can learn otherwise; those who bully can find out what others think about their behavior. The discussion process is also a space within which negativity can be accepted and queried. When this is done with genuine respect, students can begin to drop the defenses that necessitate their negativity. When the positive values under the negativity are understood and validated, a student can feel valued; gradually he or she can then experience the freedom to act differently.

In many of the LVE Activities, questions to discuss are provided. Some of these are to query about feelings; others are to open the cognitive exploration process and the generation of alternatives. Educators can use questions to delve into important emotional issues or alternative understandings. Feel free to adapt the questions to your personal style and the local usage of language.

One reason why LVE can be used in many different cultures is that the questions are open-ended. For example, "How do you give respect to your parents?" would be answered a little differently in different cultures, yet the desired outcome is the same. Within the activities there are only one or two questions to which an absolute or "right" answer is given. The most important one is: "Is it okay to hurt others?" LVE's answer is "no". If a "yes" answer is given, the educator is to explain why it is not okay to hurt others. The other questions are truly open, allowing the students to discuss the values and their application in ways that are appropriate to their culture and way of life. The reflection points, however, create a standard of dignity and respect around which the activities are built.

Exploration of Ideas

Some discussions are followed by self-reflection or small group planning in preparation for art projects, journaling, or dramas. Other discussions lead into mind-mapping values and anti-values. These methods are useful to view the effects of values and anti-values on the self, relationships and different segments of society. Contrasting the effects of values is an important step in seeing long-term consequences. Mind-mapping is also an introduction to systems thinking.

Discussions are often a lead-in to activities regarding the effects of values in different subjects. Values activities can often awaken real interests in students. To acknowledge their passion and to facilitate the exploration of the subject is the type of teaching that allows real learning and furthers intrinsic motivation. This is where a few questions from an educator can create enthusiasm: "Why do you think that happens?" "What is the relationship between . . . ?" "What value do you feel would help resolve this situation?" "What do you think should be done?" "How could you show this by Walking your Talk?"

Creative Expression

The arts are a wonderful medium for students to express their ideas and feelings creatively — and make a value their own. Drawing, painting, making mobiles, games and murals combine with performance arts. Dance, movement and music allow expression and build a feeling of community. For example, students are asked to make slogans about peace and put them up on walls, sculpt freedom, draw simplicity, and dance cooperation. As they engage in the medium they often must refer back to the value and discern what they really want to say. The creative process can also bring new understandings and insights; the value becomes more meaningful as it becomes their own. A similar process occurs as students are asked to write creative stories or poetry. The completion and beauty of the finished products can be a source of pride and act to enhance the self-esteem of students. A variety of creative arts can serve to let different students shine at different times. A school climate that can allow each person to shine at different times and through different modalities is a place where all can move toward their potential.

Music is also an important medium. Not only can it act to build a sense of community, but it can be healing. Provide the opportunity for students to create songs about values. Educators may wish to bring in traditional songs of their culture, or the cultures present in the area, and sing those with the students. Students could bring in popular songs which contain values themes or ideas.

Skill Development

It is not enough to think about and discuss values, create artistically or even to understand the effects of values. Emotional and social skills are needed to be able to apply values throughout the day. The youth of today increasingly need to be able to experience the positive feelings of values, understand the effects of their behaviors and choices in relation to their own wellbeing, and be able to develop socially conscious decision-making skills.

Personal Social and Emotional Skills — There are a variety of intrapersonal skills taught within the LVE Activities. The Peace, Respect and Love units introduce Relaxation/Focusing exercises. These Relaxation/ Focusing exercises help students "feel" the value. Educators have found that doing these exercises helps students quiet down, be less stressed, and concentrate more successfully on their studies. While there is initial resistance sometimes, usually that resistance disappears after several trials, and our experience has been that students begin to request quiet time. Once they are familiar with this strategy, they can make up their own Relaxation/Focusing Exercises. The ability to self-regulate one's emotion and "de-stress" is an important skill in adapting and communicating successfully. Self-regulation or self-modulation helps a person regain calmness more quickly when a threat is perceived and be able to stay more peaceful in daily life.

Other LVE Activities build an understanding of the individual's positive qualities, develop the belief that "I make a difference", enable exploring their own feelings and learning about the feelings of others and increase positive self-talk, and responsibility. Students are asked to apply those skills in a variety of ways.

Interpersonal Communication Skills — Skills for building emotional intelligence are included in the above set of activities and furthered in activities that build understanding of the roles of hurt, fear and anger and their consequences in our relationships with others. Conflict resolution skills, positive communication, cooperation games and doing projects together are other activities that build interpersonal communication skills. Conflict resolution skills are introduced during the Peace Unit, and reinforced during the Respect and Love Units. During the Love Unit, students are asked to think back to when the problem began and imagine what would have happened if they had used the value of love. The development of cognitive skills paired with probably consequences is aimed to help students "think on their feet" in difficult circumstances. Educators are encouraged to create the opportunity for students to be conflict resolution managers.

Students are provided the opportunity to role play different situations about which they are concerned. They may also make up their own situation cards. In the cooperation unit, students are asked to adapt their suggestions for good communication skills after games. One skill in the tolerance unit is to create assertively benevolent responses when others are making discriminatory remarks. Combining creativity with discussion and practice helps students feel comfortable in using the new skills, increasing the likelihood that they will use them.

Society, Environment and the World

To help youth desire and be able to contribute to the larger society with respect, confidence and purpose, it is important for them to understand the practical implications of values in relationship to the community and the world. One value can have a tremendous effect on the wellbeing of a community and social justice. A few activities are designed to build emotional awareness and cognitive understanding of this relationship. For example, students mind map the effects of a loving world and a non-loving world, mind map the effects of honesty versus corruption, explore the effects of corruption on the wellbeing of different countries and collect examples and stories of tolerance and intolerance.

The aim of developing social cohesion is constant throughout the material. However, the units on tolerance, simplicity and unity bring elements of social responsibility that are interesting and fun. Students explore the variety of cultures using the colors of a rainbow as an analogy. The unit on simplicity includes suggestions for conservation and respect for the earth. Further activities are in Living Green Values.

Transfer of Learning — Integrating Values in Life

"Integrating values in life" refers to students applying values-based behaviors in their life — with their family, society and the environment. For example, LVE homework activities increase the likelihood of students carrying new positive behaviors into their homes. Students are asked to create special projects that exemplify different values in their class, school and/or community. Parents and businesses can be involved as resources, for example, helping students learn organic gardening, how to clean up a stream and assist in the promotion of entrepreneurship and ethical leadership skills. Students are encouraged to share their creative dramas and music with their peers and younger students. Please do involve your students in service-learning projects. The ability to make a difference builds confidence and commitment to values.

Bringing in the Values of Your Culture

As you take LVE Training and facilitate LVE activities, you will understand the LVE methodology more deeply. At that point, you may wish to add ideas generated from your own experience, creativity, and cultural and educational resources, to help students explore, experience and express values meaningfully.

A group of teachers may want to get together before the introduction of each values unit to share their own material and ideas for students about that value — traditional stories, fiction or non-fiction articles, salient history units, web research projects, news stories, or relevant movies. Insert cultural stories at any time within the units. The students may enjoy acting out the stories. Ask the students to create their own plays and songs. They might even want to do an informal skit where the lines are improvised and are used to dramatize the situation being discussed. Perhaps older adults can tell traditional tales and teach traditional forms of music. Community based service-learning projects help strengthen students' commitment to values, and the understanding that they can make a positive difference. Educators are welcome to contribute the activities they create on the international web site. Kindly send them to content@livingvalues.net.

Making Values Education a Practical Reality

Step One:

A first step you may wish to do while considering the implementation of Living Values Education is inviting interested teachers and principals, or the leadership team of the organization, to reflect on and discuss the purpose of education. What values do you feel would benefit the students or group of people with whom you work? What values do you feel are needed in society and the world? What values would you like to be part of the culture of your school or organization?

Perhaps discuss the vision statement of the LVE Approach. Or, share that education has always been the primary method of change for society. What change would you like to see in your community and the world? Do you agree that the way to peace is peace? What would a culture of peace, respect, love, tolerance/acceptance of all, and honesty create in your community? Perhaps define together the culture or ethos you would like to create.

"At the core of values education lies the establishment of an agreed set of principles, deeply held convictions, that underpin all aspects of a school's life and work" (Hawkes).

Step Two:

Engage yourself and your entire faculty/all the adults in your community in a LVE Educator/Facilitator Workshop, to explore the kind of values-based atmosphere you would like to create, learn about skills to do such, and think about how you can make values an important, integral part of your school culture and curriculum. Plan to engage in an ongoing dialogue about values, as you make your organization one which thinks about values when making decisions about, for and with, students and teachers.

Step Three:

Find time slots to integrate LVE Activities. It is hoped that the activities in this resource generate further ideas from teachers in all subject areas, for all educators within the school can contribute to the exploration of values. Values education is most effective when the entire school community is engaged and values are integrated throughout the curriculum.

The staff of each educational community implementing LVE will need to decide how, when and by whom the LVE lessons will be taught. This is more easily done in primary schools, and with middle schools that have ample homeroom periods or dedicated periods for social skills development, citizenship, civil leadership, moral education, social responsibility or ethics. Schools without such time slots, are advised to creatively find a place to integrate two lessons a week, at least for the first several months. For example, as many of the activities for peace and respect contain discussion and writing activities, they could be integrated and/or done during literature or language classes. The lessons in the honesty unit could be done in history classes. The cooperation lessons could be done by physical education teachers.

Two or three lessons a week, suitably adapted to the age and background of students, are highly recommended during the first four months of LVE to obtain student "buy-in." This may not be possible for all educators to do, especially when only one teacher or a few teachers are implementing LVE within a school. Do not be concerned if you are the only educator doing values education. Many educators implementing LVE are in a similar situation. They have found that their way of being, and their passion for values, creates the needed "buy-in."

Implementation Details

LVE's sixteen values units are designed to allow you to easily plan values education at your site by focusing on one value a month during the school year. Book 1 includes eight values units for the first year of implementation and Book 2 includes another eight values units for implementation during the second year. A "value of focus" each month for the entire school facilitates planning for special subject areas, assemblies and special projects.

The universal values explored are peace, respect, love and caring, tolerance, honesty, happiness, responsibility, simplicity and caring for the Earth and Her Oceans, cooperation, humility, compassion, freedom and unity. Another unit is titled "Another Value We Love". This offers activities on a few values and an invitation to educators to explore a value they feel is needed locally or nationally.

There are two values units on both peace and respect as these values are so important to young people and present the opportunity to help them build important intrapersonal and interpersonal social and emotional skills. It is recommended that educators begin with the Peace I and Respect I values units in Book 1 during the first year of implementation and the Peace II and Respect II values units in Book 2 during the second year.

This book contains at least three values activities for each week and ideas for values-activities in different subject areas of the curriculum. Facilitating at least two values activities a week is highly recommended to create student "buy in". Young people also benefit by relaxation/focusing times several times a week, or daily.

If a school is planning to begin values education with *only* two grades in a school, it is recommended that you start with the older students/higher grade levels. It is much healthier for younger students to "catch" values from older students who are benefiting from values education, than to have younger students who are into values education being bullied by older students who are not in the program. However, school-wide implementation is more effective and beneficial for all.

Assemblies and Songs

When the entire educational community is exploring the same value at the same time, assemblies are an excellent way to begin or end a values unit or sustain the enthusiasm. Different classes or various clubs can take turns presenting values creatively at assemblies through drama, music, art, poetry, etc. Allow them to share their concerns about values and anti-values, and the service-learning projects with which they become involved. Assemblies are also a great way to introduce peace or an anti-bullying message to other schools or community groups.

Please begin with the Peace Unit!

Beginning each school year with a Peace Unit is always recommended. Young people are deeply concerned about peace — even those who may be externally aggressive. At the beginning of the unit, facilitators ask them to imagine a peaceful world. This allows them to look inside themselves and explore what they would like their world to be like. After a visualization, they are asked to express their ideas in words and artistically. What they create is always beautiful. The opportunity to explore what they would like in the world creates interest … and a bit of needed hope for the cynical or marginalized youth.

Older students are led in mind mapping peace and violence. Lessons with relaxation/focusing exercises and art allow students a chance to explore peace at a personal level before a series of conflict resolution activities are begun. Discussions in those lessons help build understanding of others and allow them to further their communication skills.

Throughout each values unit, reflection points educate in a universal manner, that is, in a manner which models respect for all. Usually within six weeks, with just two or three lessons a week, students are doing conflict resolution successfully. Teachers report that students find the peace unit relevant; they note reduced resistance in students often considered unmotivated.

Is there a recommended order of values units?

We suggest beginning with the Peace I and Respect I Units as they build intrapersonal and interpersonal social and emotional skills in a sequential manner. Conflict resolution and Bullying No More lessons begin in the Peace I unit and are revisited in the Respect I Unit. Mind mapping peace and conflict, relaxation/focusing exercises and conflict resolution skills developed during the Peace I and Respect I lessons are important building blocks in creating a values-based atmosphere. If students are able to solve their own conflicts, peacefully and respectfully, there is much more time for teaching.

You may wish to do further values units in the order presented in the book, or you may wish to decide a different sequence depending on perceived needs. The Love Unit continues to reinforce communication and conflict resolution skills. For example, in the Love Unit, students are asked, "What was the starting point of the conflict? How will a loving attitude change the situation?" The Tolerance Unit invites appreciating each other and other cultures.

The Honesty Unit is also important, especially as it is helpful for older students to begin to comprehend the why's and how's of corruption. Young adults are asked to engage in activities about social justice in several of the values. Each one of the values units are designed to build personal skills as well as understanding of the value and the effects of the anti-value on the self, others and the community.

If you are implementing LVE independently, it may be easier to focus on the values that fit best into your curriculum. A bit of reflection about values or an interesting discussion here and there, can help students become more engaged — and see the difference values make.

Do I need to do every activity?

No. While it is good to include a variety of values activities, educators may choose not to do some lessons or may wish to substitute material. In many of the lessons you will find scripted questions and content. This has been provided as many educators have requested such specificity. Please feel free to adapt the questions to your own personal style, the needs of the students, the culture, and your particular setting.

Incorporating Values into the Existing Curriculum

All educators are encouraged to incorporate some values exploration into the regular curriculum. As the content expert, you know which materials on hand best portray the values or their contrast. History and social studies easily lend themselves to values discussions. You may wish to stop at critical points during lessons when one individual or a group of people exercise choice. Ask students, "What is this person or group valuing so much that this choice is being made? What are the values of the other group? What are the consequences of having this value and the challenges in achieving it? How do you see a particular value or its lack being portrayed?" For example, a historical unit about independence is an ideal time to look at what kinds of freedom people want. Ask, "Did they hold that same value in their treatment of other groups?" Ask students to recognize and discuss the application of a particular value or the consequences due to lack of that value.

In literature and language classes, the teacher can select reading materials that relate to the value being explored. Ask students to react to the material they just read, write about the value, or create poems. You may wish to use journal writing to bridge students' personal experience and the experiences of characters or themes in the text or ask them to write in the role of one of the characters to see what values motivate them.

The arts are a wonderful medium in which to incorporate values while teaching skills the students need to learn. You may wish to select plays that have to do with the value of focus. In music, while teaching students how to play and harmonize their instruments, discuss, for instance, the dynamics of unity. In art class, ask students to express the values while learning how to paint, draw, and sculpt.

Ideas for values activities in different subject areas are at the end of each values unit. Or, your school may wish to create values webs. Ask the team of teachers planning the values program to discuss the value in the context of their culture and the subjects in which they are planning to teach values. An example of a value web on Freedom follows.

Values Web

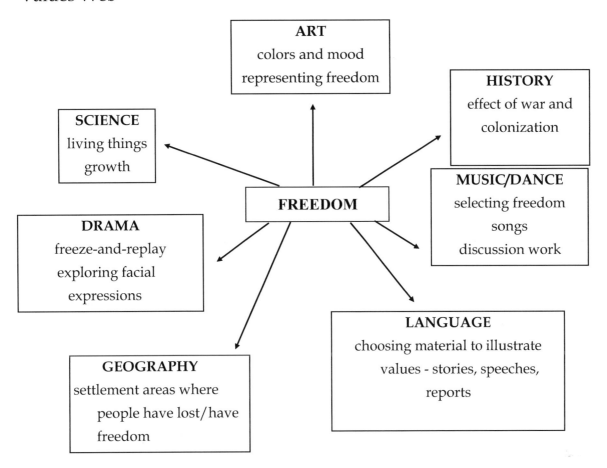

— Value web contributed by Samantha Fraser

Share Your Values Creations with the World!

Students

Students around the world are invited to share their murals, videos, poems, essays, songs, drawings, activities and experiences with students of similar age. Ask your teacher if there is an LVE social media site in your country through which young adults can share. Or send in the digital files of your artistic creation for posting on an LVE website to lve@livingvalues.net.

Educators Share

Educators are invited to share their experiences or the artistic creations of their students with other educators around the world through LVE web sites. Please send in your contribution to the national ALIVE Associate, Focal Point for LVE or lve@livingvalues.net. Country Report pages, a Success Stories page and a Research page are on the livingvalues.net site.

Annual Evaluation

An important part of any program is evaluation. Your evaluation of the program and observations about changes with students are very important. Please do request an evaluation form at lve@livingvalues.net or send us your comments.

*We hope you and those with whom you work
enjoy and benefit from Living Values Education.*

*Thank you for your dedication to young people
and nurturing hearts as well as educating minds.*

PEACE

UNIT ONE: PEACE I

Peace I Lessons

Please begin with the Peace I Unit. This is recommended as the activities in this unit create the opportunity for students to reflect on what a peaceful world would be like, contrast peace and violence, learn to relax and fill the self with peace, and learn conflict resolution skills. Our experience is that young people care deeply about peace. Beginning with this values unit creates student buy-in and builds intrapersonal and interpersonal skills which help them contribute to a values-based atmosphere. Their conflict resolutions skills will make the life of the educator easier. Even more importantly, it will provide an opportunity for them to value peace more deeply as they understand emotionally and intellectually the effects of peace versus violence in their own lives, in the community and in the larger world.

LVEAYA Book 1 is intended for the first year of implementing Living Values Education, and alternate years. During the first year, you may wish to do all the lessons on conflict resolution in this Peace unit. If your entire school is implementing LVE, for the third and fifth years, etc., you may wish to do only a couple of conflict resolution lessons and enjoy facilitating some of the other lessons and subject area suggestions.

Each lesson begins with a song, and many close with a peace relaxation/focusing exercise. Songs create a special atmosphere in which people easily experience a value and help create a feeling of community. Invite students to be on your values planning team and bring in songs that relate to the values. Some classic favorites are "Imagine" by John Lennon and "We Are the World" by Us for Africa. It is also an opportunity to learn traditional songs and music from your culture or the culture of others. Musical gatherings and peace assemblies will showcase the beauty that the students create and add to the experience.

Peace Reflection Points

- ◆ Peace is more than the absence of war.
- ◆ If everyone in the world were peaceful, this would be a peaceful world.

♦ If we have no peace, it is because we have forgotten that we belong to each other.
  — *Mother Teresa, Nobel Peace Prize 1979*

♦ World Peace grows through nonviolence, acceptance, fairness and communication.

♦ Peace is a calm and relaxed state of mind.

♦ Peace consists of pure thoughts, pure feelings, and pure wishes.

♦ Peace is a qualitative energy.

♦ Peace begins within each one of us.

♦ Worrying does not take away tomorrow's troubles, it takes away today's peace.

♦ When the power of love overcomes the love of power, the world will know peace.
  — *Jimi Hendrix*

♦ Peace is not the absence of war; it is a virtue; a state of mind; a disposition for benevolence; confidence; and justice. — *Baruch Spinoza*

♦ To stay peaceful requires compassion and strength.

♦ Serenity is not the absence of chaos, but peace in the midst of it.

♦ Compassion is a muscle that gets stronger with use. — *Mahatma Gandhi*

♦ There is no dialogue if there is not a deep love for the world and men. — *Paulo Freire, Brazilian Pedagogue*

♦ Learning to live together means combining the relationship of equality and difference. — *Xesús Jares, Spanish Pedagogue*

♦ Peace is the prominent characteristic of what we call "a civilized society."

♦ Peace must begin with each one of us. Through quiet and serious reflection on its meaning, new and creative ways can be found to foster understanding, friendships and cooperation among all peoples. — *Mr. Javier Perez de Cuellar, Former Secretary-General of the United Nations*

PEACE I LESSON 1

Mind Mapping Peace and Peacelessness

Play a peace song or a song about a better world — an uplifting song that they will like.

Discuss/Share

Say, "Today we will be starting some lessons about peace." Ask:

• Who can tell me about peace? What is peace?

- Would you like a peaceful world? Why?
- Would you like a peaceful neighborhood or community? Why?
- What are the advantages of peace?
- Is there anything else you would like to share before we explore the differences between a peaceful world and a world of conflict through mind mapping?

NOTE TO EDUCATOR

With young adults who are angry, cynical or disheartened, it is especially important to acknowledge their feelings. For example, "Yes, the world is an awful place for millions of people. There is corruption, cruelty, prejudice, horrible poverty, violence and wars. There is a saying that everything is born in the mind of men — as humans we create the bad — and the good. People can and do make a difference. For the negativity to continue — we need do nothing. It takes real courage to think about what is going on — and change the intensity of your dislike of the negativity into determination to change it. Each one of you can contribute to a better world."

Activity

Mind Map: Begin by drawing a large circle on a white board, putting Peace on the right side and Peacelessness/Conflict/Violence on the left side. If you are not familiar with Mind Mapping, you will find information in the Appendix (Item 1). Start with a branch for Self on the Peace side of the circle. Ask them what happens when there is Peace in the Self, and write a word or two of their response, repeating the whole phrase they say. After several respond, go to the Self branch on the lack of peace, conflict or violence in the Self side. The students are to supply all the answers. Also do branches for Families/Friends, Neighborhood, Society and the World.

Discuss the Reflection Points:
- Peace is more than the absence of war.
- If everyone in the world were peaceful, this would be a peaceful world.
- If we have no peace, it is because we have forgotten that we belong to each other.
  — *Mother Teresa, Nobel Peace Prize 1979*
- World Peace grows through nonviolence, acceptance, fairness and communication.

Creative Activity

Divide the students into groups of four to six. Give the groups 10 to 15 minutes to create a song or poem about peace or peace versus peacelessness, conflict or violence. It could be a rap song.

Invite them to perform their creation for the group. Lead the applause.

PEACE I LESSON 2

My Values

Begin with a song. If there was a song created during the first lesson, perhaps those in the small group that created it could present it again.

Discuss/Share

Ask:

- What two values do you think would change the world if *everyone* lived them?

Each person may have a different answer, but each one of you is right. If everyone in the world lived just two values, all the time, the world would change completely.

Ask:

- What would you like the world to be like?
- Tell me more about what you think a better world would be like.
- What would you like the environment to be?
- How would you like to feel inside?
- How would you like your relationships to be?

Positively acknowledge all responses.

Inform: The amazing thing about human beings is that we all want to be peaceful, loved and happy, and live in a healthy, clean, safe world.

It seems human beings in all cultures share universal values. We all want a peaceful world. So, why don't we have it?

Not just you, but many people around the world are concerned about the state of the world. While we share universal values, people are not living the values. You will have the opportunity to explore what values you would like to live with a course we will be doing called Living Values Education.

The premise of this project is that if we did live our values, we would create a better world. This is a program about values — thinking about them, expressing ideas, exploring what we can do to make a better world. It is a program to empower people to create more peace and happiness in their own lives and make a difference in the world.

Ask if they have any questions.

Reflection

Say, "I would like you to reflect on some of your values as I ask you to think about several things. Please write your responses."

Play some relaxing music and begin the following Reflective Exercise. Allow participants sufficient time to respond. Although approximate pausing times are suggested, each group is different. Observe when most of them are finished and then continue. Say:

- I would like you to think of a person who has positively influenced your life. (Pause for a few moments.)
- What values or qualities did you see in that person that made a difference to you? Please write the qualities or values that made it important to you. (Pause.)
- Pick one of those values or qualities. If everyone in the world had that quality, or demonstrated that value constantly, would the world be different? (Pause.)
- I would like you to think of the songs you love. What values are reflected through those words and music? Write those down. (Allow two or three minutes.)
- What images are important to you? Think of your favorite scenes, views or perhaps statues. What values and feelings are elicited by those? (Allow two or more minutes.)
- Remember a few especially positive moments of your life — what feelings were you experiencing then? What value were you demonstrating in those moments? (Allow two or more minutes.)
- Now, take a few minutes to think about six or eight values that are important in your life. Please write them down. (Allow two or more minutes.)

Activity

Step 1. Ask the young adults to form groups of four. Give them 15 to 20 minutes to share some of their experiences and values from this exercise in small groups.

Step 2. Invite each group to share a few of their favorite points with the entire group.

Step 3. Ask them to write down their definition of a value.

Step 4. Allow those who wish to do so to share their definition.

Step 5. To close, perhaps play an uplifting song that they like — on values, peace, love or creating a better world. Or, ask them to stand in a circle, each person sharing one word or one value that is important to him or her.

PEACE I LESSON 3

Imagining a Peaceful World

Play a song on peace.

Discuss/Share

Explore general concepts of peace through questions and discussion.
Ask:

- Does our world seem peaceful today?

- What would it look like or feel like to have a peaceful world?

- Who thinks peace is important?

Acknowledge all responses, including any statements about the negativity in the world or cynicism, and thank them for sharing.

Tell them that you will be giving a commentary about imagining a peaceful world. Play some peaceful instrumental music, if possible.

Imagining a Peaceful World

Please read the following slowly, pausing to allow them time to imagine. Feel free to adapt the commentary to suit your situation.

"Relax and let yourself become still. . . . Be in the present moment. . . . Focus on this moment of time. . . . Picture in your mind a beautiful bubble — this bubble is so big that you can step inside. . . . A door on the bubble opens. . . . Imagine stepping inside . . . the bubble begins to rise . . . it can travel in time or space . . . to a world where it is completely peaceful. . . . When you arrive, step out of the bubble and look around. . . . What does it look like there?. . . What is the air like? . . . How does nature look? . . . How do the buildings look? . . . You walk over to a lake. . . . Look into the lake and see your reflection. . . . How do you look? . . . How do you feel inside? . . . You can feel your body relaxing in this peaceful place. . . . As you pass by a group of people your age playing a game, notice the expressions on their faces and how they relate to one another. . . . (Pause for ten seconds.) They smile at you. . . . You continue to walk around the lake. . . . You notice a family and the way they are interacting with each other. . . . (Pause for ten seconds.) When it is time to leave, you step back into your bubble. . . . On the return journey, allow your bubble to go a little higher so you can see the peaceful world below. . . . What are the interactions like in countries . . . and between countries? . . . (Pause for 30 seconds.) What is nature like? . . . Now, allow the bubble to gently float back to this time and this class. . . . As you experience yourself seated here, let the image of the bubble disappear, and enjoy a feeling of stillness within."

Share

➢ Invite the students to form small groups of three, with people they have not spoken with in the last few days, to share their visualizations for six to nine minutes. Remind them to make sure everyone in the group gets a chance to share. Or, allow the small groups to verbally share and then make one picture together.

➢ Form one group again and invite a few students to share someone else's points about nature, the self, relationships, and/or interactions in countries and between countries. Perhaps two or three students would like to volunteer to write and draw on the board what is being shared by the group.

Activity

Ask students to silently reflect and write about their vision of a peaceful self or a peaceful world, or create a poem.

Invite any of those who wish to share their creation to do so.

Homework: Ask students to think of one small thing they can do to make their world like the world they imagined.

PEACE I LESSON 4
Feeling Peaceful and Without Peace

Play a peace song as the students enter or invite one of the small groups from the first lesson to sing a song they created.

Homework follow-up: Ask the students if they thought of things they could do to contribute to a more peaceful world. Acknowledge all responses and thank them for sharing.

Introduce the Physical Relaxation/Focusing Exercise: "Many people in the world today feel stressed. Do you experience being stressed sometimes? . . . One way to help get rid of stress and feel more peaceful is doing a physical relaxation exercise. When we get rid of some of the tension, we can be at our best. Let's try it."

Play some relaxing music, if possible.

Physical Relaxation/Focusing Exercise

"Sit comfortably . . . be aware of how you are feeling . . . and relax. . . . As you begin to relax your muscles, take in a deep breath . . . and let your body feel heavy. . . . As you breathe out, focus your attention on your feet. . . . Tighten all your muscles for a moment . . . and then relax them . . . let them stay relaxed. . . . Now become aware of your legs, letting them be heavy . . . tightening the muscles . . . and then relaxing them. . . . Breathe in slowly . . . and as you exhale, let any tension melt away. . . . Now tighten your hands for a moment . . . and then relax. . . . Be aware of your breathing, and take in a deep breath. . . . As you breathe out, let any tension melt away. . . . Breathe in deeply again . . . let the air out slowly . . . and let go of any tension. . . . Now tighten the muscles in the back and the shoulders . . . and then relax them. . . . Move your shoulders up . . . and relax as you move them down. . . . Tighten the muscles in your hands and arms . . . and then relax them. . . . Gently move the neck . . . first to one side, then to the other . . . relax the muscles . . . . Now tighten the muscles of the face . . . the jaw . . . and then relax the face and the jaw. . . . Let the feeling of wellbeing flow through the body. . . . Focus again on your breathing, breathing in deeply . . . and then letting go of any tension. . . . I am relaxed . . . I am peace . . . I am ready to be at my best."

— Contributed by Guillermo Simó Kadletz

Discuss/Share

Ask the following questions, acknowledging their replies and actively listening as appropriate.

- If every single person in this world were peaceful inside, would this world be more peaceful? How?
- How do you feel when you feel peaceful?
- What sensations are you aware of?
- When do you feel peaceless?
- What types of thoughts create a feeling of peacelessness?
- What types of thoughts help you feel peaceful?
- What activities or things do you do that help you feel peaceful?
- When do you feel most peaceful?

Discuss the following Reflection Points:

- Peace is a calm and relaxed state of mind.
- Peace is a qualitative energy.
- Worrying does not take away tomorrow's troubles, it takes away today's peace.

♦ Peace consists of pure thoughts, pure feelings, and pure wishes.

Activity

Write a short personal essay, "I feel most peaceful when . . ." or draw or paint peace. Invite those who wish to share their creation to do so.

PEACE I LESSON 5

Increasing Peace in School

Begin with a song. If you are comfortable doing so, invite everyone to stand and move peacefully during the song.

Discuss/Share

Introduction: "The other day we mind mapped some of the differences between a peaceful world and a world of conflict. Today, I'd like you to think about the differences between a Peaceful School and a School with Conflict." Ask the following questions, acknowledging their responses:

- What kinds of things would happen in each of those schools?
- What would you notice about each of these schools if you were casually walking through?
- How do the people feel who are fighting?
- How do those who they fight with feel?
- How do those who are bullied feel?
- What are the different feelings other students who watch bullying or violence in the school might feel?
- How do the people feel in the peaceful school?
- What kinds of things can they enjoy without worrying?

Say, "Just as people create their world and students create what happens on the campus, so we are creating what happens here in this class."

Activity

Step 1. Invite students to form groups of six or seven. Ask them to discuss which values or qualities would be most important to create a Peaceful Classroom or Peaceful School. Each group may choose between six to ten values or qualities.

Step 2. Ask each group to create a picture or poster on a large piece of paper with the words of the values and qualities and the words and behaviors that would happen as a result of those values and qualities in such a classroom or school. They may wish to draw or use symbols to depict some of the behaviors.

Step 3. Invite each group to share their poster/picture and their ideas with the entire class. Lead the applause for each group.

Step 4. Ask members of the groups to circle all the values and qualities and words and behaviors that are in their picture or poster that were mentioned by the other groups.

Step 5. Ask the students to name the six values or qualities that they are hearing most often that create a Peaceful Classroom or School.

Step 6. Ask the class to generate a list of practical things they would like to try based on the most frequently mentioned values or qualities.

Step 7. Ask them to select two or three of those practical things to put into practice during your time together for a week.

Close with the Peace Relaxation Exercise below. Just before the end of the exercise, please name three or four of the values or qualities the students identified earlier as the most important. For each one say: "I value _____. I am _____. I let the light of _____ enter my mind." Then pause before doing the same with the next two values or qualities.

Peace Relaxation/Focusing Exercise

"Let the body be relaxed and still. Let go of thoughts about the world outside, and slow down within. Be in the present, focusing on this moment in time. . . . Breathe in deeply . . . and let go of any tension through the bottoms of your feet. . . . Breathe in deeply again . . . and let go of any tension through the bottoms of your feet. . . . Breathe in deeply . . . and let the mind be still. Slowly absorb waves of peace. . . . Imagine being outdoors on a clear day — in a beautiful setting. . . . You may imagine being by the ocean, or in a meadow. . . . As you picture the beauty of nature in front of you, absorb waves of peace. . . . Let the self feel totally safe and relaxed. . . . Let the self feel beyond time. . . . You are full of natural tranquility. . . . You are naturally peaceful. . . . Think of your natural qualities . . . be present . . . and lovingly accept the self. . . . Surround the self with love . . . surround the self with peace. . . . When I am at peace, I am able to access my creativity and strengths . . . I am able to be part of creating a peaceful world. . . . I bring my attention back to the room . . . peaceful . . . peaceful . . . focused . . . alert. "

Evaluate the activity at the end of the week.

Ask:

- Did you create a more peaceful classroom?
- How did that feel?
- What worked or didn't work?
- Would you like to continue with that activity?
- Is there something else you would like to try?

PEACE I LESSON 6

Bullying No More — Creating
Assertive, Benevolently Assertive and Kind Responses

Begin with a song.

Discuss/Share

Share: Today, let's explore bullying. A definition of bullying is:
"unwanted, aggressive behavior . . . that involves a real or perceived power imbalance. The behavior is repeated, or has the potential to be repeated, over time. . . . Kids who bully use their power — such as physical strength, access to embarrassing information, or popularity — to control or harm others. ... Bullying includes actions such as making threats, spreading rumors, attacking someone physically or verbally, and excluding someone from a group on purpose."[1]

Ask:

- What are the different ways you've seen people bullied?
- Have you seen people bullied in different ways in other places? How?
- Have any of you ever been bullied?
- How do you feel when you are bullied?
- How do you feel when you see someone else bullied?
- Would anyone like to share anything else about bullying?

Accept and acknowledge all responses of the students. Validate, as appropriate, such as: "Yes, being bullied destroys our feelings of peace, safety and happiness."

---

[1] Stopbullying.gov

Ask:

- Do you want our class/school/club to be a bully-free zone?
- Who is the one person you can always affect? (Yourself.)
- The first step in creating a bully-free zone is to not be a bully. What belief or understanding would help you to treat all others kindly?
- What values and qualities do you think would help people to not act like a bully?
- Why do you think people sometimes act like bullies?

Say, "Thanks for sharing. Yes, often when people don't feel good about themselves, they are mean to others."

Ask:

- What can we do to feel better about ourselves when we're not feeling so good?

"Great ideas. Let's look at bullying a little more closely. Generally, when someone is mean, people react passively or aggressively. There is a third option — to be assertive.

- When someone calls you a name, what is an aggressive response?
- And what does it lead to?
- When someone calls you a name, what is a passive response? (Looking sad or looking frightened.)
- How do people bullying usually act when someone looks scared?
- How would that feel?

Explain: People who act as bullies will usually continue to be mean to someone who acts passively, that is, who looks sad or frightened. People who act as bullies want to feel they are powerful, so when the target they are bulling looks upset they feel more powerful. Other people who act like bullies are simply so miserable inside that they want others to be miserable too.

Say, "If you respond **passively** to a bully, he or she may bully you again. If you respond **aggressively** to a bully, the name calling or fighting is likely to get worse. The third type of response is an **assertive response. It begins with staying in your own power of peace and self-respect.** It might be like:"

- ☆ Looking confident, shrugging your shoulders like it doesn't matter because you know who you are, and walk away. (Please act it out for the students.)
- ☆ An assertive verbal response: "I don't like it when you do that, I want you to stop." (Please act it out for the students, stating the sentence clearly and with self-respect and confidence.)

Ask:

- What other assertive verbal responses work well? Not aggressive, but assertive!

Activity

➢ Say, "Everyone, please stand up and let me see the first 'It doesn't matter because I know who I am' response." . . . . . "Again! Great!"

➢ "Now I'm going to call all of you a name. When I do, I want you to give me your first assertive 'I know who I am' confident response. Are you ready? (Call them a not-so-bad name and positively reinforce them for their 'I know who I am' confident response.

➢ "Great. Now everyone together, which assertive verbal response, with self-respect, do you want to use?" _____ "Okay, everyone together!"

➢ "Great. Say it one more time, a little louder and with self-respect."

➢ "Well done!" And then tell them that's the last time you want to hear any name calling in your class!

Introduce benevolently assertive responses: With a benevolently assertive response, the person is deliberately not agreeing with the offending person by letting him or her know in a **non-offensive and non-defensive manner** of a different view. The comment may include an acknowledgement of the goodness of the offending person or change the direction of the interaction to values, qualities or relationship. This is can be quite effective for it communicates a lack of fear and changes the dynamic. It is also a more peaceful and respectful response.

Examples of benevolently assertive responses . . .

When someone attempts to start a fight:

- ★ Fighting stinks. Can't we think of anything better to do?
- ★ I think there's enough fighting in the world. Fighting or friends … what a choice!
- ★ Peace is a better choice than fighting.

When someone makes a discriminatory remark:

- ★ Life wouldn't be so interesting if we were all clones.
- ★ God is a great artist. I think both of our colors are beautiful.
- ★ I was hoping to be purple this birth, but it didn't work out!
- ★ I think all the religions of the world are cool.

The below examples could be used by the "target", or by another student who wants to stop the bullying of someone else and feels it is safe to do so.

- ★ Kindness is cool. Peace is cool. Come on, I know you have at least one of those inside.
- ★ All people deserve respect — that includes everyone.
- ★ The world has enough wars. Do we really need another one here?

- ➤ Ask them to generate a few more benevolently assertive responses.
- ➤ Then invite them to share examples of different situations that happen at your school or in the neighborhood. Ask everyone to generate responses to those situations as a group.

Role Play: Divide the students into small groups of three or four and ask them to role play, acting out the two assertive responses and trying out one or two of the benevolently assertive responses to the situations of their choice. Each student is to get a turn.

Discuss Bullying and Unkindness on Social Media

Ask:

- Have any of you seen someone bullied or treated badly on social media?
- What are ways people bully on social media? (Some of the students are likely to want to share some stories.)
- Are you sometimes frightened that might happen to you?
- If it has happened to you, how do you feel when someone is mean on social media?
- Would anyone like to share anything else about bullying?

"There have been a few very, very sad cases where people as young as 11 killed themselves because of what was written about them on social media."

Ask:

- What values or qualities would have prevented these tragedies from taking place? (Actively listen, as always, to their responses and reactions.)
- What guidelines can you think of that would help someone decide whether to text or post something?

Ask one of the students to write on the board the examples the students generate. Examples are:

- ★ Is this kind or helpful?

⭐ Would I like to get this?

⭐ Never hit send when I'm angry!

Closing: Play an uplifting song, and perhaps ask them to get up and move to the music, shaking out any tension and then dancing peace. End with a peace relaxation exercise.

Note to Educator: There are lessons about depression and suicide in the Love Unit if those with whom you are working are currently concerned about these issues.

PEACE I LESSON 7

Arms Are For . . . and Peace Slogans

Begin with a peace song or another uplifting song.

Discuss/Share

Ask:

• What are different ways arms are used? (Students may initially talk about the way we use the arms of our bodies.)

• How do you feel when others use their arms to hurt you or someone you care about? (Acknowledge and accept all answers, and reflect their feelings. Validating comment: "Yes, it is painful when others hurt us.")

➢ If one of the students has not already mentioned it, ask them to discuss "arms" as another word for "weapons". It is only human arms that make guns and weapons of war.

Ask the following questions, acknowledging their ideas:

• Are arms to destroy things simply an extension of the person who has the bodily arms?

• Why do you think people start wars?

• What are their goals?

• Why do they want that? What kind of life are they trying to achieve?

• Is there any other way to achieve their goal?

• What would you like to tell them?

Questions if there has been violence: If you are in a country in which there have been shootings or gun violence at schools or in the community (or any other type of violence about which the students are concerned), bring up one of the incidents and discuss it as a group. Some questions you might begin with are:

- A recent tragedy caused by violence was _____. What do you know about that? (Clarify any facts.)
- Why do you think these kinds of things happen?

➤ Discuss the particulars if the case relates to young adults their age or if they are concerned. For example, perhaps the perpetrator was a student who felt rejected or like he could never belong. In that instance, you might ask:

- Has anyone ever felt angry when someone is mean to you? (Everyone, yes?)
- When you are angry, is it right to hurt others? (No.)
- What would you like to tell the person if you could?
- What can we do to help everyone feel valued and respected?

Say, "There's a couple of slogans."
- ☆ Arms are for hugging, not for shoving.
- ☆ Arms are for helping, not for hurting.

Ask:
- Can you think of other slogans about arms?" (Give an example or two if they do not generate some — such as, Arms are for giving, not for grabbing. Arms are for use, not for abuse. Arms are for holding, not for hurting. Have fun making some up.)

➤ *Comment:* "People need to know that it is not right to hurt others."
➤ Write down what they come up with, and save it on the board for use in another lesson.

Ask:
- Can anyone think of another slogan for peace?

Activity

Invite them to form groups of two to three and make a peace poster. Examples: arms joined, a gun turning into a dove, arms of students linked across an outline of the shape of your country, etc.

End with the Physical Relaxation Exercise or the Peace Relaxation Exercise.

NOTE TO EDUCATOR

If students are not resolving conflicts in an optimum manner, conflict resolution strategies are recommended for the class or the entire school. Lessons in conflict resolution are simple, develop good communication skills that continue to be useful in life, and have been found to be successful. There are many excellent resources, each one varies to some degree. In some schools, students serve as peer conflict resolution managers or peer mediators during breaks. The room can also have relaxation/focusing commentaries available and art supplies.

The Conflict Resolution Process

First, the students in conflict are asked if they want help in resolving the problem. If they do, one or two conflict managers/mediators sit with them. One can sit by one upset student, the other by the other upset student. It is more comfortable for two conflict managers to be together so they can give each other moral support.

If one or both students say they do not want help, they are not willing to listen and talk, or they appear to be very upset, compassionately ask them if they would like a few minutes to quiet down by listening to a relaxation/focusing exercise, meditating, or doing some art work to express their feelings. If they say no, then they are choosing the standard disciplinary procedure of the school.

The "conflict resolution managers" or "peer mediators" are there to help the students who are having the conflict solve it. They are to listen to their replies, and direct them to listen to each other rather than interrupting. The peer mediators are to encourage the students to listen carefully without interruption, and then repeat to each other what they heard the other say. Their job is to appreciate the disputants' listening and problem-solving skills, and to avoid taking sides. They are not to blame, accuse, moralize, or judge. They are there to help the students resolve the conflict. It is easy to slip into old verbal patterns, so be careful!

- ❖ A conflict resolution manager starts with the more visibly upset student, asking him or her to state <u>what happened</u>.
- ❖ Ask the second student to listen and repeat back what he or she heard. (He or she is not to contradict, argue, or blame, but simply to repeat.)
- ❖ The same question of what happened is then posed to the second student, and the first student is to listen carefully and repeat.
- ❖ The next question asked of each student is, "<u>How were you feeling?</u>"

❖ Again, each listens and repeats what the other said. The peer mediator can also use active listening responses as each student talks about his or her feelings.

❖ Next, they are asked: "<u>What would you like to stop?</u>"

❖ After they each answer and have repeated back what the other said, then they are asked: "<u>What would you like to happen instead?</u>"

❖ The students are then asked if they can <u>agree to do what the other suggested</u>.

❖ If they are not happy with that suggestion, they are asked to generate other solutions.

❖ They are then asked if they can make a firm commitment to try to behave in the way they both agreed.

❖ When both have agreed on another behavior, then the conflict resolution managers may compliment them on the process and perhaps note their qualities or efforts. They may ask them if they would like time to meditate / do a relaxation exercise before they return to their regular class.

Starting Conflict Resolution in Schools: All students are taught the same communication process. Tell the students about the process, demonstrate it for them, and lead them in practice. One person may want to visit the different classes and do all the training, or teachers can be taught how to do this at a teacher training session. Post the Conflict Resolution questions/process in each class. These are listed in the summarizing steps below and in the Appendix, Item 2.

At the high school level, peer mediators often meet in a private room. They might want to take notes during the process. Let all students know that if they have a conflict, they may go to the student conflict resolution managers/peer mediators.

Conflict Resolution has had dramatic effects in teaching students how to mediate disagreements and fights. Several teams of students can rotate as conflict resolution managers or peer mediators. Adults should positively comment on the courage and qualities of the students — both of the conflict resolution managers and of the students who are willing to communicate and listen to help resolve a problem.

Conflict Resolution Process: Summary of Steps

The mediator asks each student the question:

"Are you willing to work on a solution?" If the answer is "yes," continue. Ask each student one question at a time, and wait for their response. The other student listens and repeats what was said. Then ask:

"Please tell us what happened."

"How did you feel when that happened?"

"What would you like to stop?"

"What would you like her/him to do instead?"

"Can you do that?"

"Can you make a firm commitment to try to act the way you both have agreed?"

Compliment them for the qualities they demonstrated during this peace process.

PEACE I LESSON 8

Introducing Conflict Resolution

Educator Preparation: Please become familiar with the above information and put the following on a board or poster.

Are you willing to work on a solution?

Each person has to be willing to LISTEN to each other

and repeat what the other says.

1. Please tell us what happened.
2. How did you feel when that happened?
3. What would you like to stop?
4. What would you like her/him to do instead?
5. Can you do that?
6. Can you commit to trying to act in the way you both have agreed?

Begin the session with a peace song.

Discuss/Share

Ask:

- What would happen in the world if everyone learned to communicate and solve their problems instead of fighting? . . . What would happen in your home, with your friends, in your community, and in the world? (Acknowledge their responses.)

- ➤ Say: "People all over the world are learning about conflict resolution. The more people learn it, the more there is hope for peace. I really believe that people can solve their problems."

> ➢ Inform: "These are the steps for one method of conflict resolution." Review the steps you have written on a poster or board.
> ➢ Point to the first line and the sentence under it.

Ask:

- Do you think willingness to work on a problem really helps? Why?
- What does it say about you as a person if you are willing to work on a problem? (If they have not included the following answers, please do include them: "It takes courage to work on a problem. It means that you believe you are capable of finding a solution, and it means you believe other people are capable, too.")
- What kinds of things do people fight over? (Listen and list their responses on the board. Ask one or more students to make a list of these on a large piece of paper for later use.)
- How do you feel when _____ (one event mentioned) happens?
- If the feeling is anger, ask: What feeling is underneath that feeling?
- How do you feel when _____ (another event mentioned) happens?
- If the feeling is anger, ask: What feeling is underneath the anger?
- How do you want to feel? (Accept all responses. Students often mention respect and acceptance. Ask them if they want to feel valued, respected, and loved if they have not given those responses.)

Demonstrate: Ask for two volunteers to try the conflict resolution exercise. Let them pretend to have a common conflict, or take a recent conflict. The teacher is to model asking each student the questions, and ask them to listen to each other.

> ➢ Ask for two more volunteers and demonstrate the conflict resolution process again.
> ➢ Thank the volunteers. Ask for questions or reactions.

NOTE TO EDUCATOR

As the educator, actively listen to their replies, direct them to listen to each other and repeat what the other says, and appreciate their listening and coming up with solutions. If a student blames, interrupts or accuses the other during the dialogue, say "Please listen," or "Please answer the question." Restate the question again, such as, "How did you feel when that happened?"

End with a Relaxation/Focusing Exercise. These can be found in the Appendix.

PEACE I LESSON 9

Conflict Resolution — What We Like and Don't Like

Begin with a peace song.

Discuss/Share

Say, "Yesterday, we were discussing some of the things people have conflicts over and we made a list of those. Let's look at them in relation to the questions asked during the conflict resolution process."

> ➢ Take one item from the list, for example, name calling, and ask the following questions:

- How do you feel when that happens? (If the response is anger, ask: What feeling is underneath that?)
- What would you like the other person(s) to stop?
- What would you like the other person(s) to do instead?
- What is a solution that would benefit everyone involved?
- Can you think of another fair solution?

> ➢ Repeat the above process with another couple of items from the list.

Lesson Content

Say, "In some ways, people are simple. When we get angry, there is hurt or fear or embarrassment/shame underneath. The hurt, fear or shame come first when people do not feel valued, respected, or loved. Some people stay feeling hurt and others handle it by getting angry. Some people feel hurt and withdraw while other people feel hurt and then get angry."

> ➢ Repeat the above concepts and illustrate it on the board, drawing flames above the word anger.

Anger

Hurt, Fear, Shame or feeling Unsafe

Everyone wants to be valued, respected or loved.

Apply Concept: Ask the students to think of things that happen or a time they felt this way when something happened to them. If they are not able to do this right away, use a couple of examples from the list of conflicts made previously, or use one of your own examples.

Activity

Instruct students to write two examples, applying the above concept. Ask them to use one personal example when they felt this way. Or, offer them the opportunity to gather in groups of three or four to discuss times they have seen these dynamics. Remind them that what is said in the room, stays in the room. Ask them if they are willing to promise to keep what anyone else shares private/confidential.

Reinforce Concept and add a skill: Say, "There is always hurt, fear, shame or feeling unsafe under the anger. So, if you are ever angry, be aware of that, accept it, and then ask yourself: What's under my anger? Am I hurt or afraid? Am I feeling unsafe? So be aware of or observe your emotions, accept them, and then you will be in a better place to love yourself and think of a positive way to deal with it."

End with peaceful movement to a song and/or a Relaxation/Focusing Exercise.

PEACE I LESSON 10

Conflict Resolution and Listening

Begin with a peace song.

Discuss the Reflection Points:

♦ World Peace grows through nonviolence, acceptance, fairness and communication.

♦ Peace is the prominent characteristic of what we call "a civilized society."

♦ Peace must begin with each one of us. Through quiet and serious reflection on its meaning, new and creative ways can be found to foster understanding, friendships and cooperation among all peoples. — *Mr. Javier Perez de Cuellar, Former Secretary-General of the United Nations*

Demonstrate: Invite a couple of volunteers to do participate in the Conflict Resolution process.

Discuss/Share

Say, "One of the most important things in solving problems is to listen to others and really hear what they have to say."

Ask:

- How do you feel when you try to talk to someone and they turn away?

Acknowledge: "Yes, when people don't listen and are rude, problems usually get worse. Sometimes people do other things that interfere with solving a problem."
Ask:

- What are other things people do that interfere with solving the problem?

Acknowledge their responses and add any of the following not included.

Blockers and Stoppers
- Blaming
- Name calling; telling the person he or she is silly or stupid
- Interrupting
- Accusing
- Contradicting
- Trying to make the other person feel guilty
- Getting angry because the other person is angry.
- Giving solutions

Explain: For effective listening, it is important to do two things:
1. to really (genuinely) pay attention to every word the person is saying, and
2. to let them know that you understand what he or she is saying.

Listening Activity

Form groups of three. Ask each group to count off: one, two and three. For Round 1: Person One will be the talker, Person Two the listener, and Person Three the observer.

	Person One	**Person Two**	**Person Three**
Round 1	Talker	Listener	Observer
Round 2	Observer	Talker	Listener
Round 3	Listener	Observer	Talker

- For Round 1, 2, and 3, each "Talker" is to share something positive that happened to her/him.
- Do this again, this time asking each Talker to share something that is important to her/him or something that makes her/him feel peaceful.

> Do the three rounds again, this time asking each Talker to share something that he or she feels angry or sad about. (If there is not sufficient time, continue this activity during the next lesson.)

During each round, the listener should be encouraged to listen, occasionally reflecting the emotions of the talker, or restating or paraphrasing the content of the message. The observer in each round can provide feedback.

Discuss/Share

Ask:

- How did you feel when someone really listened to you?
- Did anyone notice that anger automatically started to decrease when someone was genuinely listened to?
- Was there anything that made it difficult to listen?
- What made it easy to listen?
- How is really listening giving respect?

End with the following Relaxation/Focusing Exercise. Read the following slowly, pausing when indicated.

Peaceful Star Relaxation/Focusing Exercise

"One way to be peaceful is to be silent inside. Take a deep breath . . . and let yourself be surrounded by peace. . . . Be aware of any tension . . . and let it begin to release as you breathe out. . . . Take in a deep breath of peace . . . and slowly breathe out, letting go of any tension. . . . For a few moments, think of the stars in the sky and imagine yourself to be as still as a star in the distance. They are so beautiful in the sky . . . so quiet and peaceful. . . . Let the body be still. . . . Relax your toes and legs . . . relax your chest and your stomach . . . and your shoulders. . . . Relax your arms . . . and your face. . . . Be aware of your breathing . . . and allow the feeling of peace to come into your mind. . . . Let a soft light of peace surround you. . . . Be surrounded by peace . . . stillness . . . be peace. . . . You, the tiny star, are naturally peaceful. . . . Relax into the light of peace. . . . Let the self be still and peaceful . . . You are focused . . . concentrated . . . peaceful . . . content . . . a star of peace."

PEACE I LESSSON 11

Peaceful Hearts and a Circle of Coexistence

Begin with a peace song from your culture.

Discuss/Share

The following Reflection Points:

♦ Compassion is a muscle that gets stronger with use. — *Mahatma Gandhi*

♦ There is no dialogue if there is not a deep love for the world and men. — *Paulo Freire, Brazilian Pedagogue*

♦ Learning to live together means combining the relationship of equality and differences. — *Xesús Jares, Spanish Pedagogue*

♦ When the power of love overcomes the love of power, the world will know peace. — *Jimi Hendrix*

Activity

Step 1. Share that students in Brazil set up a "Circle of Coexistence" to resolve conflicts among students, to improve the harmony of everyone in the classroom, at school and in the community.

Step 2. Ask the students to think and practice positive feelings and actions for themselves, peers, society and the world through the following questions.

• What are some positive feelings and actions people could have for the self?

• What are positive feelings and actions people could have for others?

• In order to experience peace, would practicing the values of compassion, love and forgiveness help? How?

• How would accepting others create more peace in the world?

• What if everyone in our class/school/community accepted each other with a peaceful heart? What would that look like?

Step 3. Ask the students to form small groups and generate some practical ideas based on the themes debated and experienced in the circle.

Step 4. Invite each group to share their ideas and/or experiences.

Step 5. Close with a relaxation/focusing exercise on peace for a few minutes in which students can silently sense and share their compassionate and loving feelings.

Step 6. Suggest to the students that they practice peaceful feelings and communication for a week with peers, family and other people with whom they have contact.

— Contributed by Paulo Barros

PEACE I LESSSON 12
To Agree or Disagree?

Begin with a song. Invite the students to move peacefully with the song.

Note to Educator: This class/assembly activity was submitted by educator Lisa Jennings and her ninth-grade students at the Kuwait American School in Kuwait. The activity is related to creating Peace through effective conflict management.

They began with a quote from Stephen Moyer to help guide their thinking:

♦ Conflict is drama, and how people deal with conflict shows the kind of people they are.

Educator Preparation: One group of students, with a facilitator, pre-prepare six Peace Related statements. Examples are:

♦ Conflicts destroy peaceful relationships.

♦ Conflict should be avoided at all costs.

♦ You should stand up for what you believe in, even if other people don't agree with you.

♦ Conflict is the same in all cultures.

♦ Peace means the same in all cultures.

♦ Conflict can be healthy.

Class or Assembly Activity

Step 1. The facilitator introduces each statement to other students who are sitting in groups.

Step 2. The recipient students discuss the statement and come to a consensus as to whether they agree or disagree with the statement. Each group writes down the reason(s) for agreement or disagreement.

Step 3. The facilitator invites each group to share their consensus. A spokesperson for each group holds up a sign, either agree (green) or disagree (red).

Step 4. Where there is a difference of opinion, the facilitator opens a debate. The process continues until the whole class reaches a Peaceful consensus.

Reflection: The main outcome to consider: Peace begins with me.

— Contributed by Lisa Jennings and Grade 9 Students

PEACE I LESSON 13
Conflict Resolution — Peers as Mediators

Begin with a peace song.

Discuss the Reflection Point: Peace begins with each one of us.

Activity

Ask four students to volunteer for a conflict resolution demonstration. Two are to act as mediators and two are to pretend to have a conflict. The peer mediators will take over the role the teacher had been playing in asking the six questions and helping the students in conflict resolve the problem. Instruct each peer mediator to sit by the students who have the conflict. When one demonstration is finished, ask the four students to reverse roles.

Note to Educator: There is a Conflict Resolution sheet for the mediators to use in the Appendix (Item 2).

Contrast Poetry Activity: If time remains, ask students to brainstorm vocabulary associated with the above activities. Ask them to think of "emotion words" and write them on the board. Find antonyms and synonyms. As a group, or as individuals, students can write poetry to take the reader from one feeling or idea to its opposite. For example, a change in feelings as a conflict is resolved is below.

Anger

Hot resistance

Eyes bright, throat too tight

Nails digging deep into fists

Itching to fight

Eyes meet

A tear trickles down an inflamed check

"I'm sorry"

"Me too"

Acceptance

— Contributed by Ruth Liddle

Invite the students who wish to do so to share their poems.

PEACE I LESSON 14

Bullying No More — Peer Intervention

Begin with a song.

Discuss/Share

Summarize: We've been talking about peace in different ways. We've been exploring personal peace through thinking about when we feel most peaceful and doing the peace relaxation exercises. We've been exploring how to create peace when there's been a conflict with someone else by learning conflict resolution. We've also talked about being assertive instead of passive or aggressive as a response to bullying and we talked about kindness guidelines on social media."

Ask:

- How's that been going? What's working for you or not working for you?
- Have you generated any more benevolently assertive response? What are they?
- What differences are you noticing?

Share humor as a strategy to counter bullying: "Sometimes humor works in a bullying situation when you can be humorous with confidence. For example, a humorous response which usually disarms when delivered confidently with a smile is: 'If I had feelings, they'd be hurt!'

This works the same way as the assertive responses: When people don't get defensive and stay in self-respect, the bullying usually stops as there is no pay-off for the one bullying."

Ask:

- Have any of you tried other humorous responses that were effective in stopping bullying?

Note to Educator: Do comment if their humorous responses are mean, as the intent is not to be aggressive but to be assertive. The rule: When people don't get defensive and stay in self-respect, the bullying usually stops as there is no pay-off for the person bullying. A non-aggressive response can open the door of change for the person who is bullying."

Activity

Peer intervention — Working together to deter bullying

Share: Canadian research indicates that bullying stops 57 percent of the time within ten seconds if a peer intervenes. Bystanders passively watching bullying take place can add to the feeling of power the person who is bullying wants, so standing and watching can unwittingly reinforce bullying. Peer intervention is important as adults are rarely around when bullying occurs. Your peers are frequently around when bullying occurs: 85 percent of the time.

Introduce the intervention: When someone is bullying another person, if someone speaks up for the target, the bullying stops more than half of the time. In this lesson, we are going to look at safe things you can do that will help a person being bullied.

Say, "I am going to tell you about three different situations. I want you to think about which one you would prefer if you were the target of the person who is acting like a bully.

"**Response One:** You are being bullied and your classmates walk away from the bullying scene."

Ask:

• How do you feel? (Actively listen to their responses.)

"The good thing is that the person bullying is deprived of an audience, but the target feels unsupported and may fear the bystanders think less of him or her. It is important for the target to walk away, but to walk away alone might be difficult."

"**Response Two:** It's the same situation. You are being bullied but one of your classmates calls out to you, 'Come on, Sema. Don't listen to her.' Or, 'Come on, Tom, it's no fun listening to this.' 'Hey, Mira, let's go. This is totally uncool.' Your classmates walk away from the bullying scene *with* you."

Ask:

• How do you feel? (Actively listen to their responses.)

"The good thing is that the target feels supported by his or her classmates so does not feel as bad, and it is successful in stopping the bullying."

"In the situation, I just read there was:"

★ Come on. Don't listen to her.

★ Come on, it's no fun listening to this.

★ Hey, let's go. This is totally uncool.

Ask:

• What kinds of things could you call out to the target to let him or her know you are helping them be safe?

➢ Make a list of their statements. As the students call out a statement, ask everyone in the group to echo them. Ask half the class to read aloud alternate statements with self-respect when they have finished generating ideas.

Role Play: Ask for volunteers.

- Who wants to be the person bullying?
- Who wants to be the target?
- Who wants to be the helpful bystander? What shall we call the helpful bystander?

Say, "The rest of you will play the bystanders watching the bully and the target."
Ask:

- Person bullying, what are you going to say? …… Got it? Invite the students to generate a bullying statement and/or action they have witnessed before.

Say, "Okay, person bullying, stand here. Target, please stand a few feet away and look surprised when he says something that is bullying. Helpful bystander (or whatever name they have decided upon), stand with the group. You can pick your lines from the list we made."

Divide the students into groups of four or five so they all get to practice the helpful-bystander role. Positively reinforce efforts and encourage them to say their statements with self-respect and confidence.

"Response Three: It's the same situation. You are being bullied but one of your classmates calls out to you, 'Come on, Sema, it looks like Pam is grumpy today. Maybe she'll be nicer tomorrow!' 'Come on, Tom, it's no fun listening to this. It looks like Mack isn't his usual self today.' Then your classmates walk away from the bullying scene *with* you."
Ask:

- How do you feel? (Actively listen to their responses.)

"The target feels supported by the bystanders and you have been successful in stopping the bullying. But also, the person bullying has not been completely alienated. He or she has been offered a reason for their behavior. This opens a door for possible change."

A caution: Say, "*Sometimes* if we are a little kind a few times, the person bullying will stop bullying. *Not all the time, but sometimes*! Some people get stuck in being mean for a few years, so during that time they just get meaner. But some people who bully can feel stuck in needing to be mean. So, when someone is a little kind, it can open a door for the person bullying to change. Be a little kind — but also know your limits and move away if they even begin to cross them. The most important thing is always to stop the bullying and help the target get away feeling supported."

Ask:

- Would anyone like to comment on that? Have any of you had an experience with someone that was mean changing? Or someone who was provided many opportunities to change and didn't?

Role play again in the same small groups: Ask each group to generate real situations they encounter and practice benevolently assertive responses or any other assertive responses that stop the bullying. Allow each group to share one of their favorite role plays.

End with a peace relaxation exercise of their choice.

PEACE I LESSONS 15

How would peace effect the Sustainable Development Goals?

Begin with a song.

Lesson Content

"The 2030 Agenda for Sustainable Development, adopted by all United Nations Member States in 2015, provides a shared blueprint for peace and prosperity for people and the planet, now and into the future. At its heart are the 17 Sustainable Development Goals (SDGs), which are an urgent call for action by all countries — developed and developing — in a global partnership.

"They recognize that ending poverty and other deprivations must go hand-in-hand with strategies that improve health and education, reduce inequality, and spur economic growth – all while tackling climate change and working to preserve our oceans and forests.

The Division for Sustainable Development Goals (DSDG) in the United Nations Department of Economic and Social Affairs (UNDESA) provides substantive support and capacity-building for the SDGs and their related thematic issues, including water, energy, climate, oceans, urbanization, transport, science and technology, the Global Sustainable Development Report (GSDR), partnerships and Small Island Developing States. SDGs."

Source: https://sustainabledevelopment.un.org/

The 17 sustainable development goals (SDGs) to transform our world:

Goal 1: No Poverty

Goal 2: Zero Hunger

Goal 3: Good Health and Well-being

Goal 4: Quality Education

Goal 5: Gender Equality

Goal 6: Clean Water and Sanitation

Goal 7: Affordable and Clean Energy

Goal 8: Decent Work and Economic Growth

Goal 9: Industry, Innovation and Infrastructure

Goal 10: Reduced Inequality

Goal 11: Sustainable Cities and Communities

Goal 12: Responsible Consumption and Production

Goal 13: Climate Action

Goal 14: Life Below Water

Goal 15: Life on Land

Goal 16: Peace and Justice Strong Institutions

Goal 17: Partnerships to achieve the Goal

Activity

Step 1. Instruct the students to divide in small groups of five to seven. Ask each group to select the SDGs that would be affected by peace — individual peace, peace in the community, and peace in the country and the world.

Step 2. Facilitate each group selecting two SDGs that they feel would benefit from peace with the aim of each group working on different SDGs. If there are still SDGs that they feel would be benefited by peace and there is no group working on those, allow the groups to choose one more SDG until those they feel would be affected by peace are taken.

Step 3. Invite each group to think of specific ways peace effects the SDGs they have selected. For example, during times of peace schools can flourish and students can attend schools without interruption. This is important for quality education.

Step 4. Ask each group to write specific ways peace effects the SDGs on "Peace Leaves". They can cut out leaves on blue pieces of paper or use a crayon to color a piece of paper blue. (*Note to Educator:* Each value will be given a different color as the lessons continue so that the students can visually see which values are affecting which SDGs. Blue has been suggested for peace, but please use any color you wish.)

Step 5. Ask each group to present their Peace Leaves. They may also present a song or a poem about their findings if they wish.

Step 6. If there is time, make a display board with a representation of the SDGs on which they can pin or tape their Peace Leaves. You could use the picture the UN uses of a wheel with 17 spokes, or make a tree out of brown wrapping paper with each branch being a different SDG, or hang a string from the ceiling for each of the SDGs they have selected today and attach the leaves.

Close with a relaxation/focusing exercise.

Note to Educator: Ask each group to put their names at the bottom of their mind map or poster and keep their creations for a lesson from the Respect I values unit.

PEACE I LESSONS 16
Peace Heroes and Messages of Peace

Begin with a song.

Activity

Step 1. Divide the students into small groups and ask them to identify one or more peace heroes. Perhaps there is someone in your class that is a peace hero, or perhaps they admire a musician, artist, social worker, union leader, world leaders or environment activists. Is there an organization in your country that strives to create peace through music or community dialogue? What is her/his message to the world?

Step 2. Invite the students to reflect for a few moments on their message of peace for the world. Invite the small groups to create one or more messages for the world. They may wish to share their message through pictures, slogans, or a human sculpture.

Step 3. Invite each group to share their creation.

Close with a peace relaxation exercise of your choice.

Other Activities Options:

Perhaps the entire class, or the entire school, can create a human peace sculpture. If so, take a picture and spread your messages of peace.

You may all wish to do a peace assembly with your peers or for younger students. Share some of your songs and favorite creations and perhaps do a peace relaxation exercise together.

Peace Activities in Subject Areas

Language/Literature

Explore the theme of peace while teaching written language skills. One or more of the Reflection Points could be used to initiate discussion as a precursor to assigning an essay. The essays could be from a personal, philosophical, or societal perspective.

Young adults could read autobiographies of their country's or the world's personalities who worked to achieve peace. Read the work of or about Nobel Peace Prize winners. Make up Reflection Points based on your reading.

Study the works of anti-war poets. Listen to the songs, "Masters of War" by Bob Dylan and "The Universal Solider" by Donavan. What is their message to the world? Is this relevant today? *— Contributed by Kristan Mouat*

Write an essay on How Much Peace is Enough? *— Contributed by Caroline Druiff*

A Journal

Discuss the Reflection Point: Serenity is not the absence of chaos, but peace in the midst of it. Ask the students to use what they have learned during the classes to experiment with maintaining a feeling of peace or serenity. Students can keep a journal on what values, thoughts and qualities they use to help.

Debate

Choose peace as the topic for one or more debates. Or, debate one or several Reflection Points listed above, such as: Peace is more than the absence of war. Or: Peace is the prominent characteristic of what we call "a civilized society". Perhaps you can obtain a banner from the art students or they can create one electronically.

Consider: It is impossible to engage in peaceful activities without actually feeling peaceful. *— Contributed by Caroline Druiff*

Peace Quotes

Invite each student to select a Peace quote that has meaning for them. In turn, each student shares the quote and invites responses. Ask:

- What does it mean to you?

For example: A Grade 12 Senior Student, Fawziya Al-Baqshi at the Kuwait American School, chose a Gandhi quote for World Values Day as follows:

♦ Keep your thoughts positive, because your thoughts become your words. Because your words become your behavior. Because your behavior becomes your habits. Because your habits become your values. Because your values become your destiny.

Reflection: Inviting responses invites us to reflect and shows that we each make sense of words according to our own experiences and can show how-to live-in peace in different ways.

— Contributed by Fawzyi Al-Baqshi, Grade 12 student

History/Social Studies

Peace can be explored in a multitude of ways. For instance, the cultures of war and peace can be contrasted or the factors leading to war and peace can be examined.

Ask: "How can governments create peace through developing a culture of peace and providing for the needs of its people?"

Manifestations of Peace in the World

What are different manifestations of peace in the world? How is peace expressed through the arts, what large organizations work for peace in the world? In different subject areas, use your standard curriculum for students to explore. Or, perhaps small groups can research different manifestations of peace online and share their output.

— Contributed by Sabine Levy and Pilar Quera Colomina

Wars and Alternatives to Fighting

Research information about a couple of wars. Then talk with an adult about what the people are or were fighting about. Ask them if they feel there is an alternative to fighting. Write your thoughts. Then ask this question to two other adults or research alternatives to fighting. Ask the students to share their results in class.

— Contributed by Ruth Liddle

Economics

Ask students to study one or more of the Human Development Reports by the United Nations Development Program (UNDP). One report suggests that providing livability for all people in the world is the only sure method for peace. It does this with a look at global trade and the growing disparity between the world's richest and poorest. Another UNDP report looks at five people-friendly pillars which must govern development for a better world. It clearly states that development is not sufficient — it must be people-centered development. These excellent reports are written by teams of eminent economists.

Explore the costs of war versus the costs of peace. Calculate how many days of peace, that is, stopping all wars, would it take to provide education for all young people in the world for one year. Calculate how many days of peace it would take to feed all the people on the planet an adequate diet for one year?

Science

Science is a discipline which can be utilized in creating peace or war.
Ask:

- What would science <u>not</u> have created if humanity had held steadfast to a commitment to peace?
- Have there been more inventions for war or for peace?
- What is the physical impact of war on the environment?
- What are the long-term effects on human beings?
- What would a science of peace contribute to the world?
- What scientific advancements might you to see in a society focused on peace?

Project

If the young adults in your class had available one-fifth of the world's budget for war and could make that available for peace, what would they create? Ask them to form small groups to develop their ideas and then allow time for them to present their ideas to the entire group.

Art

Discuss with the students what they would like to put on a collaborative painting — perhaps symbols of peace, peace stars, a picture of a peaceful world, or ...? Provide students with a long piece of colorful paper, and individual small pots of paint and a brush. Play peaceful music. As they stand close to each other they can paint their own

small planned pattern. When the music stops, each student moves one step to the left or right.
                                                — *Contributed by Linda Heppenstall*

   Create a mural on peace. Focus on staying peaceful while you are creating and painting.

   Create powerful peace slogans. Or create peace banners and hang them around the school or community.

   Draw inner peace or sculpt peace.

Design a Peace Garden Wall Hanging

   Ask the students to think about the colors and shapes that would create feelings of peace and gentleness. Ask them to express those feelings on paper or fabric using a variety of available materials. Work directly from nature if possible.
                                                — *Contributed by Eleanor Viegas*

   Ask the students to write down the words to a song they like, such as "Imagine," and then glue grain on top to capture an image. It could be an image of the artist or be a symbol of the song's meaning. Or, create a song of their own.
                                                — *Contributed by Dierich von Horn*

Music

   Select your favorite songs about peace. Sing them or play them.

   What were the original instruments used in your region or culture on which songs or rhythms of peace were played? Investigate them. Is there someone in your area who has one and can play it? Can it be made with materials indigenous to your area?

   Plan a concert. Present your concert not only for your own school, but also for younger students at an elementary or middle school or another community or group. Perhaps some art students can bring peace banners or you can create some digitally.

Home Economics / Human Sciences

   Discuss the importance of peace in the home. Consider how one's ability to stay peaceful is central to peace in the home.

Enjoy one of the Peace Relaxation/Focusing Exercises from the Appendix. Reflect on what a space of peace would look and feel like in your home for a few minutes, then share in a group of three or four. Share some of the output with the larger group.

Practice cooking, sewing or woodwork while in a state of peace or contentment. What thoughts help you stay content?

Design a peaceful home environment. Ask, "What would you see in a home filled with peace? What creates a feeling of harmony and comfort?"

Create a design for peace that you can appliqué onto a T-shirt.

— *Contributed by Myrna Belgrave*

Personal Development

Discuss some of the Peace Reflection Points. Ask students to share when they feel most peaceful.

Ask students to research conflict resolution strategies and present them to the class by modeling them. Design a conflict-resolution strategy students feel will be successful in your particular setting. Present it to the school dean.

Stress Reduction

Offer a unit on stress reduction and make Peace Relaxation/Focusing Exercises part of the daily program. Learning how to make the mind stress-free and peaceful has been proven to be a major aid in reducing and controlling stress.

Song: Play, teach or sing with the students a peace song from your particular culture or share your favorite peace song.

Ask the students to make up their own relaxation exercise. The educator may wish them to write it out, record it or share it with the class. Or, small groups could create a video about peace.

Physical Education/ Dance and Movement

Play or invent a few peace games or create a peace dance. This might be a modern ballet that epitomizes peace or a dance contrasting war and peace. Be creative.

RESPECT

UNIT TWO: RESPECT I

Respect Lessons

The respect values unit builds on the concepts and intra- and interpersonal social and emotional skills in the peace unit. As before, it is suggested that each lesson begin with a song. Involve students in selecting songs. You may want them to bring in songs that relate to the theme. Many like "Hero" by Mariah Carey which is about seeing your own beauty, or "Behind the Wall" by Tracy Chapman which is about a lack of respect and physical violence. Many students enjoy learning traditional songs. Perhaps there are traditional musical instruments they could play.

Respect Reflection Points

- ◆ Every human being has innate worth.
- ◆ The first respect is to respect myself — to know I am naturally valuable.
- ◆ Respect is knowing I am unique and valuable.
- ◆ Part of self-respect is knowing my own qualities.
- ◆ Respect is listening to others.
- ◆ Respect is knowing others are valuable, too.
- ◆ Respect for the self is the seed that gives growth to confidence.
- ◆ When we have respect for the self, it is easy to have respect for others.
- ◆ Beauty is not in the face; beauty is a light in the heart. — *Kahlil Gibran*
- ◆ To know one's natural worth and to honor the worth of others is the true way to earn respect.
- ◆ Part of respect for the self is taking care of the body.
- ◆ Part of respect is knowing I make a difference.
- ◆ Those who give respect will receive respect.
- ◆ The more respect is measured on the basis of something external, the greater the desire for recognition from others. The greater the desire, the more one falls victim and loses respect for the self.

♦ When there is the power of humility in respecting the self, wisdom develops and we are fair and just to others.

♦ Everyone in the world has the right to live with respect and dignity, including myself.

RESPECT I LESSON 1
Mind Mapping Respect and Disrespect

Begin with an uplifting song.

Let the students know you will explore the value of respect for the next few weeks. Begin to explore general concepts of respect through questions and discussion.

Ask:

- What is respect?

- Imagine for a few moments what the world would be like if everyone had respect for each other. (Pause) What do you think it would be like?

- How would people feel?

- How would you feel inside if everyone only treated you with respect?

- Imagine for a moment how you would feel if you were in your self-respect all the time. . . . . . What do you think that would be like?

- Imagine if everyone in this school were in their self-respect most of the time. . . . What might that look like or feel like?

- If everyone in the world treated each other with respect and dignity, what would <u>not</u> be happening that is happening?

Say, "One of the Reflection Points upon which Living Values Education is built is:"

♦ Every human being has innate worth.

♦ The first respect is to respect myself — to know I am naturally valuable.

♦ Everyone in the world has the right to live with respect and dignity, including myself.

Activity

Say, "Today, let's explore the differences between a respectful world and a world of disrespect through mind mapping."

Mind Map: Begin by drawing a large circle on a white board, putting Respect on the right side and Disrespect on the left side. Start with a branch for SELF on the Respect side of the circle, asking them what happens when there is respect in the Self and writing in brief their responses. Then ask them what happens when there is a lack of respect in the SELF. The students are to supply all the answers. Also do branches for Relationships, Business, Community and Environment.

Creative Activity

Divide the students into groups of four to six. Ask each group to create a song or poem about respect or respect versus disrespect. It could be a rap song. Allow them to perform their creation for the group.

RESEPCT I LESSON 2

Qualities of My Heroes

Begin with a song. You may wish to have the group sing one of the songs created during the last LVE lesson.

Say, "In other lessons we will explore the effects of disrespect and why you think people choose to act without regard for others. In today's lesson we will just explore respect — and what qualities each one of you feels is most important."

"We all have many things that are the same, but one of the wonderful great things about humans is that each has a personality of his or her own. Each person comes with a unique combination of qualities. Let's start by listing good qualities that people can have."

Lead the students in brainstorming personal qualities, such as friendly, loyal, sweet, nice, kind, caring compassionate, creative, gentle, witty, cooperative, fun, honest, confident, humble, trustworthy, hardworking, industrious, benevolent, diligent, artistic, generous, economical, sensible, loving, patient, and tolerant.

Reflection

Ask the students to write down the qualities they think of as you read the following, allow them two to four minutes to respond to each question. You may wish to play music in the background. Say:

- Think about someone you admire. Write down the qualities you admire in that person.

- Think about your heroes. Who are they? Write down what qualities make them your hero or heroine.

NOTE TO EDUCATOR

If some of the students mention negative qualities or actions as something they admire in people or their heroes, acknowledge their responses respectfully with actively listening. For example, "So you admire _____ when he _____." Then ask: "What value or quality do you see in him/her that allows him/her to do that? (For example, "He is not afraid of what people think," or "She has courage to fight for what is right.")

- Write down the qualities you admire in your friends.
- Write down the qualities you like in some adults.
- Write down the six qualities that are most important to you. Six qualities that you think are most important for a person to have.
- It is said that any quality you admire is really yours. Write down six or more positive qualities that you have.

Allow the students to share in small groups of three or four for 15 to 20 minutes, each person taking a turn.

Homework suggestion: Ask them to read their list of six or more qualities to themselves every day. "Each person has wonderful qualities deep inside, and we can silently make them more present in our lives when we remember them."

End with the following relaxation exercise.

Garden of Respect Relaxation Exercise

"Sit comfortably and let your body relax. . . As you breathe slowly, let your mind be still and calm. . . . Starting at your feet, let yourself relax . . . relax your legs . . . stomach . . . shoulders, neck . . . face . . . the eyes . . . and forehead. . . . Let your mind be serene and calm . . . breathe deeply . . . concentrate on stillness. . . In your mind picture a flower . . . enjoy its fragrance . . . observe its color . . . enjoy its beauty. . . . Each person is like a flower . . . each one of us is unique . . . yet we have many things in common. . . . Picture a garden around you with many varieties of flowers . . . all of them beautiful . . . each flower with its color . . . each flower with its fragrance. . . giving the best of themselves. . . . Some are tall with pointed petals, some have rounded petals, some are big and others little . . . some have soft colors . . .

others have bright colors . . . some attract the eye because of their simplicity. . . .
Each one of us is like a flower . . . enjoy the uniqueness of each one. . . . Each adds
beauty to the garden . . . all are important. . . . Together they form the garden. . . .
Each flower has respect for itself. . . . When one respects the self it is then easy to
respect others. . . . Each one is valuable and unique . . . with respect the qualities of
others are seen. . . . Perceive what is good in each one . . . each has a unique role. . .
each is important. . . . Let this image fade in your mind, and turn your attention to
this room again."
— *Contributed by Amadeo Dieste Castejón*

RESPECT I LESSON 3
Problems of the World

Begin with a song.

Activity

Step 1. Ask the students to brainstorm the problems of the world. They might
generate ideas such as war, global climate change, terrorism, sex trafficking, drug abuse,
drug trafficking, poverty, etc. Use a whiteboard and write in a row all the problems they
call out.

Step 2. When the list is completed, ask them to choose one of the problems. Circle
that problem. Then ask what factors contribute to or cause that problem. List the factors
they call out in a second column. Note: The lists may not be mutually exclusive, for
example, poverty can be a cause of child prostitution and child labor, and it can also be a
problem in and of itself.

Step 3. Then make a third column and ask the young adults to call out which anti-
values contribute to each factor. (Such as greed, corruption, anger, racism, hate, violence,
disrespect, etc.) List in a third column, lined up with the original problem and factors.

Step 4. Now make a fourth column and ask them which values would help create
positive solutions to resolve the anti-values and factors contributing to the problem.

Step 5. As a class think of possible positive solutions based on those values that
would help resolve that problem. Many problems are years in the making because of the
deterioration of values. What are proactive or preventative things that could be done
with your age group to eliminate that problem developing in the future?

Small Group Activity

Step 6. Divide the class into small groups of four to five and ask each group to choose
one of problems they previously identified in Step 1.

Step 7. Ask them to do the same process that you did earlier with the entire class. They may choose to take up the problem the entire class did earlier. If there is time, allow them to research some of the realities of the global problem they have chosen.

Step 8. Ask them to develop one or more ideas of positive proactive solutions or positive preventative actions. Ask each group to prepare a presentation for the class. (They may need an additional period of time.)

Note to Educator: If they develop a passion for a particular topic, please allow them to research it and create a service project.

Close with one of the peace relaxation/focusing exercises.

Homework: Say, "Please continue with your homework of reading your qualities every day. I also want you to notice your tone of voice as you internally talk to yourself during the day. Check and see if your tone of voice is kind and respectful. It's important to encourage ourselves and be kind to ourselves."

RESPECT I LESSON 4

Making It Personal

Begin with a song.

Activity

Ask six young adults to stand in a row. Hand the first one in the row a pencil and ask her or him to hand the pencil to the next person, and so on down the line. Then, take the pencil and ask the first one in the row to hand the pencil to the person again, but this time handing the pencil with a lot of respect.

Ask:

- Was there a difference in the way the pencil was being given?
- How did you feel when the pencil was given with respect?
- How did you feel when the pencil was given with disrespect?
- What are different ways people give respect to each other? (List their answers to this and the next question on the board.)
- What are the different ways people "dis" each other, that is, give disrespect to each other? ("Dis" is common slang used by young adults.)
- How do you feel when that happens to you?
- How do you feel when that happens to other people?

Discuss the Reflection Points:

- ♦ The first respect is to respect my self — to know that I am naturally valuable.

♦ Respect is knowing others are valuable, too.

Ask:

- When do you feel good about yourself?
- When do you have a feeling of respect for yourself?
- When do you have respect for another person?

Students will sometimes mention specific things they do that are helpful to others as a time when they feel good about themselves. Confirm that when we do good things, we feel good about ourselves. They will often mention a time when they look pretty / handsome or have something new. If they are mostly focusing on times when they feel good when they look good or have something new, prompt for responses about how they feel when they are helpful, friendly, kind, giving, etc. Accept and acknowledge all responses.

Reflection

State the following, allowing two or more minutes for each item, and pausing for five or more seconds at the three dots. Play relaxing music during the activity if you wish.

- I want you to remember three times when you felt full of respect for yourself. What were you doing? . . . How did you feel inside? . . . It might have been doing something little for someone. Write it down. . . . Now, I want you to write down the quality you showed at that time.
- Now, remember a time when someone gave you respect. What did they do? . . . How did you feel inside?
- Now, remember a time when someone showed you a lack of respect ("dissed" you). What did he or she do? . . . How did you feel?

Share

Ask the students to form groups of three and actively listen to each other's stories and experiences. Please give them 15 to 20 minutes to do this. (Remind them of the agreement that all personal stories shared in class must be confidential, and not be retold to others.)

End with the following relaxation exercise.

I Am A Mountain Relaxation Exercise

"Allow yourself to relax and be aware of how you are feeling. . . . Take in a deep breathe . . . and release it, letting go of any tension. . . . Take in a deep breathe . . . and let the body relax. . . . Now visualize yourself as a mountain. . . . If you were a mountain what would that mountain look like? . . . . Would it be a large mountain? . . . Would it have lots of trees and foliage? . . . Would it have a granite cliff on one side? . . . . As you visualize yourself as a mountain . . . ground in your self-respect. . . . Think of two or three of your qualities or values. . . . You are stable . . . you are strong . . . you are powerful . . . . Breathe in and feel yourself to be like a mountain, stable, strong . . . connected to the beautiful Earth. . . . Sometimes in nature there are winds or rain or storms. . . . The rains are just rain, the wind is just wind . . . they do not affect the mountain. . . . Sometimes people are negative . . . they are like rain or wind when they are not happy with who they are at that moment . . . and don't know how to stay in their self-respect. . . . If there is sometimes a person who is like rain or a wind . . . ground more deeply into your self-respect. . . . Visualize the self as a mountain, stable and strong. . . . You are beautiful. . . . The rain and wind will not last forever . . . . Observe the rain . . . observe the wind . . . feel your quiet yet awesome strength. . . . As the rain stops, enjoy the warmth of the sun. . . . In the sunlight, across the valley, perhaps there are other mountains . . . family or friends. . . . Breathe in deeply . . . and relax. . . . I am a mountain. . . . I am connected . . . to me . . . to the Earth . . . to other beautiful mountains. . . . I ground in my self-respect . . . Breathe out and relax more. . . . Now . . . slowly bring your attention back to the room . . . feeling relaxed . . . and centered."

RESPECT I LESSON 5
Positive and Negative Self-Talk

Begin with a song.

Discuss/Share

Say, "Everyone talks to themselves inside. Our talk to ourselves can be positive and respectful or negative and disrespectful."

Ask:

- What types of thoughts help you stay in self-respect? (So, remembering your own qualities helps?)
- What positive or respectful things can you say to yourself?
- Would it be respectful to tell yourself you did a good job or tried your best, if you did do a good job or tried your best? (Yes.)
- What disrespectful things do people say to each other?
- Name calling is disrespectful. What names do you not want to be called?

- Is it disrespectful to call yourself a name? (Yes.)
- If you didn't do a good job, what would be a disrespectful way to talk to yourself about it?
- If you didn't do a good job, what would be a respectful way to talk to yourself about it?
- What do you say to yourself when you're afraid that you'll miss the ball during a ball game or fail a test?
- If you make a mistake, do you feel better if you call yourself "Stupid," or if you say, "It's okay to make a mistake, all I have to do is correct it"?[2]

Say, "There's no need to feel angry or sad or like a bad person when you make a mistake — mistakes are simply things through which we learn.

Ask:

- Does it help if you get angry at yourself?
- What happens to your emotions when you say, "I'll never be able to do it" or "I'll never make it"?
- Are the feelings different when you say, "This is a bit scary, but I'll do my best"?

Say, "The mistake rule is: It's okay to make a mistake, all I have to do is correct it."

Say, "You're all being asked to read or remember your positive qualities every day. We know we all have positive qualities, but sometimes when we get hurt, scared or angry, we don't use them. That doesn't mean we don't have those positive qualities, it just means that we weren't full of the strength of self-respect."

Discuss the Reflection Point:

- ♦ Respect is knowing I am lovable and capable.

Activity

Say, "Group story time. Do you remember the rules? Each person can say one, two or three sentences — no more — and then the next person continues the story. In the first group story, I would like you to create a story about someone who uses negative or disrespectful self-talk." As the facilitator, you can start: "One day there was a _____." Or, ask a student to begin. Allow the students to continue to go around until everyone who wishes to do so has contributed to the story. (Have a good time! The story can be ridiculous and create a lot of laughter.)

---

[2] Thomas R. Bingham's <u>Program for Affective Learning</u>.

Now do another group story, asking the young adults to use only positive or respectful self-talk.

Expressive Activity

Write a thought and feeling chain of positive self-talk versus negative self-talk. Starting from a mid-point on the paper, the positive chain can create an upward spiral and the negative chain a downward spiral. This can be done as an individual exercise.

End with a relaxation/focusing exercise of your choice.

RESPECT I LESSON 6

Disrespect, Discrimination and Advice

Play a song on respect as the students enter.

Discuss/Share

Write the following Respect Reflection Points on the board and discuss them.

♦ When we have respect for the self, it is easy to have respect for others.

♦ To know one's natural worth and to honor the worth of others is the true way to earn respect.

Ask:

• Why do you think people show each other disrespect?

Explore the reasons generated. You may wish to add the following: "Sometimes people give disrespect or are mean because of their own unresolved feelings of inadequacy and anger; deep inside there is a lack of love and respect for the self. They attempt to overcome that by feeling better than someone else — in order to feel better about themselves. Often these types of people have been treated with disrespect or others have been mean to them."

"Often people who give disrespect don't know better — they are ignorant. Sometimes people give disrespect because they have been taught to disrespect others because of their race, country, wealth or even their body weight."

Ask:

• How do people discriminate in our society? Do the rich get more respect than the poor?

• How else do people discriminate?

- Can anyone think of a time when they saw this happen? Can anyone give us an example?
- How do you feel about that? Do you think it is fair / kind /nice?
- What would you like to happen?
- What do people give respect or disrespect for in our school / place?
- What would you like to happen in our space?

Say, "One of the Reflection Points is: Those who give respect will receive respect." Ask:

- Can you think of examples of that?
- If you were in charge of this school / organization, what advice would you give to people who give disrespect?
- If you were in charge of a company, what advice would you give to people who give disrespect?
- How would you like people to treat each other?

Creative Activity

Step 1. Invite the students to form small groups and discuss how they would like people to treat each other, and the core values and qualities behind those behaviors.

Step 2. Ask them to create a slogan around those qualities or values. Provide the materials for each small group to artistically present their slogan.

Step 3. Invite each group to share their slogan and post it around the room.

Step 4. Ask if they would like to adopt living those slogans during this class.

End with the Garden of Respect relaxation exercise.

RESPECT I LESSON 7
Two Birds and Differences of Opinion

Begin with a song.

Read the following story by H. Otero or another story about a person taking offense because of a difference of opinion.

Share a Story: Two Birds

Two birds were very happy in the same tree, a willow tree. One of them rested on a branch at the highest part of the willow; the other one was down below, where one branch joined another.

After a while, the bird perched in the highest part of the tree said, to break the ice, "Oh, what beautiful green leaves these are!"

The bird resting on the branch below took this statement as a provocation. He replied in a curt manner, "Are you blind? Can't you see they are white?"

The one in the highest part, upset, answered, "It's you who is blind! They are green!"

The other bird, from below with his beak pointed upward, responded, "I bet my tail feathers they are white. You don't know anything."

The bird at the top felt his temper flare up and, without thinking twice, he jumped down to the same branch as his adversary to teach him a lesson.

The other bird did not move. The two birds stood eye to eye. They were so close; their feathers were ruffled with rage. In their tradition, they both looked above before they started the fight.

The bird that had come down from above said with much surprise, "How strange! Look at the leaves, they are white!" And he invited his friend, "Come up to where I was before."

They flew to the highest branch of the willow tree and this time they said together, "Look the leaves, they are so green!"

Discuss/Share

Discuss the story. Ask them if they can think of instances when conflicts arose due to poor communication or a difference in perception.

Discuss the Reflection Points:

◆ Respect is knowing others are valuable, too.

◆ To know one's worth and to honor the worth of others is how one earns respect.

Activity

Step 1. Invite everyone to close their eyes and think of their favorite color. Tell them that you will be giving them directions in accordance with their favorite color. They are to follow the directions, and stay in the position indicated until they are asked to open their eyes again. Say:

• If your favorite color is blue, stand up and keep both arms at your sides.

• If your favorite color is purple, stay in your seat and put both hands on top of your head.

• If your favorite color is yellow, stay in your seat and hold up both arms.

• If your favorite color is red, stand up and put your right hand out.

• If your favorite color is green, stand up and sway back and forth. Keep doing that please!

- If your favorite color was not named, stand up and keep turning around.
- Everyone, please open your eyes and look around you.
- Ask with a smile: "Do you all have the same favorite color?"

Step 2. Share: "I could have asked you to do these things in accordance with your favorite food, music group or political party. I asked you to do this as some people think that everyone should have the same opinion or they can't be friends or have a have a friendly conversation. It is okay for people to have different opinions and preferences. We are all different people and we have a right to a different opinion. Sometimes people want others to have the same preference as them."

Ask:

- Do you feel like that sometimes — that you want other people to feel the same about things as you do? Why do you think people feel that way?
- Are there other reasons why people feel that way?
- People feel differently about foods, music, political parties — what other things do people feel differently about?
- What other things might they have different "favorites" about?

➢ Record their answers on the board. The students might mention, depending on their age, things like: type of food, games, video games, television programs, favorite sports, sport teams, music, clothes, hobbies, hair styles, heroes, political parties, gender preference, or religion.

Step 3. Ask:

- Using the value of respect, what can you do when someone is expressing an opinion different than yours? (One answer would be to listen; another would be to say, "Cool", "Oh, that's interesting, tell me more," or "Why do you feel that way?" Help them generate respectful comments and questions and allow them to come up with answers appropriate for their age.)

Step 4. Say, "Let's practice listening with respect. Remember to stay okay with your own favorite when someone else has a different preference. We can all have different likes and dislikes and still have respect for each other."

Divide the students into groups of four. Two students are to be the Talkers, and two students are to be the Observers who can also serve as "alter egos", that is, supporting the Talker in listening and talking with respect. Ask the Talkers to pick one of the topics written on the board, taking different sides, and tell the other Talker about why that's their favorite.

Step 5. Ask the Observers to tell the Talkers how they did in terms of listening and speaking to each other with respect. Then instruct them to repeat the activity, changing roles so that the Observers get a chance to be the Talkers.

Discuss/Share

- Was it difficult or easy to listen with respect?
- Was everyone able to stay okay inside even when the other had a different opinion?
- If you weren't able to stay okay inside, what was going on?

Say, "Very often people become best friends with people who share the same favorite things. But everyone can be at least civil with everyone when there is respect for others as human beings."

Ask:

- Why is civil discourse important in a society? (Civil discourse can be defined as the ability to discuss things in a respectful manner or to engage in a conversation to enhance understanding.)
- Some people call others names or are violent when they don't like the opinions or view of others. What could that lead to?
- What can civil discourse lead to?

Allow the discussion to continue in the direction of their concerns and the situation in your country. Discuss sensible methods to approach challenges.

Mind Map

Briefly mind map respectful dialogue versus disrespectful dialogue so the large consequences of this difference in approach can be clearly seen. As usual, you the facilitator are to ask the questions for the mind map and the students are to supply all the answers.

Smile at the students and say, "Each one of you is far more important than you know. Your smile, attitude and words can create a positive difference."

End with the following relaxation/focusing exercise.

Star of Respect Relaxation Exercise

"Think of the stars . . . imagine the self in the silence the stars seem to radiate.
They are so beautiful in the sky, they sparkle and shine . . . quiet and peaceful. . . . Be

very still. . . . Relax your toes and legs. . . . Relax your stomach . . . and your shoulders. . . . Relax your arms . . . and your face. . . . Feel safe . . . and allow peace to surround you . . . . Inside you are like a star . . . peace is at your core. . . . You are capable . . . you are who you are. . . . Each person brings special qualities to the world . . . you are valuable. . . . Enjoy the feeling of respect inside. . . You are stars of respect . . . let yourself be quiet and peaceful inside. . . . Focus. . . . You are concentrated . . . full of respect . . . content. . . . Slowly bring your attention back to the room . . . feeling relaxed . . . focused . . . and ready to be at your best."

RESPECT I LESSON 8
Conflict Resolution — with Respect

Begin with a song about peace, respect or belonging.

Discuss/Share

Ask:

- How's it going with living the messages in the slogans you've put up?
- How is it going with the conflict resolution?
- What's working?
- Are there times when it isn't working? Why?

Question as appropriate to the situation, respectfully, while carefully listening to their answers.

Activity

Step 1. As you did in Peace I Lesson 13, ask four students to volunteer for a conflict resolution demonstration. Two are to act as mediators and two are to pretend to have a conflict. However, this time ask the students to pay attention to staying in self-respect and giving respect to each other.

Before they begin the demonstration, ask:

- How can you show respect to each other during the conflict resolution exercise?
- Great. Can you think of other ways to show respect?
- Great. What about your attitude? Can people perceive your attitude?

Say: "Yes, attitude is easily perceived. So, breathe in, get in your self-respect, feel respect for the other person simply because they are valuable people, and begin."

Step 2. When one demonstration is finished, ask the four students to reverse roles.

Step 3. Ask the volunteers to share their experience.

Step 4. Ask the class in general:

- Is it easy to give respect if you are feeling full of respect?
- Is it harder to give respect to others when you're feeling bad about yourself?
- What values or qualities do you recognize inside yourself that make it easier to stay in self-respect?

Step 5. Pass out uninflated balloons to the young adults. Invite them to blow them up and write one value or quality on their balloon that helps them stay in self-respect.

Step 6. Play some fun music and invite everyone to hit the balloons around the room to each other — with respect.

Step 7. When the music/song stops, ask them to try on the value or quality on that balloon for the rest of the day as well as the one they first wrote on their balloon.

RESPECT I LESSON 9
Acting, Not Reacting — Communication Skills

Begin with a song about peace, respect or belonging.

Discuss/Share

Bring out the list of things people fight about that the teacher and young adults made during Peace Lesson 9.

Introduction: Say, "Very often conflict occurs when someone shows disrespect to someone else. Today we're going to take a look at the list we made during the Peace Activities of the things people do that cause conflicts/fights. Very often when people do the things that are on this list we get hurt or angry. We feel bad when people treat us without respect. But who defines you? . . . Do you define who you are, or does someone else? . . . You are the one that knows your qualities. If someone calls you something horrible, does that mean you are? No. Are you valuable human beings? Yes. Okay, let's look at this list in the light of respect — how to act and not react."

Take one item on the list, and ask:

- Would this have occurred if the person were showing respect?
- What would you advise/like this person to do instead? What would have been a better way to handle it?
- How could that person use the value of respect?
- What would the consequences of that be?

- Would the problem have occurred then?
- If the person that this was done to stayed in self-respect, how could he or she handle it differently — so the problem does not build?

➤ Help them problem-solve. See what alternatives they generate. Ask them to generate the consequences of hurtful and kind acts — both short and long term. Ask them to come up with several ways to handle the situation. Help them create sensible strategies. For example:

✯ When someone does something you don't like such as calling you a name, what are words you can use? What can you say that is firm, clear and yet not aggressive? Perhaps, "Hey, that kind of language is out — chill," to an acquaintance your age. Or, "I love you. Why are you saying that to me?" to a family member.

➤ Help them generate statements appropriate to their culture and situation.

➤ Teach the following formula. This is a good idea to use when somebody you know does something you do not like (such as gossiping, name calling, etc.).

✯ "I feel _____ when you _____ because _____."

Give a couple of examples, such as:

✯ "I feel bad when you talk to me about Marsha that way because she is my friend. I like you, and I like her, too. I think it's okay to like both of you."

✯ "I feel pressured when you keep asking me to smoke that because I already told you I'm not interested. I know what I want to do, and not do, and I want you to respect that."

➤ Ask the students to generate an example for each item you deal with, as appropriate. Take several more items from the list made during Peace Lesson 9 and ask the same four questions above, helping the students develop strategies.

Discuss the following Reflection Point:

♦ When we have respect for the self, it is easy to have respect for others.

Say, "In the examples we discussed, the talker is sharing their feelings and setting boundaries or limits, that is saying what they want the other person to do or not do.

Some people are uncomfortable sharing their feelings and what they want the other people to do or not do, because they're afraid the other person will get angry at them and not like them anymore. But then, sometimes they feel not cared about or understood by others because they haven't shared what they want. It's much easier to share how you feel and set a limit or a boundary if you stay in self-respect and come from a space of respecting the other person.

Role Play

Small group practice: Divide the students into groups of four and ask them to role play some of the examples or strategies or create new ones. Each person is to use at least one "I feel ____, " statement during the role play.

End with a relaxation/focusing exercise of your choice.

RESPECT I LESSON 10

Different Ways of Giving Respect

Begin with a song about peace, respect or belonging.

Discuss/Share

- ♦ Respect is knowing others are valuable, too.
- ♦ To know one's worth and to honor the worth of others is how one earns respect.

Ask:

- What are the different ways we give respect to adults?
- What are the different ways we give respect to nature?
- What are the different ways we give respect to objects?
- What are the different ways we give respect to common spaces?
- What can we do to help us stay in self-respect while we are doing the things we've talked about?

Ask the students to divide into groups to analyze one or two of the topics and make suggestions. They may wish to make explanatory posters.

— Contributed by Sabine Levy and Pilar Quera Colomina

End with the Star of Respect Relaxation Exercise.

RESPECT I LESSON 11
Relationships and Setting Boundaries

Begin with a song about peace, respect or belonging.

Discuss/Share

Ask:

- How do you know when relationships are okay?

- What feelings come up when relationships are good?

- What feelings come up when you feel something is wrong?

- If appropriate: Is it ever okay for someone to hit someone else? (There is an absolute answer for this one: No. Allow the students to really discuss this if this is of concern.)

- How can we use the value of respect in the different situations you have named?

- How can you positively set a limit or boundary, that is, communicate what you would like someone not to do, and what you would like them to do instead? (For example, "I love you to come over, but would really appreciate you calling me first." Or, "I don't feel like helping you when you talk to me like that. I'd appreciate another tone of voice.")

- What are situations in which it is being self-respectful to set a limit/boundary?

- Can you communicate a limit while internally staying in a place of peace and self-respect?

Share a Story

Option One: Ask students to share stories about situations related to someone not treating them with respect.

Option Two: Read a short story pertinent to peer pressure and the situation of the young adults with whom you work.

Option Three: Read the short story, "I Can't Believe I Did That" by Pam Depoyan, or another story to which you feel the students will relate. The former in a story about a normally well-behaved girl feeling bullied into doing something she doesn't want to do is appropriate for 10- to 14-year olds. The Joy of Reading Project kindly gave their permission to post this story on the international LVE site, www.livingvalues.net. You will find it under For Schools / Young Adults / Download Free Stories.

After the story, ask:

- Why do we sometimes give into peer pressure even when we know we don't want to do something or are uncomfortable?

Activity

Step 1. Instruct the young adults to generate difficult situations in relation to the above discussion. Form small groups and generate situations.

Step 2. Then role play using communication skills and limit setting. Ask them to communicate a limit while internally staying in a place of peace and self-respect. At the same time, maintain an attitude of respect for the other person.

Close with I Am a Mountain Relaxation/Focusing Exercise.

RESPECT I LESSON 12
Bullying No More — The Art of Distraction and Nonviolence

Begin with a song.

Lesson Content

Inform: Some police departments use distraction as a method to help them deal with domestic-violence disputes. Tragically, sometimes policemen and policewomen are killed when they are called to a home to intervene. Using planned distraction, this police department was able to reduce mortality. The example given was a policeman arriving as a couple were screaming and yelling. If the couple continued the argument after the police officer arrived, he would start talking about how tired he was, go into their kitchen and start rummaging through the cupboards to find a cup and some coffee. The couple would often stop their argument to follow him and ask what he was doing. One of them would usually help the officer make a cup of coffee. It changed the dynamics and decreased the level of violence.

When a person can stay calm and act in a non-threatening way, distraction can be useful as a method to decrease violence or the potential of violence. When people are fighting, fists are flying, hormones are pumping and peace and respect aren't anywhere in the picture. Trying to restrain someone can result in the helper being hurt, sometimes quite seriously. Joining a fight to stop it is dangerous and *never* recommended. For serious violence, the first action should be to withdraw to safety and call the emergency number for police intervention.

Living Values Education has activities for street children.   is part of a series of stories about a street-children family. Distraction as an art of nonviolence is introduced as a method to stop violence. In this story, Mohammed is 17 years old, Fred is 14 and Marion is 12. Marion is a girl. They are a street-children family. Tony and Keemen are two other street children who are their friends."

Read or ask one of the students to read the following story.

Share a Story: Crazy Like a Fox

Mohammed, Fred and Marion decided to visit Tony and Keemen after their workshop at the street-children school. As they walked down the alley, they heard Tony's voice shouting, "You want to steal something? You thieves. I'll give you something!"

"Let's go," said Fred. Fred, Marion and Mohammed started running toward the sound of the yelling and fighting. Tony and Keemen were on the ground fighting three other boys as they rounded the corner. Fred, Marion and Mohammed stopped running as soon as they saw the boys.

"Hello, Tony. Hello Keemen," said Marion brightly.

"Hey guys, I got some tangerines. Want one?" asked Fred.

"You guys all look pretty good at what you're doing, maybe you can help us with our next play. We're doing it in the park on Saturday. How about it?" asked Mohammed.

"Yeah, it's a great play," said Marion. "Have you seen it, Tony? How about you, Keemen?

"I think they would fit in really well in the second act, don't you Mo?" asked Fred. "You know, right after that terrific song."

Tony and Keemen had paused. The three boys they were fighting looked up, surprise and puzzlement on their faces.

"Well," said Mohammed, "do you think you could do this in one of our plays? It's a great scene."

"Are you putting me on?" asked one of the three strangers.

"Are you crazy?" asked one of the other boys.

Fred pulled out the tangerines, "Anyone want a tangerine?"

Tony started laughing. He reached his hand up for a tangerine.

Mohammed looked down at one of the three boys who were strangers. He offered him a tangerine and sat down beside him. He started to peel another for himself. "Being a street kid is hard enough without us fighting each other."

"These are the guys that stole our guitar!" said Keemen, anger rising in his voice.

"Okay," said Mohammed. "Let's be human beings for a minute and listen. These are our brothers. They probably had a real good reason for doing what they did. Do you know their story?" He looked at the boy who had accepted the tangerine. "My name is

Mohammed. I bet you had a real good reason for taking the guitar. Would you like to share your story?"

The boy looked at Mohammed and shook his head. Another said, "Let's get out of here." The three jumped up and ran, but one paused before he rounded the corner and gave Mohammed a little nod, still holding the tangerine he had accepted in his hand.

"What's the matter with you?" Keemen asked Mohammed. "With you two we could have beat them up. I t would have been four against three instead of two."

Mohammed looked at him in silence. He slowly ate his tangerine.

Fred said, "Great tangerine, Mo."

"Yeah, Mo, thanks," said Marion.

"I don't get you guys," said Tony. "You come and help and then don't help us beat them up."

"But we stopped the fight, didn't we?" smiled Marion. "Distraction as an art of nonviolence."

Tony started to eat his tangerine and Keemen sat and just looked at them. His eyes looked like he was trying to understand something new.

"Do you want to be like them?" asked Mohammed quietly.

"I don't know what you're taking about," said Keemen.

Mohammed was silent.

"I don't want to be like them," said Tony.

"What happens when you fight?" asked Fred. "They beat you up, you beat them up. They knife you, you knife them. They shoot you, you shoot them. It only gets worse. Gangs are like that. They just gradually kill each other off."

"What comes around goes around," said Mohammed.

"But how do you stay alive if you don't fight?" asked Keemen.

"You use your head," said Fred. "You got to be smart to survive on the streets. But to do better than survive is possible. You can create beauty. You can help others to see their beauty."

"Are you crazy?" asked Keemen.

"Crazy like a fox," smiled Marion.

Translator Note: A fox is considered clever in English. Please put in the name of an animal or mythical character which is considered clever in the culture of the students.

Discuss

Ask:

- What did Fred, Marion and Mohammed do instead of joining the fight? (They said hello, offered them tangerines, and said that the fight would fit into a drama they were doing at the park.)
- What methods did they use? (Distraction. Staying peaceful. Giving respect to all. Not taking the side of one over the side of another.)
- What other things do you think people could do to avoid fighting and create dialogue instead?
- In the story, Fred explained why they did not join the fight: "They beat you up, you beat them up. They knife you, you knife them. They shoot you, you shoot them. It only gets worse." Have you seen or read of examples of that?
- Mohammed said: "What comes around goes around." What do you think that means?
- What values did Fred, Marion and Mohammed use?

Inform: Distraction can be used as to tool to stop low-level fighting and bullying, if you are comfortable doing so — and it is safe. Your protection is acting in a clearly nonthreatening manner. You are de-escalating tension, not increasing it. "

> Say, "I'd like one of you to read out some examples of distracting things to say, then I'll ask you to make up some of your own." Ask one or more students to read the following.

When someone at a distance is bullying someone you know — Call out to the target in a loud voice:
- ✮ Dana, could you come over here? I need your help right away!
- ✮ Hey, Dana! Mr. Murphy (name of a teacher) wants to see you right now!
- ✮ Dana, have you seen Mrs. Tey? I can't find her anywhere!
- ✮ Hey, did you see the really cool _____ Sam has?
- ✮ Hey, guys, is that a snake over there?

When someone close by is bullying someone you know — Call to the target:
- ✮ I can't find my phone! Have either of you seen it? If I lose it my father's going to be soooooo upset. I'll probably be working for a year to get another one. Have either of you lost your phone? Have you seen mine? Harry, would you help me look for it?
- ✮ Hey, have you guys seen that really cool new movie, _____? The part I like best was _____.

⭐ Did you see the raccoon over by room 3? Awesome! Today it was just one, but the other day I saw one with two cubs....

⭐ Do either of you remember what Mrs. Rami said about the _____?

To strangers:

⭐ Do you know where _____ is?

⭐ Excuse me. I'm trying to find _____.

Activity

Divide the students into small groups and ask each one to select a situation that they would like to portray, and generate statements, questions or dialogues which could work as a distraction and allow them to be safe. Facilitate a learning process, helping them learn how to be safer in their local setting. Discuss their concerns and help them generate some practical, non-violent solutions.

End with a respect relaxation/focusing exercise.

RESPECT I LESSON 13
Nonviolence — Keeping Your Head in the Face of Danger

Begin with a song.

Read or ask one of the students to read the following story.

Share a Story: Samosas and Peace in the Face of Danger

Nelson, Marion, Joe, Fred and Mohammed enjoyed putting on the AIDS skits at the park on Friday nights and at the community center on Saturday nights. The teacher thought that it was making a difference. Joe had a part in the play and was happy that he was part of helping. After the play, they walked home — a bit tired but happy. "Do we have enough money for something from the vendor tonight?" asked Joe. "I'm hungry."

Marion whispered to her younger brother so only he could hear, "That was a nice way of asking, Joe. You have learned to ask without whining. Wow!"

Nelson said, "I think this is your lucky night, Joe. Fred and I had lots of customers today."

Their favorite vendor stall was just up the street from the big tree. They had just reached the big tree and were just beginning to eat the hot corn on the cob and the samosas (Translator Note: Please substitute a common local hot food that is not expensive.) when the feeling of danger intruded. Two youths came up out of the dark shadows with knives in their hands.

110

"Give us all your money," one said in a menacing tone.

"Quick," added the other. "Or you'll be sorry."

Marion took in a sharp breath. She tried to stay calm. What if they hurt Joe? She didn't move. Just stay peaceful she told herself. Be still. Be peace. Give peace. Be still, she repeated to herself. Be peace. Give peace.

The others must have been doing the same. Mohammed and Fred had trained them well.

Mohammed said quietly, "We just got some hot food from the vendor. We have enough to share. Would you like some?"

"Just give us your money," said the first youth in a threatening tone of voice.

"You look a little hungry," said Fred softly. "Please, do sit down and join us."

Joe surprised Marion, "You can have mine," he said. "My sister always shares with me."

"I'm not taking no food from a little kid," said the first youth angrily.

"It's a little cold out and the food is hot," said Fred. "Where are you from? Have you been living on the streets long?" Fred lifted up a samosa. The second youth grabbed it and stuffed part of it in his mouth. He wolfed down the samosa hungrily.

"It's tough living on the street. It's good you have each other as friends," said Mohammed.

"You guys are really strange," said the first youth and he sat down. He put his knife on the ground. "I'll have one too."

"Great," said Nelson. To the other youth he said, "Here, have another."

Marion smiled to herself as the boys started to chat. She had seen this happen many a time. But it worked. It always worked. Their street-children family must have more friends than anybody, she thought. When they treated others how they wanted to be treated — it seemed they were protected.

After the two youths left, fed by the warmth of the food and the company, Marion asked, "Mo, does that always work? It always seems to work out when you're around."

"Well," said Mohammed, "I guess I'm lucky. I avoid trouble if I can. I think if you can truly stay peaceful and give them real respect almost all people come around. I think people get all nervous inside when they are about to rob you and are threatening you. So, if you get nervous or scared or angry it makes them feel more nervous. That's when they can get violent. If you don't get all scared — but stay peaceful and steady . . . and they don't feel threatened . . . then they usually calm down."

"That's the hard part," said Nelson, "staying all peaceful inside — and not losing your head."

"Yes. If you can stay peaceful then your head works better. Then you can watch them. Be steady inside. You got to use your head and watch them — make sure they aren't wound up too tight," Mohammed said thoughtfully. "If they are too high on drugs and crazed — and have a knife or gun in that state — sometimes the best thing to do is to run. See how they are first. But if they get crazy or are mean through and through (Translator note: "through and through" means completely mean.) the best thing to do is run. Most people miss when they shoot when you're running."

"Another reason to eat well and not take drugs," laughed Marion, "so you can run fast."

"Great samosas and corn," said Fred with a little light in his eyes. "I think I'll run up and get some more. Imagine, we still have our money!"

"Great," said Joe with a happy laugh.

Discuss

Ask:

- What did Marion think to herself to stay calm when the two boys with the knives appeared? (Just stay peaceful. Be still. Be peace. Give peace.)
- What do you say to yourself to keep calm or stay in your respect in difficult situations?
- What did Mohammed say happens with him when he stays calm and gives respect when someone threatens him? (The threatening one calms down.)
- What things can someone safely do to give time to others to calm down?
- What did Mohammed say happens when you get nervous, scared or angry at the threatening one? (It makes them feel more nervous. That's when they can get violent. If you don't get all scared — but stay peaceful and steady . . . and they don't feel threatened . . . then they usually calm down.)
- What did Mohammed suggest doing if they get "crazed" or are mean through and through? (Run.)
- What other things can you do to stay safe?
- When did Mohammed say your head works better? (When you can stay peaceful.)
- Have you ever had anyone threaten you before? How did you feel?
- What happens when you get scared or angry? Would anyone like to tell a story about that?
- What can happen when the threatening person gets angrier or more scared? (They get more dangerous and likely do something that is more violent.)

- Have you ever seen anyone stay calm in a dangerous situation and have it get better?
- What can you do better when you stay calm? (You can think better.)

Explain: "Your brain has a thinking part and an emotional part. The cortex, the thinking part, stops working when your emotions get all excited. If you stay calm and full of respect for yourself and the other person — your mind will be able to think clearly. When you can think clearly, you are more likely to be able to get out of a dangerous situation."

Ask:

- What are the dangerous situations that you have encountered or are likely to encounter on the streets around here?

Activity

Step 1. Divide the students into small groups and ask them to think about a situation they have encountered or are afraid of encountering.

Step 2. Invite them to create a beginning scene and then role play three different ways to respond to the situation:

a. with anger;

b. with fear; and

c. staying calm and using their head.

Part of staying calm and using their head may be knowing when it is time to flee or protect themselves in another way. Ask them to apply a value if they can!

Step 3. Facilitate a learning process, helping them learn how to be safer in their local setting. Discuss their concerns and help them generate some practical, non-violent solutions.

End with a relaxation/focusing exercise.

RESPECT I LESSON 14

Dealing with Difficult Situations
with Peace and Respect

Note to Educator: The following eight situations provide students with the opportunity to discuss various alternatives in dealing with real life situations. "Situation Six" allows students to make up their own situation.

Many classes really enjoy this activity as it provides another forum for students to discuss their real concerns, and apply the practical skills they have been learning through the values activities. The teacher is to act as a facilitator. Avoid moralizing and telling them what they "should" do. (Sometimes this is difficult.) Instead, listen and encourage them to respond.

Ask them about the consequences, both positive and negative, when their answers are appropriate and inappropriate. They will end up teaching themselves and each other. If their answers continue to be inappropriate ask them how they would feel if they were the other person. Ask them to role play the situation, and then exchange roles. Ask the class if a "fair" solution has been generated.

Activity

Step 1. Read Situation One to the class and encourage them to generate responses. Additional questions are:

- What do you think would happen then?
- What else could you say or do?

Step 2. Read another situation or two and enjoy the class discussion.

Step 3. Then allow students to form small groups and discuss further situations. The students can take turns reading the situations and giving oral responses or role play the solutions. If the groups find one situation difficult, the class can share their solutions and discuss it as a whole group.

Situations

Situation One: An acquaintance has told you that someone else has been saying awful things about you. What they have said is not true.

Ask:

- How do you feel?
- What could you do?
- How can you apply the value of peace?
- If you decide to talk with him or her, what would you say?
- What can you say to the "acquaintance?"
- How can you apply the value of respect?

Act it out.

Situation Two: Your Mom is a single parent. She has been working long hours at her job. She always seems to be in a bad mood and it feels like she never has time for you. You are spending more and more time with your friends, but there's a nagging feeling that perhaps you could do something to improve the relationship with your mom.

Ask:

- How do you feel?
- What are different things you could do?
- Which value(s) would help? How?

Situation Three: Two of your friends are really angry with each other. They are not talking to each other now, but both of them are talking with you. Now one of them is pressuring you to not talk to the friend with whom she (he) is angry.

Ask:

- How do you feel?
- What can you do? What might help?
- If you decide to talk with the one who is pressuring you, what would you say?
- What value would help resolve the situation?

Act it out using the "I feel" formula.

Situation Four: Another student at school is being rude and mocking you.

Ask:

- How do you feel?
- How could you respond using the value of peace?
- How could you respond using the value of respect?

Act out your responses.

Situation Five: Your best friend's father has just died.

Ask:

- How do you think your friend feels?
- What can you do to help him or her?
- Do you think your other friends could help too? How?

Situation Six: Make up your own situation.

Situation Seven: You've just failed an important exam.

Ask:

- How do you feel?
- Are you still a good person? (There is a "right" answer to this question: YES.
- How would you have liked to do on the exam?
- What can you do next time to do better?
- What kinds of things do you say (to yourself) that discourage you?
- What kinds of things can you say (to yourself) to encourage yourself?
- What other things can you tell yourself to "keep this in perspective"?

Situation Eight: There is a student in your class who sometimes criticizes you. He or she has just criticized you again.

Ask:

- How do you feel?
- What value(s) will help you resolve the situation?
- What thoughts can you say (to yourself) that will help you stay in self-respect?
- What could you say to the criticizing person while staying in self-respect?

Act it out.

Extension Activity

Students can make up their own situation cards and later exchange them with other groups.

— Contributed by Trish Summerfield

End with a song or a relaxation/focusing exercise.

RESPECT I LESSON 15
A Me Tree

Begin with a song.

Instruct each person to make a tree in which she writes her personal qualities and talents in the roots, the positive things she does in the branches, and successes of those things in the leaves and fruits. The trees could be drawn on paper or made of other available materials. Each student could share his or her drawing in a group of five or six, the other students listening with respect and perhaps adding things that the creator had not included.

— Contributed by Sabine Levy and Pilar Quera Colomina

Close with a relaxation/focusing exercise.

RESEPCT I LESSON 16

Respect for All

Begin with a song.

Activity

Step 1. Ask students to remember and share good experiences they have experienced with mates, family and other people they have made contact with during the week. Listen to them with respect and consideration.

Step 2. Read the poem Peace of Mind by Robert M. Hensel from Spain. You may also wish to share other poems from your country or culture.

> **Peace of Mind**
>
> Carry me out to the ocean,
>
> where my drifting thoughts flow free.
>
> Guide them to a far distant land,
>
> that only the mind can see.
>
> There I shall paint a great portrait,
>
> of what this world should be.
>
> A place without senseless wars,
>
> and human poverty.

Step 3. After reading the poem, reflect on the statement:

- ♦ Recognizing the uniqueness, wonder and beauty of our own being enables us to treat ourselves, others, animals and nature with consideration and care.
- ♦ There are many forms of life. All deserve our respect, compassion and love.

Step 4. Invite students to come together in groups of three and produce poems, drawings, songs, mind maps and prose on the theme of respect for all.

Step 5. Invite each group to share their creation with the class.

— Contributed by Paulo Barros

RESPECT I LESSONS 17

How would respect effect the Sustainable Development Goals?

Begin with a song.

Lesson Content

"The 2030 Agenda for Sustainable Development, adopted by all United Nations Member States in 2015, provides a shared blueprint for peace and prosperity for people and the planet, now and into the future. At its heart are the 17 Sustainable Development Goals (SDGs), which are an urgent call for action by all countries — developed and developing — in a global partnership."

Source: https://sustainabledevelopment.un.org/

The 17 sustainable development goals (SDGs) to transform our world:

Goal 1: No Poverty

Goal 2: Zero Hunger

Goal 3: Good Health and Well-being

Goal 4: Quality Education

Goal 5: Gender Equality

Goal 6: Clean Water and Sanitation

Goal 7: Affordable and Clean Energy

Goal 8: Decent Work and Economic Growth

Goal 9: Industry, Innovation and Infrastructure

Goal 10: Reduced Inequality

Goal 11: Sustainable Cities and Communities

Goal 12: Responsible Consumption and Production

Goal 13: Climate Action

Goal 14: Life Below Water

Goal 15: Life on Land

Goal 16: Peace and Justice Strong Institutions

Goal 17: Partnerships to achieve the Goal

Activity

Step 1. Invite the students to form the same groups they were with during Lesson 15 in the Peace I unit on SDGs. Ask them to work on the same SDGs that they did in that previous lesson. Are there other SDGs that no one included last time that would be positively affected by respect? Gender equality, for example, might be one. Allow the groups to add any SDGs that they feel would be affected that were not previously chosen.

Step 2. Ask each group to create purple Respect Leaves on specific ways respect would affect the SDGs they had selected.

Step 3. Invite each group to present their Respect Leaves to the class. They may also present a song or a poem about their findings if they wish.

Step 4. Invite each group to attach their purple Respect Leaves to the class artistic presentation of the SDGs which already has the green Peace Leaves.

Close with a relaxation/focusing exercise.

RESPECT I LESSON 18
My Qualities

Begin with a song.

Discuss the Reflection Points:

◆ Part of self-respect is knowing my own qualities.

◆ Respect for the self is the seed that gives growth to confidence.

Activity

Pass out paper to everyone. Ask each student to write her or his name at the top of the paper. The objective is for the students to pass around the paper, each writing the quality he or she sees in the person whose name is at the top. Everyone's paper should be passed to everyone else before being returned to the rightful owner. Allow the students to read their list of qualities for a minute or two in silence before continuing.

Discuss/Share

- What did you learn during the respect unit?
- What would you like to do with what you learned?

Listen to their ideas. Would they like to do something with what they learned inside or outside the school? Would they like to create a video about the importance of respect for social media? Would they like to encourage people to be able to have more civil dialogue? Would they like to create an assembly for their peers or younger students?

Expressive Activity

Create a respectful world commentary and paint a respectful world in the state of self-respect and respect for others. Or, put on music and dance respect for a few minutes, then disrespect, then respect, then peace. Perhaps perform a couple of the favorite songs or skits.

End with the Garden Image Relaxation/Focusing Exercise.

Respect Activities in Subject Areas

Language/Literature

Throughout the week, the teacher might quietly approach each student and note one of the student's qualities.

Young adults in literature class may read and contrast stories of people with self-respect and people without regard for the self. Discuss different aspects of the story. Some of the following questions may be pertinent.

- How did the characters give disrespect?
- How did the protagonist feel?
- How would you have felt if that happened to you?
- How could the other characters in the story have given respect?
- What would you have liked to do if you were there?

Read stories of your culture's heroes.

Discuss one or more of the Respect Reflection Points every day. Write poems or essays on these points.

Respect for Friends: Discuss the Reflection Point: Everyone in the world has the right to live with respect and dignity, including myself. Create a cartoon or a story on respect for friends, or write an essay.   — *Contributed by Marcia Maria Lins de Medeiros*

Ask students to list as many adverbs and adjectives as they can think of to describe positive traits of human beings. Ask each student to select from each list eight characteristics that describe him or her. Use those words in a written description of the self.

Divide the group into small groups. Keep the lists of positive adverbs and adjectives on the board. Ask each student to recognize and state three qualities in every other student in the small group.

Write a poem or an essay expressing feelings and reactions to respect or disrespect.

Add to the list of Reflection Points using favorite sayings from your culture, from legends, or quotes from respected individuals.

Write a personal or experiential essay addressing the following:
- What makes you respect your friends?
- What makes you respect certain adults in your life?
- What qualities do they have that you respect?
- What causes a loss of respect?
- When do you respect yourself the most?

Instruct students to write a short story on the difference someone made in their life, how they made a difference for someone else, or a story on the person they interviewed.

History/Social Studies

Look for examples in history or social studies lessons currently being studied, identifying ways governments or cultures give respect and disrespect. Correlate the different practices with economic development, distribution of wealth, education for all and/or human rights for all.

Science

Imagine that you live in a world where humanity respects all the peoples of the world as well as all animals and the environment. Ask, "What type of things would you create? What would you not create?"

Think of 10 ecological practices you can do to show respect for the environment.

Art

Paint respect. Perhaps add a theme that is especially important in your school or community . . . or a need you see in the world.

Discuss respecting your own art work and that of others. List qualities that can be seen in your work and in the work of artists throughout history. Each period of art has its own qualities and worth. Ask, "How can we maintain our self-respect as artists?"

Make a collage or wall hanging about who you are. Include symbols of what you believe in, your favorite pastimes, your qualities, perhaps your favorite foods and animals. Make it bright or subtle, big or small, dramatic or conservative, plastic or adorned with feathers.

Collect articles and pictures about people who have made a positive difference and make a collage.

Drama

Make up a skit on respect and disrespect.

Music

Ask students to bring in songs about respect. Play them in the group.

Home Economics / Home Sciences

Explore the theme of homemakers of the world being the keepers of the world — those who nurture and who are the first teachers. Look at the importance of the role of homemakers and caregivers. Ask, "How do they maintain self-respect?" Ask students to identify four values important to homemakers and caregivers. Stay in the feeling of self-respect while doing the homemaking assignment.

Physical Education / Dance / Movement

Discuss respect for our own body and what that means. Discuss how we take care of the body.

Discuss the rules of good sportsmanship — of having respect for other players and other teams. Discuss the statement: Those with respect always give respect to others. Ask, "If you could create any type of league you wanted, what would your relationship be with the other players and the other teams?" Ask students to observe their team's words and actions the next time they compete.

Have a group dance, with each dancer being fully aware of maintaining self-respect and having respect for every other dancer. Ask, "What happens to your eye contact and hand motions? What is your experience?"

LOVE

UNIT THREE: LOVE AND CARING

Love and Caring Lessons

Love is at the core of the human being and an essential part of our human experience. Nurturing love in the home helps children thrive. Educators are valued and prized by untold millions around the world as providers of not only knowledge but love, and creators of nurturing, caring and safe places to learn.

In this updated book, we have retitled the Love Values Unit as the Love and Caring Values Unit. While caring and kindness are always part of love, in some cultures it is easier to talk about love by using the word "caring". Please feel free to use the word that you feel is most appropriate for your culture or the culture of the young people with whom you work. You may simply wish to substitute the word "caring" for "love".

Songs: Play songs about love, caring, belonging or harmony each morning as students are entering class or at the beginning of values time. Pick out songs about love which students like or ask them to select songs. There are lots of wonderful songs and videos of young people singing on YouTube. Some students enjoy learning traditional songs.

Please include a relaxation/focusing exercise during "values time". Many students greatly value this time to relax and "be", hence you may wish to do one daily. You may wish to use relaxation/focusing exercises from the Peace and Respect units. All of the exercises can be found in the Appendix.

Love and Caring Reflection Points

- In a better world, the natural law is love; and in a better person, the natural nature is loving.
- Universal love holds no boundaries or preferences; love emanates to all.
- The real law lives in the kindness of our hearts. If our hearts are empty, no law or political reform can fill them. — *Tolstoy*
- Self-love is not selfish; you cannot truly love another until you know how to love yourself.

- If you are gentle with yourself, you can be gentle with others. If you are harsh with yourself, your harshness will spill onto others.

- When you care for yourself, you will naturally be able to care for others.

- To love yourself is to accept yourself unconditionally.

- To love yourself is to understand you don't need to be perfect to be good.

- To love yourself is to know you are naturally good.

- A flower does not think of competing to the flower next to it. It just blooms.

- The opposite of fear is love.

- Love is not simply a desire, a passion, an intense feeling for one person or object, but a consciousness which is simultaneously selfless and self-fulfilling.

- Our task must be to free ourselves . . . by widening our circle of compassion to embrace all living beings and all of nature. — *Albert Einstein*

- Love can be for one's country, for a cherished aim, for truth, for justice, for ethics, for people, for nature.

- Love is the principle which creates and sustains human relations with dignity and depth.

- Love means I can be kind, caring, and understanding.

- Love is the basis for a belief in equality and goodwill toward all.

- When we feel strong inside, it's easy to be loving.

- Love is a catalyst for change, development, and achievement.

- Love is seeing each one as beautiful than the next.

- Real love ensures kindness, caring, and understanding and removes jealous and controlling behaviors.

- No one is born hating another person because of the color of his skin, or his background, or his religion. People must learn to hate, and if they can learn to hate, they can be taught to love, for love comes more naturally to the human heart than its opposite. — *Nelson Mandela*

LOVE LESSON 1
Imagining A Loving World

Begin with a song of love for humanity or love for the world.

Explore general concepts of love through questions and discussion:

Ask:

- Why is love important?

- Do you think love is a universal value? Why, or why not?

- Do you think love is a human need?
- Would it be a different world if everyone were loving or caring towards everyone else?
- What do you think it would be like?

Imagining a Loving World

Commentary: Lead the students in this imagining exercise, adapting it to your situation.

"Today, I would like you to think about someone who is loving and kind. It can be a real person in your life now, or a person who helped you before, or it can be a person that you have seen in the movies. Think about that person's attitude. . . . Picture that person helping. . . . Now, I want you to imagine that everyone in the world was that loving and kind. . . . What would the world be like?. . . . Step into your imaginary plane of the mind, and fly through the blue sky. . . . Imagine leaders of different nations and how they would treat each other. . . . How would they be with the citizens of their countries? . . . . Picture friends spending time together. . . . Imagine their faces as they have fun together. . . . Picture people in your neighborhood interacting. . . . See people in corporations . . . picture scientists and what they are working on. . . . Fly the plane over this country, and across the borders of nearby countries . . . now fly over this school. . . . Imagine what would be different. . . . Now the plane circles and lands, and you are relaxed and in your place here again."

Discuss/Share

➢ Give the students time to share in small groups what they pictured and experienced.
➢ Allow each group to share a few of their comments with the entire group.

Discuss the Reflection Points:

♦ Love means I can be kind, caring, and understanding.
♦ In a better world, the natural law is love; and in a better person, the natural nature is loving.
♦ Love is the principle which creates and sustains human relations with dignity and depth.
♦ Love is the basis for a belief in equality and goodwill toward all.

Ask:

- How would the world be different if the natural law was love?
- In a loving world, would anybody be interested in war? Why or why not?
- In a loving world, what would the all leaders and rulers want for their citizens?

Activity

Ask the students to draw a symbol of a loving world or make up a poem. Invite those who wish to share to do so.

Close with a relaxation/focusing exercise.

LOVE LESSON 2
Mind Mapping "Laws"

Play a song about love for the world.

Say, "In one of the Reflection Point from the last lessons, it stated: In a better world, the natural law is love."

Ask:

- What types of laws do you feel we have in society or the world now? The law of love? The law of greed? The law of power over others? The law that the one with the most possessions wins?

- Encourage students to generate as many "laws" as they wish, writing the "laws" on the board. Acknowledge the problems and concerns that they perceive in the world.

Comment if there is cynicism: If you find the students are expressing a lot of cynicism, ask why they are cynical and/or state the following: Say, "Sometimes people your age are cynical. I think cynicism develops when someone really wants a peaceful world or a just world, a better world for all — and they are disappointed. So, in a way it means cynical people really care — they're just disappointed."

"You are the future generation. Other people have made the world the way it is now. What kind of world do you want? You need to deal with the present reality, but you are part of creating the future. What kind of world do you want? Each decision a person makes is choosing a value."

Activity

Divide the students into groups of six to eight and invite them to mind map the rules for the "law of love" and another type of "law" they have generated. Provide large pieces of paper so they can show their work. Save these for the next lesson.

Creative Activity

Ask each small group to create a song or poem about the law of love versus the other law they have mind mapped. Invite each group to share the "law" they have mind mapped and then perform their creation for the entire group.

LOVE LESSON 3
Values and Anti-Values Continuum

Begin with a song of love for humanity.

Discuss the Reflection Points:

♦ No one is born hating another person because of the color of his skin, or his background, or his religion. People must learn to hate, and if they can learn to hate, they can be taught to love, for love comes more naturally to the human heart than its opposite. — *Nelson Mandela*

♦ Universal love holds no boundaries or preferences; love emanates to all.

♦ Our task must be to free ourselves . . . by widening our circle of compassion to embrace all living beings and all of nature. — *Albert Einstein*

♦ The real law lives in the kindness of our hearts. If our hearts are empty, no law or political reform can fill them. — *Tolstoy*

Values and Anti-Values Continuum

Step 1. Ask the students to gather into the small groups they were in during the previous lesson and analyze the effects noted on their mind maps. Are these effects the results of values or a lack of values, that is, anti-values?

Step 2. Instruct them to write down the values and anti-values next to the relevant items on their mind maps.

Step 3. Gather all the students together as one group and draw a line several meters wide on the board, if possible. Facilitate the following process as you ask the questions below and write or have students help you write on the line, the continuum.

Ask, acknowledging their responses:

- This end of the continuum is the values end and the other end is the anti-values end. What values did you talk about in your discussion that you think are the most important?
- What other values did you discuss that you would like at this end of the continuum? Where shall we put them on the line?
- This end of the continuum is the anti-values end. What anti-values did you talk about in your discussion do you think cause the most harm? When you tell us the anti-value, please tell us why it causes so much harm. (Great answers.)

➤ Say: "Each group, please write your anti-value 'law' in large letters on a piece of paper and ask one member of your group to come to the front of the room to hold that piece of paper."

➤ Say: "Now class, please make your case for which 'law' should be nearest the anti-values end of the continuum." Ask the individuals holding the signs to change places along the continuum in accordance with the discussion about the effects of the "law". Actively listen to the discussion, acknowledging with respect all responses, and see if the group can reach consensus about the order of the "laws". Once the order is agreed upon, the persons holding the paper can write the law on the appropriate place on the continuum. It may be that they decide three out of four are equally negative, or perhaps they will come up with a line order.

Ask:
- What are the effects of the "law of love"? Invite the students to list some of the effects on the continuum, putting the most important toward the value end.

Ask:
- What part of the continuum reflects today's Reflection Points?
- What happens when the circle of compassion is very small or does not exist?
- How can we widen that circle of compassion?

Close with a relaxation/focusing exercise.

Homework: Invite them to look for and bring in songs, poems, symbols or pictures that represents widening a circle of compassion. Or, interview one of your favorite people and ask them about this topic. These items can be displayed when they bring them in; they will be used after a few lessons.

LOVE LESSON 4
Love for the Self

Begin with a song.

Discuss/Share

Note to Educator: As always when you ask questions, be mindful of the pacing. Allow several young adults to answer the question when they are eager to do so, then continue.

Ask:

- Do you think most people love themselves? Why or why not?
- What do you think makes it hard for some people to love themselves?
- What types of experiences make us feel not loved?
- What types of experiences make us feel loved?
- What types of experiences make it easy to love ourselves?
- What would the world be like if everyone loved themselves?

Share the Reflection Points:

- ◆ Self-love is not selfish; you cannot truly love another until you know how to love yourself.
- ◆ If you are gentle with yourself, you can be gentle with others. If you are harsh with yourself, your harshness will spill onto others.
- ◆ When you care for yourself, you will naturally be able to care for others.
- ◆ To love yourself is to know you are naturally good.
- ◆ To love yourself is to accept yourself unconditionally.
- ◆ To love yourself is to understand you don't need to be perfect to be good.
- ◆ A flower does not think of competing with the flower next to it. It just blooms.

Activity

Step 1. Divide the class into small groups and ask them to pick one or more of the Love and Caring Refection Points listed for this lesson.

Step 2. Ask them to discuss the points they have chosen and present a two to three-minute presentation from their small group about why that/those reflection points are true or not true and how to bring more love and caring into daily life.

Step 3. Invite each group to give their presentation.

Step 4. If there is time, invite each group to make and decorate a slogan and display it.

Close with the following relaxation/focusing exercise. Please read it slowly and play relaxation music, if possible.

Lovingly Accepting the Self Relaxation/Focusing Exercise

"Let the body be relaxed and still. Let go of thoughts about the world outside, and slow down within. . . . Allow yourself to be in the present, focusing on this moment in time. . . . Let the mind be still, and slowly absorb waves of peace. . . . Imagine being outdoors in a world where everyone is kind and caring. . . . Imagine a garden or a meadow . . . or an ocean or river . . . whatever you wish. . . . And in the picture of your mind imagine a world where everyone knows they are love . . . and are loved . . . and are capable. . . . Breathe in slowly and relax. . . . Let a light of love surround you. . . . Each child comes into the world with love and beauty. . . . Sometimes people around us forget to remind us of our love and beauty because they are stressed . . . or busy . . . or mean . . . or have too many burdens. . . . Or maybe they just don't have enough love inside themselves to let others know they are gorgeous and worthy of love. . . . I may not like what others do, but for now I let that go . . . and I go into the truth that I have love at my core. . . . (Please pause for at least eight seconds.) Allow yourself to breathe in love. . . . Allow yourself to know that you are good . . . you are worthy of love. . . . Lovingly accept the self . . . your positive qualities . . . and even your negative emotions. . . . Accept yourself exactly as you are. . . . Breathe in that loving acceptance of the self. . . . Each person comes into the world to bring a special gift of his or her qualities . . . and his or her talents. . . . Be still . . . quiet within . . . focused . . . and enjoy feeling full of love and peace. . . . As you begin to bring your attention back to this place . . . allow yourself to feel loving acceptance of yourself. . . . Wiggle your toes and move your shoulders . . . and bring your attention fully back to this place, fresh and alert."

LOVE LESSON 5

Dealing with Anxiety

Begin with a song.

Discuss/Share

Share: A lot of people experience anxiety. When we think of love and caring, we usually think that the opposite of love is hate. That is true. People can either love or hate something. But the opposite of fear is love.

Ask:

- Describe anxiety to me. What does it feel like emotionally?
- What does it feel like physically?
- Any other answers?
- How does anxiety interfere with life?
- How does it interfere with thinking?
- Do people with anxiety worry?

Activity and Lesson Content

Step 1. Divide the class into small groups and ask them to make a list of the things which people their age have anxiety about.

Step 2. Ask them to go through the list as a small group and decide which ones they can do something about and which ones they cannot do anything about.

Step 3. Ask:

- Can you let go of the things you can't do anything about?
- If not: What is a thought you can think of that will counter/decrease your anxiety?

Step 4. *Present Lesson Content on common ways to decrease anxiety.*

- ❖ Breathe and become present.
  Take deep slow breaths and count from ten to one, visualizing yourself as a balloon with too much air with the excess pressure being released as you gradually count down. Let the pressure of fear go and turn the remaining air in the balloon into love. Love dissolves fear. Invite them to practice this with you.
- ❖ Make a list.
  Make a list of the practical things you need to do to make a task about which you have anxiety to be more manageable. Building a wall is done one brick at a time, one row at a time. Divide the task into manageable units. If the anxiety is great, make it ten minutes at a time and make the environment pleasant. Would music help you work? What positive thoughts would help?
- ❖ Eat.
  Make sure you are not hungry when you are tackling a stressful task. Eat something healthy. Sugar will make your anxiety worse in 20 minutes.

❖ Move.

Dance for three minutes or do 50 jumping jacks and then do the task. While doing that, tell yourself: I can do this. I am good. I can do this. I am good.

❖ Positively affirm you and your values.

If you are feeling anxious about what someone thinks of you or has said about you, think of one of your favorite values. For example: I am one who believes in peace. What goes around, comes around. When I stay in my values, everything will be okay.

❖ Talk to a friend or a loving responsible adult if something is troubling you.

❖ Communicate.

In today's world, a lot of people are stressed, and when they are stressed, they put pressure on others. For example, sometimes people your age feel that parents or other adults put a lot of pressure on them to succeed. In response, people your age sometimes feel that they are not measuring up when they are not meeting those expectations and they feel they are not good enough. Sometimes when a parent is adding pressure, it may be useful to tell them how you are feeling and suggest a behavior that would be helpful. Example:

"Mom, it doesn't help me when you yell at me about studying. It would help me if you just gave me a hug and told me, 'I know you can do it.'"

Ask:

• What other things might you say to a parent to point to a more helpful behavior than what they are doing?

Step 5. Ask them to come up with short skits about different situations people their age feel anxious about. Perhaps in the skit, one person voices an anxiety and two or three others help him or her deal with it by sharing a different perspective or breathing with them, etc., or one plays the young adults and another the parent.

Close with the following relaxation/focusing exercise.

Dissolving Stress with Love Relaxation/Focusing Exercise

"Be aware of your surroundings . . . be mindful of your emotions . . . and take in a deep breath of the light of love. . . . As you exhale, let any tension go out the bottoms of your feet. . . . Breathe in the light of love . . . breathe out any tension through the bottoms of your feet. . . . As you breathe in the light of love, let your muscles relax. . . . Sometimes we experience stress or tension or anxiety. . . . Be aware of where you hold that in your body. . . . Now breathe in the light of love . . . relaxing that area . . . and lovingly accept your emotions. . . . Perhaps that area has a dull gray light. . . . Accept that gray light and know that sometimes fear makes us doubt our ability or our worth. . . . Let the light of love begin to surround that area of gray . . . and begin to dissolve the edges. . . . I am good . . . I am worthy of love . . . I am worthy of respect . . . all will be well. . . . I acknowledge my goodness . . . and the vulnerability of myself . . . and all others. . . . Each of us desires peace . . . and love . . . and sometimes we are not sensitive to our own needs . . . or the needs of others. . . . The light of love surrounds all of me . . . and this area of gray . . . and that area of gray becomes smaller. . . . I lovingly accept my stress and my beauty. . . . I now let the light of strength mix with the light of love. . . . I am capable to facing my challenge. . . . I have the strength to stay in the present and enjoy doing one thing at a time. . . . I am loving, I am strong, I am powerful . . . I am light. . . . Breathe in . . . and now gradually bring your attention back to this space, feeling light and refreshed."

LOVE LESSON 6
Advice to the Self

Begin with a song.

Discuss/Share

♦ Real love ensures kindness, caring, and understanding and removes jealous and controlling behaviors.

♦ Love is a catalyst for change, development, and achievement

Ask:

• What do you love in yourself?

• How can people be loving or kind to the self?

• How is your self-talk going?

• What kinds of things can people say to themselves when they are discouraged to encourage themselves?

• Is there anything you would recommend avoiding if you wanted to be loving to the self?

Activity

Write a short letter to yourself, saying what you appreciate about yourself and giving yourself your best advice.

— Based on a contribution by Marcia Maria Lins de Medeiros

Close with one of the relaxation/focusing exercises from the last two lessons.

Homework: Do loving good deeds at home for a week. Give your brothers or sisters an extra hug every day, spend ten minutes a day playing with a sibling, sew a tear in a torn stuffed animal, share your dessert, or _____?

LOVE LESSON 7

Widening the Circle of Compassion

Begin with a song.

Discuss/Share

The Reflection Points:

♦ Love is the principle which creates and sustains human relations with dignity and depth.

♦ Love means I can be kind, caring, and understanding.

♦ Love is viewing each one as more beautiful than the next.

Share Homework: Ask the young adults to share with the class the songs, poems, symbols, pictures and/or stories about widening a circle of compassion that they brought. There is time in the next lesson for sharing more of those.

Ask:

• What would a place feel like if it always had a circle of compassion?

• What do you think about widening the circle of compassion in our school/at school/at our facility?

• What do you think are some things that could be done?

• What problems do you see that the value of love would take care of?

• Would you be willing to try an experiment for a week?

Accepting Environment Experiment: Tell the students that you would like them to experiment with something — to create the feeling of a circle of compassion at school. It might be in the form of maintaining good wishes for everyone. Or, of simply accepting everyone.

Activity

Ask them if they would be willing to create a completely accepting environment at school; to be aware of others and create an atmosphere where everyone feels they belong. Ask what they can do to create such an environment. They may suggest being sensitive or helping others, being mindful of words or using positive or encouraging words with everyone. Encourage them to express their ideas on how to achieve this.

Ask:

- Do you want to try this just in our classroom and with those of us in this class or would you like to experiment with this with everyone in the school?

Make a plan.

End the lesson with the following Relaxation/Focusing Exercise. You may wish to say, "Many people around the world live in difficult circumstances. The new relaxation/focusing exercise is one in which we send love."

Sending Love Relaxation/Focusing Exercise

"Allow yourself to be aware of how you are feeling at this present moment. Be aware of your breath and any tension in your muscles. Let yourself be surrounded by the light of peace. Breathe in the light of peace and relax. . . . Breathe out any tension. . . . Breathe in the light of peace and let that peace sink into your muscles. . . . You are a peaceful and powerful light . . . full of love. . . . Be a star of peace for a few minutes and send love to people all over the world. . . . Let the self be full of loving energy. . . . We can all send love and peace any time we want. . . . Concentrate on increasing the experience of the light of love . . . let the self relax more. . . . As you relax, that love will automatically extend to people all over the world. . . . Let the body relax more. . . . Take in more love. . . . You are focused . . . you are contributing to a better world. . . . Let the mind be still . . . . Now, move your shoulders, wiggle your toes and bring your awareness back to your surroundings."

LOVE LESSON 8

Listening with Love

Begin with a song.

Share Homework: Ask the young adults to share with the class the symbols, poems, songs, news articles and/or stories about widening a circle of compassion that they brought.

Discuss/Share

Ask:

- How is the experiment going?

- What is going well?
- What do you like about it?
- Have you noticed a difference?
- Is there something that someone did that really stood out for you?
- Is anything difficult?
- If there are difficulties, ask: What might help with that challenge?

Discuss and problem solve regarding any difficulties.

Note to Educator: If someone complains that she or he does not want to be "best friends" with someone else, the following statement is appropriate: "Accepting or having good wishes does not mean that everyone has to be your best friend. They can stay acquaintances. It means you are not rude or rejecting on the outside, and have clear or positive feelings for them on the inside. A simple smile, a hello, or a nod, and good feelings communicated through the eyes — wow — that alone would create a great, and accepting, atmosphere."

Activity

Step 1. Mention to the students that in an earlier lesson, they practiced listening. Today, you want them to think of a time someone really listened to them. Ask if anyone would like to share a story about a time when someone really listened to them.

Step 2. Ask the students to form groups of three with others they do not know very well. One student is to share something she enjoyed doing when she was younger, or something that interested her. The other two students are to listen. They then exchange roles, giving each person a chance to share.

Step 3. Invite each person to share one or two qualities, values or virtues they observed in the person to whom they listened.

Close with a relaxation/focusing exercise of your choice or play a song and move with the music.

Homework: Listen to someone in your family and stay full of love as you listen. Listen to an adult one day and to a sister or brother another day. Listen to a friend.

— Contributed by Marcia Maria Lins de Medeiros

LOVE LESSON 9

Conflict Resolution and Love

Begin with a song.

Discuss the "Accepting Environment Experiment."

Ask:

- How did it feel?
- Was it easy to maintain good wishes?
- What helped?
- Are you happy with the results?
- Would you like to continue the experiment for another couple weeks?
- Are there any changes you would like to make? If so, what?

Discuss the ideas, and make a plan as a group. Try for consensus.

Activity

Step 1. Invite the students to form small groups of five or six and to make up three Situation Cards about current or imagined conflicts.

Step 2. Ask one of the groups to role play the situation using the conflict resolution skills in the Peace 1 unit.

Step 3. At the end of their conflict resolution role play, ask them to think about the value of love and come up with a loving action that would have stopped the conflict at an earlier stage or prevented it altogether.

Step 4. Ask all the groups to create a short skit about a conflict relevant at school or in the neighborhood. Ask them to introduce a "freeze-and-replay" element into the skit — in which the actors return to the actions and words in the play when the conflict started and when a loving attitude would have affected the outcome. They are then to inject that loving attitude into the replay.

Step 5. Invite each group to perform their skit for the class.

If another problem arises the next day or week, ask them to have a "replay." Ask, "What was the starting point of the conflict? How will a loving attitude change the outcome?"

Close with the Lovingly Accepting the Self Relaxation/Focusing Exercise.

LOVE LESSON 10
Love is Kindness — and Social Media and Suicide Link

Begin with a song.

Discuss/Share

Discuss the following Reflection Point: Love is caring, love is sharing.

Ask:

- What helps people feel cared about in our classroom?
- What helps people feel included or that they belong?
- How do you think people feel when they feel left out?
- How does it feel when everyone in the class is valued and safe?
- Is there anything you would like to suggest that would make our classroom a kinder place? (Follow-up on their ideas as appropriate.)
- What are kind things we could do in our school, in the community or at home?
- What percentage of the time do you see kindness in social media postings?
- What do you see that you feel is harmful?

Inform: "In recent years, the numbers of young people being depressed has increased. Suicide rates for young people eleven years old and older have also increased. Some of this is attributed to negative attacks on social media. Suicide is always a tragedy and is never ever an answer.

Love and kindness are essential food for all human beings. Being a teenager or a young adult is hard already, as at this age people are trying to figure out who they are and self-doubt is common. I think it is really, really important to support each other and be kind."

Ask:

- Your comments, thoughts?
- Have you or a close friend been affected by meanness on social media?
- How do you recover from that?
- What kindness guidelines would you like everyone to use on social media?" (Actively listen to their experiences and allow them to discuss what is currently happening locally.)
- What would you advise others your age to do when they are reacting to something mean that someone did and are tempted to respond with meanness?

Activity

Social Media Guidelines: Invite the students to form small groups and discuss what kindness guidelines they recommend for young adults. Invite them to create posters and present their creation to the class.

Close with a relaxation/focusing exercise.

LOVE LESSON 11
Trust, Friendship and Helping Those with Suicidal Thoughts

Begin with a song.

Discuss/Share

Talk about the following Reflection Points:

♦ Love is being a trustworthy friend.

♦ Love for others means I want what is good for them.

Lesson Content

Comment: In our last lesson we spoke a little about the fact that many young people struggle with depression and that suicide rates are increasing even for children as young as eleven. Attempting suicide can be a cry for help or an effort to get intense emotional pain to stop. Love and emotional support from friends is incredibly important. Suicide is never the answer.

Ask the following questions, actively listening and validating as appropriate.

• Do you know someone who has committed suicide?

• *If the answer is yes:* Is there anything you wish you had said to them? (List their replies on the board.)

• What would you like to say to any young person thinking about suicide? (List their replies on the board.)

• When someone is considering killing themselves, what kinds of things might they say to others?

• What would you like to tell them?

• I'm going to say the things that we have listed on the board. Thumbs up if you think this would help you feel better. (Read the list created during the second question and/or third question above.)

• What else can we do to help when someone is thinking of hurting themselves?

Allow them time to really talk about any concerns. Depending on the situation, friends can also apply the methods discussed earlier — listening, good wishes, identifying their good qualities. Other things to do to help follow.

❖ Listen to their concerns and offer loving support.

❖ Tell them they are valued and loved.

❖ Tell them you will support them through this and things will get better.

❖ Give them hope. Let them know that they can feel very differently about things soon.

Activity

Ask them to draw a picture of what happens when people die. Allow them five to ten minutes to do so, calling time when almost all of them are finished.

Discuss/Share

Ask:

- What happens when people die? (If there are students of different religions in the room, listen respectfully to those of each religion.)

Comment: "In some traditions, the body of the person is buried, in other traditions the body is cremated." (Add what happens in other traditions if there are different rites that have been mentioned.) "So that is what happens with the body."

Ask:

- Is there another part of the human being? (Even children of eight will say yes, there is a spirit or a soul. Accept whatever term they say and use it in the rest of the discussion.)
- What happens to the spirit/soul? (Accept all answers with respect.)
- Which part of the human being feels emotions, the body or the spirit/soul?

Lesson Content Comment: "Yes, it is the spirit/soul that feels. **If someone kills themselves, they won't feel better, they will feel the same way.** So, it is very, very important to live. People's view of what is happening changes. It is very important for people to know that things can and will change, and they will feel better again. It is also important for people to know that you love them and they are important."

Share Information: Some students have a common misperception that part of being trustworthy is to hide information from adults when a friend is in serious trouble. Friends who are trustworthy also want what is good for their friends. That means if a friend is in serious trouble, one should take action to help. This would mean contacting a a responsible adult if suicide is a concern or if the person has a plan for killing themselves.

Ask:

- Who could you tell or call for help? (Help them come up with a few appropriate people they could contact. This may include their parent, the parent of the friend, a teacher, a school counselor or psychologist, the local emergency number or . . . ?

❖ Don't be sworn to secrecy — confidentiality doesn't ever apply to suicide.

Ask:

- How would you feel if you didn't reach out for help and your friend killed him or herself?

❖ Stay with the person if you consider the risk of suicide to be high or try to arrange that someone to be with them while they get through the immediate crises.

Creative Activity

Instruct the students to form small groups of five to eight and create a song or poem about the importance of living.

Close with a relaxation/focusing exercise.

LOVE LESSON 12
Appreciating the Self

Begin with a song.

Discuss/Share

Ask, actively listening as appropriate.

- Is love the natural nature of children?
- Is love your natural nature?
- What do you think makes some people hardened, not able to feel their love?
- What would our behavior be like if we experienced love in our minds all the time?
- If you could feel any way you wanted to any time you wanted to, what value or feeling would you like to feel?
- What kinds of things can you do that create those feelings?
- What kinds of things can you say to yourself to help you feel this way?

Share a Story

Read the short story or ask the students to read "Ginger Beer" by Louise Johnstone. This is a story about being belittled, forgiveness and appreciation of the self. The Joy of Reading Project kindly gave their permission to post this story on the international LVE site, www.livingvalues.net. You will find it under For Schools/Young Adults/Download Free Stories.

Small Group Activity

Step 1. Invite students to discuss any of the questions in small groups of four or five, making a list of thoughts and a list of actions that promote the feeling of staying valued and full of love — or another feeling or value they would like to feel.

Step 2. Ask each person to write a sentence of appreciation about each other person in the small group, noting a positive quality, action or value. Each person is also to write two sentences of appreciation for the self. This can be on one piece of paper or on small slips of paper.

Step 3. If there is time, paint an abstract picture of feeling valued and full of love on one part of a sheet, and feeling inadequate or angry on another part.

Close with a relaxation/focusing exercise of their choice. Ask them if they would like to experiment with a relaxation/focusing exercise on forgiveness. This can be found in the Appendix.

LOVE LESSON 13

Understanding and Managing Depression

Begin with a song.

Lesson Content

Share: We human beings are interesting. We all need to be loved. Sometimes people of all ages feel sad because they don't feel they are loved or respected. We all like to be loved and respected and we all like to be successful. Yes?

When people feel sad or low for a few weeks and don't feel like they want to do their usual activities in life, that is what is usually called being depressed.

Depression is a major concern around the world, affecting about 300 million people at a time, according to the World Health Organization. There are mild, moderate and severe degrees of depression.

"The Diagnostic and Statistical Manual of Mental Disorders (DSM-V) defines a **major depressive episode** as at least two weeks of a depressed mood or loss of interest or pleasure in almost all activities, as well as at least five other symptoms, such as:
- Sleep issues on an almost daily basis (either difficulty sleeping or sleeping too much)
- Changes in appetite and weight (change of more than 5 percent body weight in a month) or a decrease or increase in appetite nearly every day
- Decreased energy or fatigue almost every day

- Difficulty concentrating, making decisions, and thinking clearly
- Psychomotor agitation or retardation that is observable by others (slow physical movements or unintentional or purposeless motions)
- Recurrent thoughts of death or suicide, a suicide attempt, or a specific plan for suicide"

To be considered a major depressive disorder, "the symptoms must cause significant distress or impairment in a person's social, occupational, or educational functioning. There's no single cause of depression, according to research. It can be the result of brain chemistry, hormones, and genetics, as well as life experiences and physical health.

'A great deal of mental health conditions are both preventable and treatable, especially if people start looking after their mental health at an early age.'" (Mr. Guterres)

Source: https://www.verywellmind.com/depression-statistics-everyone-should-know-4159056

Share a Story

Read "Can I catch it like a cold? coping with a parent's depression" by the Centre for Addiction and Mental Health. The Joy of Reading Project kindly gave their permission to post this story on the international LVE site, www.livingvalues.net. You will find it under For Schools / Children Ages 8–14 / Download Free Stories / Happiness 8–14.

Discuss/Share

Invite the students to discuss the story, ask any questions and share whatever they wish. Actively listen and validate as appropriate.

Share: We all feel sad sometimes. Sometimes we are reacting to something someone said that was mean, or feel sad about a friend moving away or another loss. That is completely normal. But to have a persistent feeling of sadness and feel down for a couple of weeks at a time, to the extent that it is causing a change in sleep and an inability to think clearly and not wanting to do anything is considered depression.

Usually people who tend to get depressed have a negative view of themselves, others or the world. So, one of the things we can do, and are doing during these lessons, is to develop an ability to see our own qualities, values and strengths.

Ask:
- We all feel sad sometimes. Yes?

- How can we make ourselves feel better when we are sad? (Reinforce concepts learned/presented previously, such as talking to the self in an encouraging and kind way, knowing that you are lovable and capable, talking with a friend, doing relaxation/focusing exercises and surrounding yourself with love, telling a safe adult about the difficulty, eating healthy foods, etc. Please write them down on the board, repeating each suggestion as it is written.)

❖ Daily exercise also helps. 30 minutes of walking a day helps the neurotransmitters in the brain rebalance when they get out of balance with negative thinking or too much sugar.
❖ Eating healthy foods is a wonderful way to avoid getting depressed. Refined sugars rob your body of needed B vitamins.
❖ Another thing we can do when we are feeling sad if to lovingly accept our emotions. When we accept what we are feeling, we are accepting the self. If is important to love the self and to accept the self.

Ask:
- When you are feeling sad, what have others done that help?
- Do you have any other ideas about how friends or family could help when you or someone else is depressed?
- What doesn't help?
- Do you like to receive a friendly smile?
- Would you like a friend to listen to you if you wanted to talk?
- If you don't want to talk, do you want them to tell you that you must talk? (No)
- Would you sometimes like a hug from a special friend?
- Would you want people to include you and just act normal around you?
- Is there anything else you would like people to do or not to do?

Activity

Ask the students to write a journal entry, essay or poem on "When I am feeling sad, it helps me feel better to . . ." Invite those who wish to share their poems, or a few ideas from their journal or essay.

Play some relaxing music and close with the relaxation/focusing exercise below. You may wish to play this special healing music published by ZenLifeRelax on YouTube. It is a Solfeggio frequency of 528Hz. https://www.youtube.com/watch?v=tnKBUdVh02s

Taking Care of Me Relaxation/Focusing Exercise

"Let the body be relaxed and still. Slow down within. . . . Breathe in deeply . . . and as you exhale, begin to relax. . . . Be aware of how you are feeling. . . . Breathe in deeply. . . and relax as you exhale. . . . Are your arms tight or your chest? . . . . Is there a feeling of sadness or hurt inside? . . . Allow yourself to feel where you are holding emotion in your body . . . perhaps in your throat . . . perhaps in your chest . . . perhaps in your stomach . . . perhaps in your gut. . . . Breathe in deeply . . . and exhale slowly. . . . Lovingly accept your emotions. . . . Be in the present . . . and lovingly accept how you feel. . . . Pay attention to that feeling . . . accept it with love . . . and it will quiet down a little. . . . Surround your sadness or hurt with the light of love. . . . Visualize the light of love surrounding that pain . . . and feel that love. . . . Breathe in . . . and relax as you breathe out. . . . Let the mind be still . . . and absorb the light of love. . . . Perhaps that area of pain is getting smaller as you absorb the light of love. . . . Feel that light of love. . . . You are lovable and capable. . . . Breathe in slowly and relax. . . . Know you are lovable and capable. . . . Allow yourself to breathe in love. . . . Think for a moment of what quality or value would help you now. . . . Imagine that quality or value taking the form of a jewel and let that jewel appear in front of you. . . . It may be a jewel of love . . . or courage . . . compassion for yourself . . . or others . . . patience . . . or fearlessness. . . . You are a beautiful jewel. . . . You have the courage to be kind to yourself . . . and to live your truth. . . . Be still . . . quiet within . . . focused . . . absorb the light of love and peace. . . . Gradually begin to bring your attention back to this place . . . Wiggle your toes and move your legs . . . and bring your attention fully back to this place."

Close with a nurturing song of peace or love and invite everyone to stand up and move around the room with the song.

Note to Educator: An Additional Lesson on Depression and/or Suicide

If some of the students are concerned about depressed parents or friends, or the suicide of someone they know, perhaps take another period to allow them to draw a picture of what happened, discuss it, and ask any questions. You will need to lovingly and sincerely active listen to and/or validate their comments. Creating a safe and understanding space for them to share is important.

Share: "It is very important for people to know that they are important, they are good, they are special to you, they are loved — and that it is very, very, very, very important to not kill themselves. If anyone ever tells you that they want to kill themselves, please tell them how important they are, and ask them to promise not to kill themselves. Promise them that things will get better."

Also, it is essential to tell a responsible adult so they can get help."

Ask:

- Can we change things for the better if we are alive? (Yes)

Promise them that you will work with them with whatever the concern is to make it better. Know what resources are available and ask the school or organization for help from the school counselor, psychologist or social worker if needed — or an outside organization.

Expressive Activity: Invite them to paint their feelings. Allow them to share their artistic creations.

Close with the Taking Care of Myself When I Feel Sad Relaxation/Focusing Exercise.

LOVE LESSON 14
Dating Violence

Begin with a song.

Lesson Content

Inform: Today our topic is dating violence. Very, very unfortunately young people from 12 to 19 years of age experience the highest rates of rape and sexual assault. Dating violence may be emotional, physical, sexual or stalking. Many adolescent girls are subjected to physical, emotional or verbal abuse from a dating partner.[3] Dating violence is always wrong.

Let's read a story and then we can discuss it.

Share a Story: A Wolf in Sheep's Clothing

Read this short story or ask the students to read on line "A Wolf in Sheep's Clothing" by Kristine Elias. The Joy of Reading Project kindly gave their permission to post this story on the international LVE site, www.livingvalues.net. You will find it under For Schools/Young Adults/Download Free Stories Or, read "Real Men Do Not Hit" by Beatriz Moncó.

Discuss/Share

Allow them to share and actively listen and validate as appropriate. Ask:

---

[3] http://www.futureswithoutviolence.org

- Would anyone like to comment about the story?
- Do you know someone who has been subjected to physical, emotional or verbal abuse from a dating partner?
- Would anyone like to share?

Lesson Content

Inform: There is a usually a pattern in abusive relationships. Initially, the abuser is very nice. The first warning sign is that the abuser attempts to control the social activities of the victim. Beware if someone you are dating tries to control who you talk to and tries to keep you away from your friends. They may even try to get you to not like your friends by saying bad things about them.

Step One of the three-step abuse cycle: Tension builds. The abuser may call names or threaten violence. The victim may try to get the abuser in a good mood by avoiding the situation where the abuser gets upset.

Step Two of the three-part abuse cycle: Abuse. The tension grows and the abuser explodes with verbal and/or physical violence. Usually the abuser blames the victim, making it sound like it is her or his fault. "If you hadn't done _____, I wouldn't have _____."

Step Three of the three-part abuse cycle: Honeymoon Phase. The abuser excuses his own behavior, sometimes apologies and often says it won't happen again. He/she is usually extra nice and wants to be close. The steps then repeat.

Discuss/Share

Comment: Abuse is always wrong. The abuser tries to fool the victim into thinking that he or she is to blame. For example, "If you hadn't talked to him, I wouldn't have hit you." You have the right to speak to anyone. No one has the right to hit you.

Let's look at some Love and Caring Reflection Points.

- Love is the principle which creates and sustains human relations with dignity and depth.
- Love means I can be kind, caring, and understanding.
- Love is the basis for a belief in equality and goodwill toward all.
- When we feel strong inside, it's easy to be loving.
- Real love ensures kindness, caring, and understanding and removes jealous and controlling behaviors.

Ask:

- Comments? Questions? Thoughts?
- What is the first warning sign of an abuser?
- What are the three stages or steps of the abuse cycle?
- What would you like to tell all abusers?
- If you are in a relationship with an abuser how would you be able to exit safely?
- Where are safe places to go when you want to protect yourself from an abuser?

Activity

Step 1. Divide the class into small groups and ask each group to create a skit based on some the things happening locally, and role play what things they can do to avoid being trapped in a relationship with an abuser. Inform them that it is important to recognize the warning signs of an abuser and to leave the relationship as soon as possible.

Step 2. Invite each group to act out their skit/drama.

Step 3. Invite them to share their feelings.

Close with a relaxation/focusing exercise.

LOVE LESSON 15 — Optional

Trust, Friendship and Drinking and Driving

Note to Educator: This lesson may or may not be relevant to the culture or circumstances of the young adults with whom you are working.

Begin with a song.

Discuss/Share

The following Reflection Points:

- ♦ Love is being a trustworthy friend.
- ♦ Love for others means I want what is good for them.

Ask:

- What do you want in a friend?
- What makes a friend trustworthy?
- What makes us think we cannot trust someone?
- How do you show you are a trustworthy friend yet still do what is good for others?

Share: "Friends don't let friends drink and drive" incorporates the above two points. (Or, use an example that is relevant to your situation.)

Ask:

- Is part of trust helping your friend make good choices and helping them get the help needed when he or she is in danger?
- What can happen when friends drink and drive?

Share a Story – Choices

Read the short story or ask the students to read "Choices" on line by Makaila Fenwick. A true story about drinking and driving, Makaila's friend is killed. The Joy of Reading Project kindly gave their permission to post this story on the international LVE site, www.livingvalues.net. You will find it under For Schools/Young Adults/Download Free Stories

Ask:

- How would you feel if a friend died?

➢ *Comment:* Each one of you is very, very important. Your lives are precious. Take care of yourselves.

Note to Educator: If the young adults have known someone that has died because of someone being under the influence of alcohol or drugs and want to discuss it extensively, allow them to do so. Stay steady and actively listen.

Activity

Invite them to form small groups and make slogans to post. Or, perhaps a group would like to make a card or send a letter to the parents of one of the young people that was killed.

Close with a relaxation/focusing exercise.

LOVE LESSON 16 – Optional

Love Never Includes Abuse

Begin with a song.

Share a Story

Read the short story about abuse that you are familiar with or read or ask the students to read on line "Real Men Do Not Hit" by Beatriz Moncó. The Joy of Reading Project kindly gave their permission to post this story on the international LVE site, www.livingvalues.net. You will find it under For Schools / Young Adults / Download Free Stories

Discuss/Share

Ask:

- Why is domestic violence always wrong?
- How would you feel if your partner hit you?
- In an ideal world, how would you like all families to show their love to their partners and children?
- Would abuse of children exist in such a world?
- Is abuse of children ever right? There is a correct answer for this question: No. Abuse of children is never right.
- What types of abuse are there? (Yes, physical abuse like beating a child, sexual abuse, and emotional abuse.)
- What are the danger signals of a toxic relationship?
- What boundaries can you set when someone is behaving badly?
- Is each of you worthy of real love? (There is a correct answer to this question — "yes." If they say "no," discuss why or why not, but tell them each one is worthy of real love.)
- What does real love look like? How would a parent give real love?
- How would a boyfriend/girlfriend, husband/wife give real love?
- How can you give real love to others?
- How can you give real love to yourself?

Activity

Step 1. Form small groups and ask the students to generate several examples of inappropriate, toxic or abusive behavior they have encountered. They are to prepare a skit/drama of one of those situations and how it usually proceeds, then call a stop and re-play, enacting a protective strategy such as setting boundaries or another action to stay safe.

Step 2. Ask each group to present their skit/drama. After each skit, lead the applause. Then ask the audience if they have other ideas of other boundaries to set or other strategies.

Step 3. If there is time, ask all of them to enact another situation, doing steps 1 and 2 again.

Close with a relaxation/focusing exercise of their choice.

LOVE LESSON 17

Loving Relationships

Begin with a song.

Discuss/Share

Discuss the Reflection Point:

♦ Love is the principle which creates and sustains human relations with dignity and depth.

Ask:

- Think about the people you love and that love you for a few moments. . . . How do the people you love show they love you?
- People in different roles in the family often show their love different to different people. How do(can) different people in the family show love?
- How would you like to show love to your children if you were a parent?
- How can you show love to your family?
- What are the common ways we show love in all loving relationships?
- What are the effects at home of doing loving deeds during the week?
- What interferes with loving relationships? Does blame interfere? What else?
- Do put-downs help or hinder?
- Do constant corrections help or hinder?
- What helps?
- What else helps?
- What are you grateful for?

Lesson Input

Research by Dr. John Gottman shows happy couples have five times as many positive interactions as negative interactions. When there are more negative interactions than positive, divorce is usually the result.

This message is true for all relationships. Relationships thrive with positivity and become bitter, sad or full of anger with frequent negativity. The message: be positive, spend time with each other, tell each other what you appreciate.

If those you are in a relationship with are negative, then let's talk some more about how to limit that and keep safe. Comments or questions anyone? (Allow them time to share and discuss and explore boundaries and options. Actively listen and validate as appropriate.)

Activity

Step 1. Ask them to list ten things they are grateful for in life, including in their family. Begin each sentence with: "I am grateful for . . ."

Step 2. Ask them to reflect on very small positive actions they can do during the next week at home. What would a loving or caring thing be to do in your family? It might be simple things such as saying good morning if they are not already saying good morning, it might be helping make dinner or helping with something else.

Step 3. Write a card or a note of appreciation to someone you love.

Close with a relaxation/focusing exercise.

LOVE LESSON 18

How would love effect the Sustainable Development Goals?

Begin with a song.

Lesson Content

Goal 1: No Poverty
Goal 2: Zero Hunger
Goal 3: Good Health and Well-being
Goal 4: Quality Education
Goal 5: Gender Equality
Goal 6: Clean Water and Sanitation
Goal 7: Affordable and Clean Energy
Goal 8: Decent Work and Economic Growth
Goal 9: Industry, Innovation and Infrastructure
Goal 10: Reduced Inequality
Goal 11: Sustainable Cities and Communities
Goal 12: Responsible Consumption and Production
Goal 13: Climate Action
Goal 14: Life Below Water
Goal 15: Life on Land
Goal 16: Peace and Justice Strong Institutions
Goal 17: Partnerships to achieve the Goal

Activity

Step 1. Invite the students to form the same groups they were with during Lesson 17 in the Respect I unit on SDGs.

Step 2. Ask them to explore the effect of love on the SDGs they have already looked at in terms of peace and respect. Would love make a difference?

If everyone in one country had love for everyone else, what policies would be different, for example, on hunger and poverty? Do any more SDGs need to be added?

Step 3. Ask them to write specific ways holding the value of love and caring would affect the SDGs on which their group is focused and write those on green Love Leaves.

Step 4. Invite them to create a song or poem about love and the fulfillment of one of the SDGs. They may wish to contrast it with the lack of love and the current need.

Step 5. Invite them to share their Love Leaves and creation with the entire group.

Step 6. Invite the groups to attach their Love Leaves to the class artistic presentation of the SDGs.

Close with a relaxation/focusing exercise.

LOVE LESSON 19
If I could . . . Selfless and Self-fulfilling Love

Begin with a song and the Sending Love Relaxation/Focusing Exercise.
Discuss the Reflection Point:

♦ Love is not simply a desire, a passion, an intense feeling for one person or object, but a consciousness which is simultaneously selfless and self-fulfilling.

Ask:

• If you could pick anything to do in the world, and there were no barriers to doing it, what would you like to do that would be selfless and self-fulfilling at the same time?

• What kind of actions do you think might create those feelings?

Activity

Step 1. Invite the students to write a paragraph or two about their thoughts of doing something selfless and self-fulling in the world if there were no barriers of access or money.

Step 2. Invite the students to share their ideas. They could either share briefly to the entire class or in groups of eight to ten.

Step 3. Ask them to think of one thing they could do as a class that would generate benefit to others. The understanding is that when we are benefiting others, we create the feeling of being selflessness and self-fulfillment. Perhaps there is something they could do for a younger class or those in need. (Note: A real need in many schools and colleges is setting up a pantry with food items so that students can access food for themselves and their families.)

Step 4. Mention that when we do something selfless, it is also important to take care of the self. What things are they doing to take care of the self?

Close with a relaxation/focusing exercise of their choice.

LOVE LESSON 20
A Collage or a Skit/Drama

Begin with a song.

Activity Options

Option One: Allow students to work on the project they identified in the previous lesson.

Option Two: Divide the class in groups of ten to twelve and invite them to make skits/dramas of something they felt was important during this love and caring unit. It could be about preventing dating violence or a comedy about healthy and caring relationships. Invite them to share their skits. Are there groups that would benefit by seeing these skits/dramas?

Option Three: Ask students to write five sentences beginning with the words, "Love is . . . ." Use some of the shared symbols and pictures that they brought in earlier in the unit and those sentences to make a collage.

Option Four: While some of the students are arranging items for the collage on the board, others can design small cards on various qualities and values. Paint one side and write a sentence about the quality on the other side. Share them with your family and friends or on social media.

Close with a relaxation/focusing exercise of their choice.

Love and Caring Activities in Subject Areas

Language/Literature

Write a Love Reflection Point on the board every day for students to reflect on as they enter the room. Perhaps play a song on love during those few minutes. Discuss for a few minutes. Assign essays and continue to teach writing skills and develop vocabulary at the same time.

Literary Works

Invite students to think of characters in literary works they have been studying recently. What actions of the characters create a loving world, and what actions destroy?

Ask which of those characters they would like to join them in their world now, and why. Write a short essay on this topic.

Ask the students to bring in their favorite stories about people's love serving as inspiration to do something special. Allow them time to read a few passages.

Rainbow Flower

In Zimbabwe, Natalie Ncube's class of high school boys read the short story, Valentin Katayev's "Rainbow Flower." This story is about a girl who became lost and met an old woman. The old woman gave her a magic Rainbow Flower that could make any wish come true. The flower had seven petals, each allowing a wish. The girl wasted six of them and used the seventh, the last one, to cure a crippled boy.

Mrs. Ncube noted: "After the story had been read in class, the development of the girl's character was discussed. The pupils noticed that with the first six petals the girl's character deteriorated because of jealousy, envy, and unnecessary pride. Only when she was left with one petal, did she become more thoughtful and try to use the petal 'wisely.' While she was wishing for material things, she felt unhappy, dissatisfied and unfulfilled. When she saw the lame boy, many values emerged."

Follow-up Activities

Class Debate: Do selfish desires bring satisfaction and happiness in life? What is selfish and what is taking care of the self?

Draw a table of the negativities and virtues of the girl (or the central character in a story selected by the teacher).

Homework: Write a story, "What I would do if I had the Rainbow Flower." Draw the Rainbow Flower and write your words on the petals.

Different Kinds of Love

Ask students to generate a list of different types of love (paternal, maternal, fraternal, romantic, platonic, universal love, love for humanity, love for animals, love for nature, love for your country, etc.) Ask students to read short stories on at least three kinds of love and then write a couple of poems depicting at least two types of love.

Discuss the Reflection Point:

- ◆ Love can be for one's country, for a cherished aim, for truth, for justice, for ethics, for people, for nature.

Romantic versus Platonic Love

Relate "romantic love" and "platonic love" to works recently studied in literature, or refer to classics, or literature, or oral stories from the culture of the students.

If the teacher is comfortable, ask the students what they think the rules of platonic love should be now. What do they think the rules of romantic love should be? What should people never do? (This is an opportunity to confirm that any violence toward a boy or girl friend is wrong.) How old do they think people should be when they get married? (Students usually give answers older than one would expect!) What are the advantages of waiting to get married? (Students have more time for school; with a better education they can provide more for their families, etc.)

The Chaser

Read "The Chaser," Part One. Draw attention to the words: "Young people who need a love potion very seldom have five thousand dollars. If they had, they would not need a love potion." Ask: "What do these cynical words tell us about the old man's attitude towards love?"

Discuss: "Can money buy love?" "What is real love?"

Continue the discussion after playing the songs, "Can't Buy Me Love" by the Beatles and "As Long As You Love Me" by Back Street Boys.

To conclude the lesson, the undersigned teacher brought the attention of her young adult students to the words from Deepak Chopra's book *Ageless Body, Timeless Mind*: "Being unattached means that you are free from outside influences that overshadow your real self. This lesson isn't something our culture teaches. Most people place higher value on being committed, excited, passionate, deeply involved and so forth, failing to realize that these qualities are not the opposite of non-attachment.

To be committed to a relationship, ultimately means having the love and understanding to let the other person be who they want to be. The paradox that is to get the most passion from life you must be able to stand back and be yourself. Finding your own freedom is necessary and it involves letting go of expectations, pre-conditioned outcome and egoistic point of view."

— Contributed by Natalie Ncube

Love Is Letting Go of Fear

Ask the class to read a book about love. The teacher may want to read excerpts from Gerald Jampolski's book, *Love Is Letting Go of Fear*.

Debate one or more of the Love Reflection Points.

History/Social Studies

As the class reads about different cultures, the teacher can point out different ways of showing love. Have a discussion, asking students to point out how love is shown in different cultures.

The Principle of Love

Pose these questions to the class:

- What differences would there be in the world if all governments operated on the principle of love?
- How would the current government change in our country if everyone in the government operated from the principle of love for all?
- How would we change if we operated from the principle of love for all?
- There is the saying: There is enough for man's need, but not for man's greed. How would you create fairness for all?
- What are a few things we could do that would reflect this love and fairness for all?

Science

Love has played an interesting role in science. At times it has been one person's love for another which motivated a person to research a disease and find its cure. It has been humanity's lack of love which has led to the invention of horrible instruments of war.

Ask:

- What other examples of love and science can you think of?
- Is there a role for love in science?
- Do scientists have a moral responsibility for what they create? Why or why not?

Art

Slogans

Do the Imagining a World of Love exercise in Love Lesson 1, then ask: "Can art play a role in bringing the quality of love into the world?" Create slogans about love and incorporate those words into a poster. Stay in the feeling of love as you create the poster.

Do kind, loving things artistically. Examples: Make cards for your parents, grandparents, or friends; make a card for a friend who has moved or a child in the hospital; etc.

Mural

Tell the students that they get to make a quick, spontaneous mural as a group. Divide the class into teams of students. One team can be responsible for the sky, another for the ground and trees, another for buildings, another for animals and another for people. Play some music and do the Imagining a Loving World exercise again, inserting a little more dialogue on the beauty of the sky, meadows, trees, buildings, and animals. Tell them to pretend they are in that world while they are painting.

– Contributed by Diana Hsu

Museum

Visit your local museum or art gallery to look at paintings and sculptures that express the quality of love. Or, ask local artists to come to the class to show some of their work. Using clay or plaster make a model of a figure which expresses love.

– Contributed by Eleanor Viegas

Music

Learn songs about love for each and every person, including the self. Select your favorites. Visit an orphanage or hospital to share your songs.

Study love songs from different decades. Do the messages and sentiments differ decade to decade for romantic love? Do songs about love for humanity differ decade to decade?

Song: Someday

Chorus: ^CSomeday on the ^Fplanet,

^{Emin7/C}There will ^{Dmin7/D}be ^{Emin7/c}perfect ^{Dmin7/c} peace and ^{Emin7/c}harmony.

And ^{Eb}all the ^{F/G}people every ^Cwhere

Will ^{Eb}love each ^{F/G}other without ^Cfear.

Verse 1: ^{Bb/F F}I know the ^{Bb/F}day is ^Fcoming soon

^{Ab/Eb}When there ^{Eb}is no more ^Fhate

^{Bb/F}And we ^Fsee ^{Bb/F}every ^Fone with love

^{Ab/Eb}I know ^{Eb} it's not too ^Flate.

Verse 2: Bb/FThere won't Fbe a Bb/Fneed for Fguns
Ab/EbAnd we'll Eb have no more Fwar.
Bb/FAnd we Fcan just Bb/Fplay to-Fgether,
Ab/Eb'Cause that's Eb what life is F for!
(Repeat chorus and verse 1)

Verse 3: Bb/FSo let's Ftalk our Bb/Fproblems Fout,
Ab/EbPut our Eb anger a- Fway.
Bb/FIf we Fall can Bb/Fjoin to-Fgether,
Ab/Eb'We'll get Eb close to some F day.
(Repeat chorus two times)

— Contributed by Max and Marcia Nass

Home Economic

Do one of your home-economic projects in your own home. For instance, cook a meal or prepare a dessert with lots of love. Surprise your parent(s) with it!

Discuss the central role of love in the home. How can we maintain our level of love in order to be able to give?

Dance/Drama

Create a dance of universal love.

Lead the students through the above World of Love visualization exercise. Use the "replay" process as part of a drama.

TOLERANCE

UNIT FOUR: TOLERANCE

Tolerance/Acceptance Lessons

The Oxford Dictionary defines tolerance as "The ability or willingness to tolerate the existence of opinions or behavior that one dislikes or disagrees with." The Random House College Dictionary, defines tolerance as "a fair and objective attitude toward those whose opinions, practices, race, religion, nationality, or the like, differ from one's own; freedom from bigotry." What we are aiming for in this values unit includes this meaning and adds the broader dimension of actively respecting and appreciating other cultures.

Tolerance is used by the United Nations and in political arenas as the name of the value which allows people of different cultures to coexist with mutual understanding, dignity and respect. November 16 is celebrated by the United Nations and many Member States as the International Day of Tolerance. "The United Nations is committed to strengthening tolerance by fostering mutual understanding among cultures and peoples. This imperative lies at the core of the United Nations Charter, as well as the Universal Declaration of Human Rights, and is more important than ever in this era of rising and violent extremism and widening conflicts that are characterized by a fundamental disregard for human life."

On November 16, 1995, "UNESCO's Member States adopted a Declaration of Principles on Tolerance. Among other things, the Declaration affirms that tolerance is neither indulgence nor indifference. It is respect and appreciation of the rich variety of our world's cultures, our forms of expression and ways of being human. Tolerance recognizes the universal human rights and fundamental freedoms of others. People are naturally diverse; only tolerance can ensure the survival of mixed communities in every region of the globe." (*Source:* United Nations website)

Your school may wish to use the word Tolerance. However, some educators have shared that students relate more easily to the word Appreciation. Please feel free to use either word for this value.

While in this unit on tolerance the above is the primary focus, a couple of lessons also take up another meaning: the ability to endure a hardship, or something unpleasant or difficult.

When studying different cultures, perhaps bring in some of that culture's songs and music at the beginning of the lesson. Some students enjoy learning traditional songs. Perhaps sing or listen to songs that speak of the world's peoples as family. For example, "One Family" by Red Grammer speaks of the human world family as "sisters and brothers, a coat of many colors."

Tolerance/Acceptance Reflection Points

- Peace is the goal, tolerance is the method.
- Tolerance is being open and receptive to the beauty of differences.
- Tolerance recognizes individuality and diversity while removing divisive masks and defusing tension created by ignorance. It provides the opportunity to discover and remove stereotypes and stigmas associated with people perceived to be different because of nationality, religion, or heritage.
- Tolerance is mutual respect through mutual understanding.
- The seeds of intolerance are fear and ignorance.
- The seed of tolerance is love; its water is compassion and care.
- When there is lack of love, there is a lack of tolerance.
- Those who know how to appreciate the good in people and situations have tolerance.
- Tolerance is also an ability to face difficult situations.
- To tolerate life's inconveniences is to let go, be light, make others light, and move on.
- Through understanding and open-mindedness, a tolerant person attracts someone different, and by genuinely accepting and accommodating that person, demonstrates tolerance in a practical way. As a result, relationships bloom.

TOLERANCE LESSON 1

Intolerance — Its Effects and Possible Origin

Play a song about peace or love for humanity.

Discuss/Share

Explore general concepts of tolerance through questions and discussion.

Inform: Tolerance is defined as 'a fair and objective attitude toward those whose opinions, practices, race, religion, nationality, or the like, differ from one's own; freedom from bigotry.' (Random House College Dictionary)

Tolerance as a value is even more beautiful, for it is being open to understanding, respecting and appreciating other cultures, races and nationalities."

On November 16, 1995, "UNESCO's Member States adopted a Declaration of Principles on Tolerance. Among other things, the Declaration affirms that tolerance is neither indulgence nor indifference. It is respect and appreciation of the rich variety of our world's cultures, our forms of expression and ways of being human. Tolerance recognizes the universal human rights and fundamental freedoms of others. People are naturally diverse; only tolerance can ensure the survival of mixed communities in every region of the globe." (*Source:* United Nations website)

➢ Please consider the following Reflection Points. Discuss them in relationship to the questions below.

♦ Tolerance is being open and receptive to the beauty of differences.

♦ Tolerance is mutual respect through mutual understanding.

♦ Peace is the goal, tolerance is the method.

Ask:

• Tolerance has been called an essential factor for world peace. What is the relationship between world peace and tolerance?

• What do you think would happen in the world if everyone respected the religion of everyone else?

• What do you think would happen in the world if everyone respected the culture and race of everyone else?

Read the following short story which is said to be real. It occurred in Switzerland in a self-service restaurant. From the collection of stories by the Colectivo No Violencia y Educación. Reprinted with permission of Manual para Educadores II, Valores para Vivir: Una Iniciativa Educativa, Actividades.

Share a Story: A Bowl of Stock

An elderly lady, about 75 years old, took a bowl and asked the waiter to fill it with stock. She then sat down at one of the many tables in the self-service restaurant. She had hardly sat down when she realized she had forgotten her bread. So, she stood up, took a bun to eat with her stock, and returned to sit down.

Surprise! Before the bowl of stock, she found a black man calmly eating. "That's the last straw!" thought the lady, "but I am not going to let myself be robbed of my soup." She sat herself down by the black man, divided the bun into pieces, put them into the bowl in front of the black man and put her own spoon into the bowl.

The black man, obliging, smiled. Each one had a spoonful until they finished the soup. All in silence. Once the soup was finished, the black man stood up, approached the bar and a little later came back with a large dish of spaghetti and . . . two forks. They both ate from the same dish, in silence, taking turns. At the end, the man left.

"See you," the lady said as he left. "See you," answered the man, with a smile in his eyes. He seemed satisfied for having done a good action, and went out the door.

The lady followed him with her eyes. As her surprise diminished, she reached back with her hand for her purse which she had left on the back of a chair. But, to her astonishment, the bag had disappeared. "That black . . ." she thought. She was about to call out, "Stop that thief!" when her eye caught her bag hanging from a chair two tables behind where she sat. On the table there was a tray with a bowl of stock, already cold.

She realized immediately what had happened. It was not the African man who ate her soup. It was she who was at the wrong table — and she, the grand lady, who had eaten at the expense of the African.

Discuss/Share

Discuss the story, then ask:
- What assumptions do you think each of the characters in the story had?
- What assumption did you have in the middle of the story?
- Who demonstrated real tolerance in the story?

Comment: In this story there is some prejudice, but there was also some civility. Discrimination, that is, lack of tolerance, causes many kinds of problems, some of them are disrespectful, disempowering and rude, others are cruel, inhumane and life-threatening.

Ask:
- What are examples of disrespectful, disempowering and rude discrimination?
- What are examples of cruel, inhumane and life-threatening discrimination?
- In the world today there are many instances of a relationship between war and extreme intolerance. What are recent instances, or instances you can think of in history?

➢ Start with a situation from their examples.

Ask:

- What factors led to that conflict?
- What have been the consequences of that conflict?
- What are the material costs?
- What are the human costs?

> Take another example of a war because of extreme intolerance. Ask the same four questions.

Then ask:

- Do you think there is a relationship between personal peace and tolerance?
- If yes: What do you think that might be?

Discuss the Reflection Points on the board:

♦ The seeds of intolerance are fear and ignorance.

♦ The seed of tolerance is love; its water is compassion and care.

Comment: In the unit on love and caring, a quote from Nelson Mandela was shared.

♦ No one is born hating another person because of the color of his skin, or his background, or his religion. People must learn to hate, and if they can learn to hate, they can be taught to love, for love comes more naturally to the human heart than its opposite.

The quote from Mr. Mandela speaks of the current state of intolerance of most people, that is, they are taught intolerance and become intolerant through acquired ignorance.

Activity

Step 1. Instruct the students to form small groups of four or six. Ask them to explore the origins of intolerance. They might want to ask: Who created the myth that some races or cultures are better than others? Did those people have ulterior motives? What were the advantages to those who convinced others they were superior? Ask them to cite one or more historical examples.

Step 2. Ask them what they would like to say to the people who created intolerance for their own advantage.

Step 3. Invite each group to briefly share their findings, and their advice to the perpetrators of intolerance.

Close with a relaxation/focusing exercise.

Homework: Ask the students to watch the news or find articles about examples of tolerance and intolerance in the newspaper during the next week or two. Ask them to keep their eyes open for symbols, pictures, songs, stories and poems about tolerance.

TOLERANCE LESSON 2
Walking in Your Shoes

Begin with a song.

Write the following Reflection Points on the board as a song on peace or love is played.

 ♦ Tolerance is mutual respect and mutual understanding.

 ♦ Tolerance is being open and receptive to the beauty of differences.

Activity

Step 1. Tell members of the class that you will be asking them to pair up with someone they do not normally play or work with and to decide who is going to be A and B. This is a silent exercise to discover what it is like to pretend to be somebody else.

Explain that the A's are going to go for a walk for ten minutes (the A's keep time). The B's are going to follow them and copy everything they do — from the length, speed, and rhythm of their stride and the way they place their feet to the way they hold their hands and swing their arms. They will look and listen to whatever the A's look at and listen to. In other words, B is going to spend ten minutes discovering what it is like to be A.

Step 2. Invite them to walk as explained above. After ten minutes they can stop and talk, and B can tell A what he or she discovered — what changed when pretending to be A.

Step 3. Reverse roles and walk for another ten minutes. Follow this with sharing. repeat the above.

Step 4. When you all return, invite them to share their discoveries and put them up on the board.

— Contributed by Diana Beaver

Discuss the following Reflection Points, and ask the young adults to think of examples of this that they have encountered in their lives.

 ♦ The seeds of intolerance are fear and ignorance.

 ♦ The seed of tolerance is love; its water is compassion and care.

Close with a relaxation/focusing exercise.

Homework: Ask them to bring in symbols, pictures, songs, stories and/or poems about tolerance of the next lesson.

TOLERANCE LESSON 3
News of Tolerance

Begin with a song.

Activity

As the students bring in news items of tolerance, symbols, pictures, songs, poems, and stories they have found, ask them to share with the class. Use the collected items to make a Tolerance Collage on the wall. Perhaps the class would like to make the entire collage in a shape that is a symbol of tolerance. Students could artistically present their news items as part of the collage. With news of intolerance, mark the instances on a world map.

— Contributed by Pilar Quera Colomina and Sabine Levy

Close with a relaxation/focusing exercise.

TOLERANCE LESSONS 4 to 7
Learning about and Appreciating Two Different Cultures

Note to Educator: Think about which cultures you would like the students to explore. Perhaps the first year, you may wish to explore two cultures that exist in the class, school or local area in order to create more tolerance/appreciation, taking two lesson periods for each culture. If you have students that are recent immigrants, deepen their welcome by learning about their culture. Another year, choose different cultures that they may not encounter frequently. If LVE is being implemented schoolwide, make this decision as a school.

Daily Sequence of Activities

Step 1. Song

Begin with a song. Perhaps play music or songs from the culture you are studying.

Step 2. Reflection Points

Discuss the following Reflection Points each day prior to doing the main content activity.

Lesson 4:

- Tolerance is respecting and appreciating the culture of others.
- Tolerance recognizes individuality and diversity while removing divisive masks and defusing tension created by ignorance. It provides the opportunity to discover and remove stereotypes and stigmas associated with people perceived to be different because of nationality, religion, or heritage.

Lesson 5:

- Tolerance is mutual respect through mutual understanding.
- Through understanding and open-mindedness, a tolerant person attracts someone different, and by genuinely accepting and accommodating that person, demonstrates tolerance in a practical way. As a result, relationships bloom.

Lesson 6:

- Tolerance is an act of humanity which we must nurture and enact, each in their own lives every day, to rejoice in the diversity that makes us strong and the values that bring us together. — UNESCO Director-General Audrey Azoulay

Lesson 7:

- Those who know how to appreciate the good in people and situations have tolerance.
- Peace is the goal, tolerance is the method.

Step 3. *Lesson Content, two time periods for each of the two cultures*

Option One: Share a Story — Relate informative stories about various cultures, selecting fiction or non-fiction stories appropriate for young adults. Discuss the information afterwards.

Option Two: Learn about different cultures through guest speakers

Invite teens or adults from the chosen cultures to come and talk with the students. Ask them to discuss their heritage and tradition, and the values behind them. They may be willing to bring in a traditional treat, or share a song, poem, or piece of art from that culture. Perhaps one or two of the guests can teach a dance, or share their vision of a peaceful world.

Option Three: Study and research about the culture in small groups

Study the history of the culture, including contributions to art, nature or science.

Step 4. *Discuss/Share*

Invite the students to ask the guest speaker questions.

Ask your students:

- What did you learn about this culture that you didn't know before?
- What values are important to this culture?

- How do they show that?

Step 5. Activity

If possible, do an artistic or cultural activity from the culture of focus during Lesson 5 and Lesson 7, such as a dance, a song, creating symbols, engaging in a ceremony or making something.

Step 6. Close with a relaxation/focusing exercise

Perhaps name some of the values cherished by that culture. A small group of students could be responsible for creating a different relaxation/focusing exercise each day.

Homework: During these lessons begin to watch the news and/or find pictures and articles in the newspaper or on-line about examples of intolerance and tolerance.

NOTE TO EDUCATOR

The teacher is responsible for providing a tolerant atmosphere in which the students can thrive. Be attentive to all forms of exclusion, selfishness, and meanness that mask fear and ignorance. Establish the spirit of tolerance through dialogue and understanding.

Please help students put an end to intolerance by encouraging them to appreciate the beauty of diversity and the richness it brings. Emphasize that listening to others is the first step towards tolerance. Help them listen, be tolerant, and have the aim of understanding and achieving a positive and accurate solution. Continue to reinforce respect while helping them understand others.

When conflicts arise that have a hint of intolerance, discuss them.

Ask:

- What are little things that people do that indicate prejudice or intolerance?
- What can we do to change that?

Share:

◆ Tolerance is the ability and art to face situations and offer creative solutions.

— *Contributed by Pilar Quera Colomina and Sabine Levy*

TOLERANCE LESSON 8
Refugees

Begin with a song.

Lesson Content

The United Nations notes that there are more refugees now than since the end of World War II: 60 million. As civil, religious and regional wars continue, millions have fled their lands seeking freedom from conflict, persecution and violence. Tens of millions languish in refugee camps across the globe, while many other millions are displaced by war in their own countries without access to proper food, clean water, shelter and basic care. Other become refugees in an effort to escape violence and persecution in their own countries. Tens of thousands of refugees have lost their lives attempting to cross deserts, mountain ranges, seas and oceans to safer places.

This humanitarian crises has overwhelmed resources, and frightened citizens concerned about the economic wellbeing of their own lives and that of their country. Some fear an increase in violence from refugees who might be extremists. While some countries have risen to the occasion and welcomed refugees, others have severely limited the numbers allowed or closed their borders. Others confine them in situations with very limited resources, negatively impacting their physical and emotional wellbeing and educational opportunities.

Under the 1951 Refugee Convention of the United Nations, someone is acknowledged to be a refugee if the person is "outside his or her country of nationality or habitual residence; has a well-founded fear of persecution, or serious harm or threat to life or freedom, or other serious human rights violations, due to his or her race, religion, nationality, political opinion or membership of a particular social group; and is unable or unwilling to avail him or herself of the protection of that country, or to return there, for fear of persecution." Examples of persecution include: death; torture, rape, slavery, arbitrary arrest or detention; deprivation of legal personality or citizenship; or deprivation of freedom of thought, conscience, or religion." A migrant, in comparison, may leave his or her country for many reasons that are not related to persecution, such as for the purposes of employment, family reunification or study. A migrant continues to enjoy the protection of his or her own government, even when abroad."

Share a Story

Option One: If some of your students are refugees themselves, talk to them in advance to see if they would be willing to share their stories. Please ensure there is a caring and safe classroom atmosphere and use active listening and validation as they share.

Option Two: Provide the opportunity for students to learn more about the incredibly difficult struggles of many refugees. You may have a favorite story of refugees. Or, on the livingvalues.net site, the story "Brothers in Hope — The story of the lost boys of

Sudan" by Mary Williams is outstanding. The Joy of Reading Project kindly gave their permission to post this story. You will find it under For Schools/Young Adults/ Download Free Stories/ Tolerance 12–YA.

Option 3. Ask the students to research stories of refugees in different areas of the world.

Share/Discuss

Ask the students to share their response to the stores they have heard.
Then ask:

- How do you think you would feel if you needed to flee your country because of the violence?
- How would you want to be treated if you did that?
- How would you want your family to be treated?
- What would you like to tell the people in your new land?

Activity Options

Consider doing one or more of the following options.

Option One: Ask students to research the conditions for refugees in your own land or another country.

Option Two: Invite students to form small groups and discuss the following: What is the attitude toward refugees in your country? What is the percentage of people who are welcoming versus the percentage who are not welcoming? What values do you think the refugees in your country would like to be met with? Create messages that encourage understanding the plight of refugees (or all) and the importance of extending acceptance, understanding, tolerance and kindness. Perhaps put them together artistically and post them on social media.

Option Three: Think of volunteer opportunities to help refugees in need, or be mindful of including migrants and refugees when doing special projects. Be aware that you are not the only ones with skills and talents; learn about their skills, talents and culture. Perhaps share music together or cook together.

Close with a relaxation/focusing exercise.

TOLERANCE LESSONS 9

Intercultural Respect for All

Begin with a song.

Lesson Content

Auxiliadora Sales and Rafaela Garcia, Spanish authors on intercultural education, emphasize a dynamic relationship between cultures. They advocate a process of mediating dialogue to create new cultural forms which can be shared by all in school and in a multicultural society. Interculturality emphasizes that evolution and change only take place when different cultural groups interact and blend. Enriching one's culture with elements of others creates open cultures with complementary and contrasting elements.

Discuss the Reflection Points:

♦ All cultures have unique characteristics that make them different from others, as well as have common traits with other cultures.

♦ Respect for cultural differences is essential for a democratic society.

♦ Respect, love, tolerance, cooperation and solidarity are core values for a culture of peace in social relations.

Activity

Step 1. Instruct students to search for distinct cultural groups in their schools, communities, city, or country.

Step 2. Ask them to identify their origins (regions, countries), distinctive cultural traits and points in common with their cultures.

Step 3. Invite students to do interviews, videos or photograph cultural manifestations of these groups (dance, music, language, food etc.) and make an exhibition in the school. If possible, members of the groups searched should be invited to take part in the exhibition and interact with students.

– Contributed by Paulo Barros

Close with a relaxation/focusing exercise of their choice.

TOLERANCE LESSON 10

Love and Its Lack

Begin with a song.

Discuss the Reflection Point:

♦ When there is a lack of love, there is a lack of tolerance.

Note: This reflection point can be taken two ways.

1. When there is a lack of love for another culture or race, there is a lack of tolerance.

2. When there is a lack of love within an individual, there is a lack of tolerance for others.

Ask the young adults what the above reflection point means. Affirm both answers (or more!). Then ask the following questions, making a list of factors they generate:

- People discriminate in a variety of ways — what are they prejudice against? Let's see how many we can name. People discriminate based on _____. (People will often name: race, religion, skin color, and culture.)
- Can you think of any more? How about money?
- Or beauty?
- Are you disdainful if someone is poor?
- Or ugly?
- Or not too smart?
- What other factors can you think of? (Other factors might be education, age or position.)
- Why do people do this? Is there an inherent need to be better than or superior to someone? . . . Or, do you think people compare themselves because they are trying to feel good (or better) about themselves?

Lesson Content

Inform: People often compare themselves with others as they are trying to feel good about themselves. This is a very natural thing to do, and most of us do it. But there is always someone smarter, less smart, more handsome, or less pretty. If one accepts the self as valuable — there is no need to compare for the purpose of feeling good about the self. There is then no need to act superior.

Babies are not prejudice. Bigotry is taught. In history classes, some of you may be exploring economic reasons why slavery and other forms of discrimination have taken place. Economic sanctions were effective in stopping apartheid in South Africa.

While there has been change, it is taking time to change people's attitudes. Some people were prejudice simply because they were taught that that was how things were. Some were not even aware that they were being discriminatory. Being indifferent to the feelings of others was accepted. Raising awareness of human rights, and understanding the importance and value of each human being has been important in changing attitudes.

There is another factor I want to bring up today and that is some people in the world have very limited thinking. They are dedicated to spreading hate. This goes beyond learned indifference. Some of you may wish to study this further, but sometimes people have a lot of hurt. When that hurt continues, it can manifest as anger. When people express that anger, they are trying to free themselves of it. Hate groups allow them a convenient outlet in which to do that. However, the anger brings more anger, and the hurt only grows. They end up in a very self-destructive — and other-destructive — cycle. It is damaging to the self, and others.

➤ Discuss any reactions the young adults might have.

Share: Research studies show that people with high self-esteem are more tolerant than people with low self-esteem. This supports today's reflection point.
Ask:

• Which value or reflection point supports the concept that each one of you is unique, and valuable?

Activity

Ask the young adults to create a rap song, or a song to a traditional tune, about their thoughts on the lesson. Or, write a short story about prejudice.

End with a song and/or a Relaxing/Focusing exercise.

TOLERANCE LESSON 11
Inner Peace and Tolerance

Begin with a song.
Ask:

• What is the relationship between inner peace and tolerance?

Then discuss the following Reflection Point:

♦ The seed of tolerance is love; its water is compassion and care.

Activity

Paint, draw or dance tolerance, peace, love, compassion and care. Perhaps read a couple of your favorite items on the Tolerance Collage.

Close with a relaxation/focusing exercise.

TOLERANCE LESSON 12
Current Intolerance

Begin with a song.

Discuss/Share

Because of sensitivities concerning prejudice, the teacher may want to set a context for the next discussion, such as: "In today's discussion, people may share things about prejudice that have upset them. If students share things of a personal nature, are you willing to honor and respect your fellow students by not repeating their personal stories outside of class? . . . .

Today we will be talking about the lack of tolerance of differences you have noticed at school or in our society."

Ask:

- Are some people discriminated against in our society?
- Are some people discriminated against in our school?
- On what basis?
- Have you ever been discriminated against?
- How did it feel?
- How old were you when you first experienced discrimination? (Only ask this question if there is a high trust level in the class.)
- Why do you think people discriminate against others?
- How do people learn to discriminate against others?
- How old were you when you learned to discriminate?
- What attitude would you like everyone to have toward each other?

Activity

Ask students to write a personal essay contrasting being discriminated against versus being included — or paint the feelings of alienation versus inclusion.

Invite the students to share any paintings.

Close with a relaxation/focusing exercise.

TOLERANCE LESSON 13

Message to the World

Begin with a song.

Review some of the information from the day before, allowing those who wish to continue the discussion. Then ask:

- If everyone was tolerant what would the world be like?
- What message would you like to give the world?
- What can we say to ourselves so we have more tolerance, that is, real acceptance of others? Create a list on the board.

Activity

Ask young adults to write their message to the world. Each student may choose to whom they wish to address their advice — to the leaders of the country, to the leaders of the world, to other students, or to the people of the world? The students could read their advice in small groups and each group could then make a slogan. Draw the slogans on posters or long pieces of paper and place them on the walls.

Alternate Activity for those who hate another group

If there are young adults in your group voicing dislike or hate toward other racial or religious groups, ask them what their goals are. (Stay matter-of-fact as you question them.) Keep asking them why they want that. In the professional experience of the author, all people will eventually say that they want to be safe and/or valued if questioned in a respectful way. Affirm the desire to be loved, safe, have enough, etc.

Once you have a value-based goal, then ask them to open their mind to a more constructive way to achieve that.

Ask:
- What is the result of anger? (More anger.)
- What is the result of violence? (Death, more anger, grief, retaliation, etc.)

➢ If they have mistaken information about the group they dislike, please provide them with accurate information. Perhaps provide humanizing stories, videos or films about that group.

Mind Map or Consequence Line: Ask them to Mind Map or make a consequence line of the actions of tolerance and the actions of intolerance towards this group if enmity were to continue. Continue to keep your relationship clear and respectful.

Close with a relaxation/focusing exercise.

Follow-up Activity: Find something positive for them to do with members of the group they dislike or hate. Perhaps they can work with them on a special project, an environmental project or even cook or make music together. Perhaps arrange for a special outing.

TOLERANCE LESSON 14
Disarming Prejudice

Begin with a song.

Discuss/Share

Ask:

- What discriminatory things have you heard from your peers? (List those quickly on the board.)

- What usually happens when that type of thing is said?

Summarize what has been said, such as: "So, sometimes when someone says something aggressive, feelings are hurt, and things get even worse. Sometimes when one is aggressive, the other person says or does something aggressive back."

If they talk about the insulted party going away and saying nothing, say, "Sometimes when someone says something aggressive, the other person goes away. Their response appears passive."

Ask:

- But how do they feel inside? (Acknowledge their responses.)

Explain: Say, "When someone says something mean, there are generally three types of responses. You have described aggressive responses and passive responses. The other type of response is called an assertive response.

"You are being assertive during conflict resolution when you say to someone, with respect:

- ❖ I don't like it when you _____. I want you to _____.
- ❖ Or, you might say: I don't really like that kind of joke.
- ❖ I'm uncomfortable when you _____
- ❖ You are also being assertive when you use the one we practiced in the unit on respect: I feel _____ when you do _____ because _____.

Ask:

- Can anyone take an example given and see if you can think of something to say using that last sentence, the 'I feel' sentence?

➢ Give the students time to try and do the above. Positively remark on their efforts and help them as needed.

Say, "Very often we only want to share our feelings with people who are friends, or people we know very well. So sometimes you will be uncomfortable using the 'I feel' statement, and will choose not to use it. However, sometimes people say mean things and we just want to say something back."

Ask:

- What happens if we say something back aggressive? (Acknowledge their responses. Some may say: people become even angrier; there is more resentment; sometimes people fight; and retaliation begins.)
- What happens when we are passive? (Some may say: People have no respect for you and treat you worse; you feel like you have no power.)

Activity

Step 1. Ask the students to form small groups, and then role play for the rest of the class situations that they have encountered that are particularly difficult. Then "re-play" the situation with a tolerant "benevolent" response.

Step 2. Next, ask students to generate remarks that could be said in response — remarks that offer a more tolerant view, which could be considered assertive, "cool," and benevolent — not aggressive, or wishy-washy. Examples are:

- ❖ Yeah, it wouldn't be such a neat world if we were all clones.
- ❖ I feel a lot better practicing peace.
- ❖ What would you do if you were in her place?

Step 3. Ask for a couple volunteers to model the responses. Lead the applause.

Step 4. Ask students to make a list of the best supportive comebacks.

Close with a relaxation/focusing exercise.

TOLERANCE LESSON 15

Increasing Tolerance

Begin with a song.

Discuss the Reflection Point:

- ◆ Those who know how to appreciate the good in people and situations have tolerance.

Follow-up Activity: Generate and practice supportive comebacks for ten minutes or more, to practice the skill introduced in the last lesson. The teacher or students can say comments they have heard. Others can offer replies which are assertive and full of self-respect. Practicing these until they are comfortable makes them more likely to be used. Role play a couple of scenes, and tell them what a wonderful job they are doing.

Activity

Step 1. Ask students to individually create a list of things that help create tolerance.

Step 2. The students can discuss their choices in small groups.

Step 3. Then instruct each group to select the one item on their list that is especially important for tolerance. Ask each group to present their finding to the class. Why is that item the most important?

Step 4. Ask the class: "Are you able to stay full of tolerance, appreciating the viewpoint of each group even when they have a different opinion? What can you think that makes it easy to do that?"

Close with a song, a relaxation/focusing exercise or with a cultural dance that you have learned.

TOLERANCE LESSON 16
Tolerating Difficulties

Begin with a song.

Talk about the other meaning of tolerance: to endure. The Reflection Points for this are:

- ◆ Tolerance is the ability to face difficult situations.
- ◆ To tolerate life's inconveniences is to let go, be light, make others light, and move on.

Share a Story

Select a biography of someone who has demonstrated exceptional tolerance in her or his life. Read aloud passages that illustrate the value of tolerance or have the students tell stories of tolerating or research people they admire who have tolerated. Or, students could write a short story or personal essay on something they have tolerated.

Discuss/Share

Ask the students to share "self-talk" or methods that help them face or accommodate difficulties. Positively reinforce their sharing. Perhaps ask them to share what things are difficult now and what might help them cope with it by positive or encouraging self-talk.

Close with a relaxation/focusing exercise.

TOLERANCE LESSON 17

How would tolerance effect the Sustainable Development Goals?

Begin with a song.

Lesson Content

Goal 1: No Poverty
Goal 2: Zero Hunger
Goal 3: Good Health and Well-being
Goal 4: Quality Education
Goal 5: Gender Equality
Goal 6: Clean Water and Sanitation
Goal 7: Affordable and Clean Energy
Goal 8: Decent Work and Economic Growth
Goal 9: Industry, Innovation and Infrastructure
Goal 10: Reduced Inequality
Goal 11: Sustainable Cities and Communities
Goal 12: Responsible Consumption and Production
Goal 13: Climate Action
Goal 14: Life Below Water
Goal 15: Life on Land
Goal 16: Peace and Justice Strong Institutions
Goal 17: Partnerships to achieve the Goal

Activity

Step 1.   Invite the students to form the same groups they were with during the previous SDGs lessons.

Step 2. Ask them to explore the effect of tolerance on the SDGs. If everyone in the world had tolerance/appreciation for every culture and religion, what would be positively affected? Do any more SDGs need to be added?

Step 3. Ask them to write specific ways holding the value of tolerance/appreciation would affect the SDGs on which their group is focused and write those on Red Leaves.

Step 4. Invite them to create a song or poem about tolerance and the fulfillment of one of the SDGs. They may wish to contrast it with the lack of tolerance and the current need.

Step 5. Invite them to share their Tolerance Leaves and creation with the entire group.

Step 6. Invite the groups to attach their Love Leaves to the class artistic presentation of the SDGs.

Step 7. Put on some music and ask everyone to be the embodiment of appreciation as they move/dance around the world and greet others.

Close with a relaxation/focusing exercise.

TOLERANCE LESSON 18
An Ending Note

Possible Activities

Cultural Celebration: If you would like a celebratory finish to the Tolerance Unit, help the students plan a celebration of different cultures, with song, dance and food from a variety of cultures. You may wish to have this as a classroom activity, a school-wide activity or an assembly. If greater cultural appreciation and integration is needed in your community, please involve community members to involve more parents and families.

Special Project: If there is discrimination in the community, ask the students what they think they can do about it as a class. Perhaps they would like to create a skit/drama about students who have prejudice learning to appreciate each other's culture, race or religion. Perhaps other students in the class can provide music and poems. Share it at an assembly in your school and perhaps in other schools. When creating the skit, ask them to review some of their suggestions for tolerance/appreciation and some of their benevolent assertive response. Perhaps some of these can become part of the skit, or slogans that the students share. As a follow-up, ask: "Would you like to share some of these slogans with others in our school or community?" "How could we do that?" Students may wish to share their slogans on social media.

Tolerance Activities in Subject Areas

Language/Literature

Write a Reflection Point on the board daily. Ask students to reflect and then discuss for a few minutes.

Select works of tolerance and the struggle to overcome the effects of intolerance. There are many stories, classical works, historical novels, and autobiographies about discrimination and the effects of intolerance. When students have read one work as a class, ask:

- How did the protagonist feel?
- How would you have felt in his or her situation?

- Pretend you are the protagonist. Give a message to the perpetrator and the world.

If the students have read individual works, have them share with the class, answering the same questions. Assign a paper discussing the theme of one work; ask them to write a poem about another reading.

Read parts of Nelson Mandela's Walk to Freedom or another work from your language arts Tolerance Lesson curriculum.

Talk with students about their feelings regarding the story they have read. Ask them to write a few lines and illustrate their thoughts, or write a short personal essay.

A Rainbow

Compare the variety of races, cultures, and individuals to a rainbow. The rainbow would not be nearly as beautiful if it were missing one or two colors — in fact, it would not be a rainbow with only one color. The human family is like a rainbow; it comes with a rich variety of colors. Each culture and tradition have something important to contribute.

Activity: Ask students to make a rainbow. If the class is reading one work, have them make a large rainbow on the wall, filling in each ray with different aspects of the story and paying particular attention to the positive attributes of the culture depicted. If they are reading different books, they could make individual rainbows for each work they have read.

Ask students to make up a poem or a song about the human world family or the family of their particular country as a rainbow.

Walking in Your Shoes

Ask students to identify a character who is different than they. To develop understanding, ask them to write a short story as if they were that person, explaining the beliefs and reasons behind the character's actions.

Interview a person from a culture other than your own. Write his or her story.

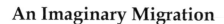

An Imaginary Migration

Ask students to make up a story about migrating to another country — as a minority race different than their own. Perhaps research some of the difficulties currently experienced by refugees in one or more areas of the world as a basis for the story. What obstacles are they likely to find? Are these different than the obstacles minorities encounter in your country? End the story with their protagonist giving advice to others about how people should be treated — especially him or her.

Tolerating Difficulties

Another definition of the word tolerance is "the act or capacity of enduring; endurance: My tolerance of noise is limited." (Random House College Dictionary)

Reflection Points for this kind of tolerance are:

♦ Tolerance is also an ability to face difficult situations.

♦ To tolerate life's inconveniences is to let go, be light, make others light, and move on.

In this form, tolerance is facing difficult situations by seeing them from a different perspective: as molehills, not mountains. Adopting that perspective, of course, would depend on the nature of the situation. Express to the students that sometimes what appears as a formidable challenge — "a mountain" — may, in retrospect, have only been "a molehill." It's a matter of seeing the circumstance in the overall scheme of things.

Discuss: Ask the students to share "self-talk" or methods that help them face or accommodate difficulties. Positively reinforce their sharing.

Activity: Select a biography of someone who has demonstrated exceptional tolerance in her or his life. Ask students to select and read aloud meaningful passages that illustrate the value of tolerance.

History/Social Studies

The Year of Tolerance

Background: The year 1995 was observed as The Year of Tolerance by UNESCO (United Nations Educational, Scientific and Cultural Organization) on the grounds that tolerance is an "essential factor for world peace." The United Nations General Assembly made this decision . . . "in the light of the resurgence of: ethno-nationalist conflict; discrimination against minority groups; acts of xenophobia, particularly against refugees and asylum-seekers, migrant workers, and immigrant racist organizations and ideologies; and acts of racial violence . . . intolerance expressed through marginalization and exclusion from society of vulnerable groups, or violence and discrimination against them

. . . . Intolerance . . . is the rejection of differences among individuals and cultures. When intolerance becomes collective or institutionalized, it erodes democratic principles and poses a threat to world peace . . . It is essential to recall that the basic human values that unite us are stronger than the forces that pull us apart." (From International Year of Tolerance, 1995, UNESCO)

Factors Leading to Intolerance

Activity: Look at several current and recent conflicts in the world where intolerance was a major factor. For example, genocide, as an extreme form of intolerance was a major factor in conflicts in Rwanda and Kosovo. Identify several conflicts.

- ➢ Form small groups and ask each group to talk about a different conflict. Each group is to explore the factors that lead to the explosions of intolerance.
- ➢ As the groups report their findings to the entire class, make a list of all contributing factors. As the teacher, add a few more if they have left some out. Are the same factors operating in each conflict?
- ➢ After the list has been made, look at the lack of values or anti-values behind each factor.
- ➢ Ask each small group to work together again to develop alternative ways to deal with precipitating factors. What methods would have resolved the factors leading to the explosion of intolerance?

Ask:

- Do any of these factors exist in our school? What are they?
- What positive things can we do to build tolerance?

A Sense of Belonging

Review the Tolerance Reflection Points and identify words and actions which would help create a sense of belonging for all people at your school.

A Skit

Ask students to read the work of one person's personal struggle against intolerance during the period of history the class is currently studying. The next day read a story about tolerance and inclusion. Form small groups to create a skit, allowing each group to select the particular scene they wish to portray. After the skits, discuss. Ask each group to give a message to the perpetrator: What we want you to stop doing, what we want you to do instead. Ask for feelings about each story.

Making History Real

Invite people from the cultures you have been studying to visit your class and tell their story.

Generating Cultural Bias

Information: In the last 2,000 years, history has recorded many wars and conquests. The victor has often used cultural bias as a method to maintain control. The conquerors would establish themselves as "superior," relegating an inferior status to those conquered. This lack of regard permitted lack of equal treatment and at times inhumane treatment. Often, while insisting they were superior, the conquerors would destroy evidence of the natural skills of those conquered. The myths and misinformation generated by the conquering peoples have persisted over time, making it more difficult to change intolerance and prejudice.

Ask:

- Can you think of historical examples of this?
- Are there examples of this in our own country?

Provide examples with local or regional relevance. For instance, when the Spaniards conquered Mexico, they destroyed the advanced forms of writing and the advanced astrological and mathematical information of the Mayan people.

Ask:

- What common prejudices exist in this country?
- What was the state of the original people of this land?
- Were they happy? Did their culture flourish?
- What are the current cultural biases?
- How can we promote understanding and tolerance?

Practicing Tolerance/Acceptance

Study the Reflection Points. Ask students to practice tolerance every day during the week. Generate ideas to promote tolerance every day at the beginning of class. Journal about tolerance/acceptance for ten minutes a day. What examples do you see of intolerance? What have you done to generate tolerance/acceptance during the day?

Science

Skewed Results

At times in man's history, science has contributed to intolerance and prejudice through individuals trying to substantiate a cultural bias. Sometimes intolerance was inherent in their culture and they were not even aware they were biased. (Refer to preceding activity.)

One example in psychology is intelligence tests which ask cultural questions or questions with which one particular ethnic group would not be familiar. People not exposed to that culture or area of questioning do not fare well and are therefore labeled "less intelligent." Some of us would do very poorly if tested by Eskimos on the characteristics of ten different kinds of snow!

Ask:

- What questions can we ask ourselves if we want to design a scientific study free of cultural bias? Ask students to create a list of questions they would ask. You might want to ask them to form small groups.

Economics

Promoting Intolerance through Fear of Scarcity

Discuss economic factors in relation to prejudice. For example, ask:

- Is the fear of scarcity promoted to increase intolerance? To what end?
- Is there often a relationship between discriminatory working practices and monetary gain?
- If so: What are the different forms this takes?

Activity: Look up economic statistics to support your hypothesis.

Loans to Those in Poverty

For years, large banks refused to loan money to the poor, perpetuating a cycle of poverty and prejudice against the poor. The Grameen Bank in Bangladesh disproved the stereotypical belief about loaning money to poor people and proved when the poor are given the chance to borrow, they can live up to and exceed expectations. Their rate of repayment was better than at the average bank. You may have a similar project. Study this practice in relation to tolerance.

Is it time for reparation?

In many countries around the world, discriminatory practices toward certain races, religions or "classes" has added to their impoverishment. During wars, the possessions of people are stolen or their land is taken. Have any discriminatory practices based on intolerance taken place in your country? If so, and you have the power to do so, what would be fair reparation? Perhaps it would need to take place county by county, family by family to be completely fair.

Art

Study the art of different cultures. Make replicas of items from several cultures and display them at an art show for the rest of the school. Make a display card for each item, describing its background.

Draw figures wearing traditional dress from different cultures. Perhaps some students would like to draw children, others older people, others families. They could make groupings of one culture or one poster of many cultures.

Create a mural of cultural diversity which has an accepting and loving quality.

Artistic Diversity

Providing textured paper, instruct students to make a careful drawing of a plant or any object of their choice. They can color it if they wish.

When the drawing is finished, ask them to take a larger sheet of paper of the same texture. Instruct them to create a semi-abstract work by ripping up their drawing into various sized pieces and carefully reassembling their drawing on the larger sheet of paper while leaving some space between each piece. Ask them to check the extent to which they are using tolerance. Ask the students if they think their final pictures are more interesting than the original drawings.

– Contributed by Eleanor Viegas

Music

Sing songs that speak of the world's peoples as family. "One Family" by Red Grammer speaks of the human world family as "sisters and brothers, a coat of many colors."

Learn five musical pieces or songs from five different cultures.

Home Economics

Study one area from the standpoint of five different cultures, including those in your part of the country. For example, if you are studying food, select a cross-cultural sampling of recipes, or if you are studying textiles, look at cultural examples of weaving or embroidery. Invite people skilled in those areas to talk and display their work in class. Ask students to write down three positive things about the work of each culture and to tell the people what they appreciate.

Electronics

Produce an anti-bullying display at school using the value of respect or tolerance. The students can practice their electronic skills through the use of flashing lights.

— Contributed by Mick Jones

Dance

Do a dance dressed in different cultural costumes. Retain the integrity of that culture's dance, having interplay between the dancers at times and showcasing each type of dance at other times.

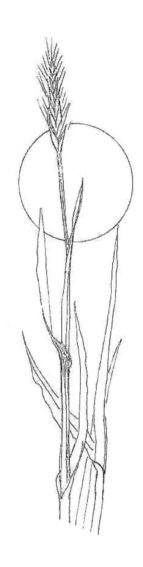

SIMPLICITY
AND CARING FOR THE
EARTH AND HER OCEANS

UNIT FIVE: SIMPLICITY AND CARING FOR THE EARTH AND HER OCEANS

Simplicity and Caring for the Earth and Her Oceans Lessons

Each value is important, but the importance of simplicity and taking care of our Earth and her oceans at this point in time is paramount as human demands on the planet's resources increase and global climate change imperils human existence.

Simplicity as a value is addressed in a few ways: enjoying the simplicity and beauty of nature, valuing the simplicity and wisdom of indigenous cultures, simplicity as a value that helps us create sustainable development and simplicity as a way to reduce our material demands on the planet.

The Caring for the Earth and Her Oceans lessons begin with an article by United Nations Secretary-General António Guterres, responding to the concerns of youth on climate change. The key provision of the Paris Climate Change Agreement, to try to keep the global temperature to rising only to 1.5 degrees Celsius above the pre-industrial age, and definitely below 2 degrees Celsius, is used to branch into the variables creating the increase in temperature. Young adults are presented with specific scientific information about greenhouse gases, what is causing them, and the harmful effects of human actions on the ocean, rivers, animals, air and ground — and on human beings themselves. Students are encouraged to explore daily options to reduce their carbon footprint, reduce their use of plastics, to research an area of interest and do a service-learning project to benefit the environment. Please add your own ideas and help them do what is most needed in the local community. Please allow them to go with their interests, motivation and project ideas — allow them time to research, do projects and be constructively creative.

Paulo Barros contributed several activities to this unit for young adults. He has highlighted the importance of exploring the effects of not only man on the environment but how social prejudice, anti-values and injustice impact us all, and our Earth, a concept reinforced by the UN Global Assessment on Biodiversity and Ecosystems.

Enjoy doing the activities with the students. We will be happy to post news of your projects, poems and songs in our newsletter or on the international website.

Thank you for helping take care of our Earth and her oceans.

Simplicity and Caring for the Earth and Her Oceans Reflection Points

- Simplicity is natural.
- Simplicity is learning from the earth.
- Simplicity is beautiful.
- Simplicity is relaxing.
- Simplicity is being natural.
- Simplicity is staying in the present and not making things complicated.
- Simplicity is learning from the wisdom of indigenous cultures.
- Simplicity is giving patience, friendship, and encouragement.
- Simplicity is appreciating the small things in life.
- Simplicity is freedom from material desires and emotional desires — permission to simply "be." — *Contributed by students at West Kidlington School*
- Simplicity is putting others first with kindness, openness, pure intentions — without expectations and conditions. — *Contributed by students at West Kidlington School*
- Simplicity avoids waste, teaches economy, avoids value clashes complicated by greed, fear, peer pressure, and a false sense of identity.
- Simplicity is appreciating inner beauty and recognizing the value of all actors, even the poorest and worst off.
- Simplicity helps create sustainable development.
- Simplicity teaches us economy — how to use our resources keeping future generations in mind.
- Simplicity calls upon people to rethink their values.
- Simplicity asks whether we are being induced to purchase unnecessary products. Psychological enticements create artificial needs. Desires stimulated by wanting unnecessary things result in value clashes complicated by greed, fear, peer pressure, and a false sense of identity. Once fulfillment of basic necessities allows for a comfortable lifestyle, extremes and excesses invite overindulgence and waste.
- Simplicity helps decrease the gap between "the haves" and "the have nots" by demonstrating the logic of true economics: to earn, save, invest, and share the

sacrifices and the prosperity so that there can be a better quality of life for all people regardless of where they were born.

SIMPLICITY AND CARING
FOR THE EARTH AND HER OCEANS LESSON 1
Simple Things

Begin with a song about the beauty of nature or a melody from a native musical instrument.

Write the following Reflection Points on the board.

♦ Simplicity is natural.

♦ Simplicity is learning from the earth.

♦ Simplicity is beautiful.

♦ Simplicity is relaxing.

♦ Simplicity is being natural.

♦ Simplicity is staying in the present and not making things complicated.

Explore general concepts of simplicity through questions and discussion:

• What is simplicity?

• What simple things do you enjoy?

• What things do you enjoy that cost very little or no money?

• What can we learn from the Earth?

• When can life be too complicated?

• In what ways can life be simplified?

Activity

Do a simple activity. If possible, take a walk at a nearby park or go to a place of natural beauty. While there, ask them to walk slowly in silence for 15 minutes and observe the simple things in nature, such as the light on a leaf, bubs or tiny flowers, clouds, birds, the bark on trees, etc. If it is not possible to for a walk, perhaps invite them to paint something simple or write a poem to themselves from a bird or another animal — advising them about the simple beauties of life.

Invite the students to share if they would like to do so.

Close with a relaxation/focusing exercise of your choice.

Homework: Give the students the following Simplicity-Is-Relaxing and Simplicity-Is-Not-Making-Things-Complicated homework. Ask them to spend ten minutes every day for one week relaxing, without electronics. They may wish to focus on a tree, a flower, or a light as they relax. Or go for a walk and observe simple things. Perhaps lie under a tree and watch the leaves or lie on the ground and watch the sky. For a few minutes, simply be an observer, free from desires. Focus on the beauty of what is natural. Think about what it would feel like to know that the natural you is beautiful.

SIMPLICITY AND CARING
FOR THE EARTH AND HER OCEANS LESSON 2
Simply Being

Begin with a song and a Relaxation/Focusing Exercise.

Discuss/Share

Ask about their experiences doing the Simplicity-Is-Relaxing and Simplicity-Is-Not-Making-Things-Complicated homework. Listen with interest and respect and acknowledge their experiences.

List the Reflection Points on the board. Ask the students to form small groups and discuss the points.

♦ Simplicity is staying in the present and not making things complicated.

♦ Simplicity is freedom from material desires and emotional desires — permission to simply "be."

♦ Simplicity is putting others first with kindness, openness, pure intentions — without expectations and conditions.

Ask:

• Many people overthink and worry about things. When that happens, what are simple things we can do to help ourselves relax? (Such as take a deep breath, take a walk, tell yourself that everything will be okay, talk to a close friend, etc.)

• Sometimes people say that we walk around like "human doings" rather than "human beings". Do you feel like that sometimes? If so, what simple things help you relax and "be", easing the stress of doing?

Activity

Each small group can choose to write one of their own Relaxation/Focusing Exercises or make up a slogan on simplicity. Allow them different options to decorate the slogan. They might wish to use things from nature.

Close with one of the relaxation/focusing exercises they created.

SIMPLICITY AND CARING
FOR THE EARTH AND HER OCEANS LESSON 3
Learning from Indigenous Cultures

Note to Educator: Do one or more lessons about indigenous cultures. Educators who teach anthropology or social studies will be great resources. Or, have the educators in those departments simply focus on simplicity and honoring the wisdom of indigenous cultures when doing the regular curriculum. The United Nations Global Assessment Report on biodiversity and ecosystems acknowledges the positive contributions of Indigenous Peoples to sustainability and suggests learning from Indigenous Peoples.

Purpose: To get in touch with the wisdom of indigenous cultures in your own country or in other countries. In ancient traditions, natural simplicity, wisdom, and respect for the earth were inherent in almost every practice. The needs of the people and the methods to satisfy those needs were simple and without waste.

To explore this, look at the natural simplicity in the lives of your country's Indigenous Peoples. Discover ways in which Indigenous Peoples have used resources by reading a story, visiting a museum or a library with an exhibit, or viewing films or videos. Invite members of the community who can share artifacts or crafts from your heritage. Perhaps invite someone from the community who can share about an indigenous culture and the relationship of their people to the environment. It seems each indigenous culture has a way to honor the Earth.

Begin with a song about the beauty of nature, or a melody from a native musical instrument.

Discuss the Reflection Points:
- Simplicity is learning from the Earth.
- Simplicity teaches us economy — how to use our resources wisely, keeping future generations in mind.
- Simplicity is learning from the wisdom of indigenous cultures.

Activity

Step 1. Invite the students to form small group and study one indigenous culture. All the groups could study one culture or different cultures around the globe.

Ask each group to explore:

❖ The practices of the indigenous culture being studied.

❖ How the people of indigenous cultures were wise in their use of resources.

❖ How they honored the Earth or her ocean.

❖ Which values were inherent in their different practices?

❖ Which aspects of their wisdom they think would be beneficial to practice in today's world.

Step 2. Invite each group to share their findings. They may wish to showcase one or more elements of the culture, such as sharing music, art, shelter, attitudes toward nature, etc.

Close by sharing some music from an indigenous culture and a few reflective statements about the values within that culture or one of the relaxation/focusing exercises created by students during the last lesson.

Advanced Study Option: Explore some of the following questions.

• What factors contributed to the destruction and/or decline of native cultures?

• Have these same factors negatively affected other elements of our current society or the environment?

• What values were behind their beliefs and practices? How did those become affected by the imposition of the current culture?

• What practices would have been beneficial to the perseverance of that culture?

• Which of those practices would serve to help other segments of society or the environment now?

SIMPLICITY AND CARING

FOR THE EARTH AND HER OCEANS LESSON 4

Climate Change: Let's listen to the world's young people

Begin with a song about nature, indigenous music, recordings of whales or another choice related to nature and/or simplicity.

Lesson Content

United Nations Secretary-General António Guterres, in an op-ed article in The Guardian (15 March 2019), featured as "The climate strikers should inspire us all to act at the next UN summit," said leaders need to listen to the concerns of youth on climate change and presented plans for the Climate Action Summit in September (2019) for concrete and ambitious solutions. He wrote:

"Tens of thousands of young people took to the streets on Friday with a clear message to world leaders: act now to save our planet and our future from the climate emergency.

These schoolchildren have grasped something that seems to elude many of their elders: we are in a race for our lives, and we are losing. The window of opportunity is closing – we no longer have the luxury of time, and climate delay is almost as dangerous as climate denial.

FacebookTwitterPinterest Photograph: Neil Hall/EPA

My generation has failed to respond properly to the dramatic challenge of climate change. This is deeply felt by young people. No wonder they are angry.

Despite years of talk, global emissions are reaching record levels and show no sign of peaking. The concentration of carbon dioxide in our atmosphere is the highest it has been in 3m years. The last four years were the four hottest on record, and winter temperatures in the Arctic have risen by 3-4°C in the last 50 years. Sea levels are rising, coral reefs are dying and we are starting to see the life-threatening impact of climate change on health, through air pollution, heatwaves and risks to food security.

Thankfully, we have the Paris agreement – a visionary, viable, forward-looking policy framework that sets out exactly what needs to be done to stop climate disruption and reverse its impact. But the agreement itself is meaningless without ambitious action. That is why I am bringing world leaders together at a climate action summit later this year. I am calling on all leaders to come to New York in September with concrete, realistic plans to enhance their nationally determined contributions by 2020, in line with reducing greenhouse gas emissions by 45% over the next decade, and to net zero by 2050.

The summit will bring together governments, the private sector, civil society, local authorities and other international organisations to develop ambitious solutions in six areas: renewable energy; emission reductions; sustainable infrastructure; sustainable agriculture and management of forests and oceans; withstanding climate impacts; and investing in the green economy.

The latest analysis shows that if we act now, we can reduce carbon emissions within 12 years and limit global warming to 1.5C. But if we continue along our current path, the consequences are impossible to predict.

While climate action is essential to combat an existential threat, it also comes with costs. So action plans must not create winners and losers or add to economic inequality: they must be fair and create new opportunities for those negatively impacted, in the context of a just transition.

Business is on our side. Accelerated climate solutions can strengthen our economies and create jobs, while bringing cleaner air, preserving natural habitats and biodiversity, and protecting our environment.

New technologies and engineering solutions are already delivering energy at a lower cost than the fossil-fuel driven economy. Solar and onshore wind are now the cheapest sources of new bulk power in virtually all major economies. But we must set radical change in motion.

This means ending subsidies for fossil fuels and high-emitting agriculture and shifting towards renewable energy, electric vehicles and climate-smart practices. It means carbon pricing that reflects the true cost of emissions, from climate risk to the health hazards of air pollution. And it means accelerating the closure of coal plants and replacing jobs with healthier alternatives so that the transformation is just, inclusive and profitable.

Momentum is building, people are listening and there is a new determination to unleash the promise of the Paris agreement. The climate summit must be the starting point to build the future we need.

I will close with a message for those who marched on Friday. I know young people can and do change the world.

Many of you are anxious and fearful for the future, and I understand your concerns and your anger. But I know humankind is capable of enormous achievements. Your voices give me hope.

The more I see your commitment and activism, the more confident I am that we will win. Together, with your help and thanks to your efforts, we can and must beat this threat and create a cleaner, safer, greener world for everyone."

Discuss/Share

Inform: Protests by millions of school children and young people around the world are bringing attention to the urgency of dealing with climate change.

Ask:

- How did you feel about UN Secretary-General António Guterres' comments?
- Are there any other thoughts you'd like to share about his article?
- Have you been part of the protests?
- What are the main concerns of those protesting?
- What are your concerns about climate change?
- What would you like to tell leaders of governments about this?
- There is a saying: Think globally, act locally. How does this relate to climate change?

Activity

Divide the students into small groups and ask them to research information about climate change and prepare a presentation to the class.

Group One: Invite them to study the effects of climate change. There are some interesting videos available on UN sites and other internet sites.

Group Two: Invite them to study the Paris Climate Change Agreement, and subsequent UN Climate Action Summits.

Group Three: Invite them to study the Global Assessment Report produced by the Intergovernmental Science-Policy Platform on Biodiversity and Ecosystem Services. A three-year study released in May 2019 it includes information that one million animal and plant species are now threatened with extinction within decades unless there is transformative change. (Item 4 in the Appendix includes information about this report.)

Allow time for each group to present.

Close with the relaxation/focusing exercise which follows the Resources/Information section.

Resources/Information

Science related to climate change:

Source: https://www.ipcc.ch/sr15/

The Intergovernmental Panel on Climate Change (IPCC) is the United Nations body for assessing the science related to climate change. Their extensive report: "Global Warming of 1.5 °C".

UN Climate Action Summit:

Source: https://www.un.org/en/climatechange/

"The impacts of climate change are being felt everywhere and are having very real consequences on people's lives. Climate change is disrupting national economies, costing us dearly today and even more tomorrow. But there is a growing recognition that affordable, scalable solutions are available now that will enable us all to leapfrog to cleaner, more resilient economies.

The Paris Agreement adopted in 2015, was an essential step to address climate change. It has the central goal of keeping global average temperature rise this century to well below 2 degrees Celsius above pre-industrial levels and as close as possible to 1.5 degrees Celsius.

The 2015 Paris Agreement marked a historic turning point. World leaders from across the globe clinched a new, universal agreement under the umbrella of the UN Framework Convention on Climate Change.

Last December at the UN Climate Change Conference COP24 in Poland, governments set to agree the implementation guidelines of the Paris Agreement, thereby unleashing its full potential.

As of November 2018, 184 states and the European Union have joined the Agreement, which entered into force with record speed."

Global Assessment Report:

Source: https://www.un.org/sustainabledevelopment/blog/2019/05/nature-decline-unprecedented-report/

Produced by the Intergovernmental Science-Policy Platform on Biodiversity and Ecosystem Services. "UN Report: Nature's Dangerous Decline 'Unprecedented'; Species Extinction Rates 'Accelerating'."

"PARIS, 6 May – Nature is declining globally at rates unprecedented in human history – and the rate of species extinctions is accelerating, with grave impacts on people around the world now likely, warns a landmark new report from the

Intergovernmental Science-Policy Platform on Biodiversity and Ecosystem Services (IPBES), the summary of which was approved at the 7th session of the IPBES Plenary, meeting last week (29 April – 4 May) in Paris.

"The overwhelming evidence of the IPBES Global Assessment, from a wide range of different fields of knowledge, presents an ominous picture," said IPBES Chair, Sir Robert Watson. "The health of ecosystems on which we and all other species depend is deteriorating more rapidly than ever. We are eroding the very foundations of our economies, livelihoods, food security, health and quality of life worldwide."

"The Report also tells us that it is not too late to make a difference, but only if we start now at every level from local to global," he said. "Through 'transformative change', nature can still be conserved, restored and used sustainably – this is also key to meeting most other global goals. By transformative change, we mean a fundamental, system-wide reorganization across technological, economic and social factors, including paradigms, goals and values."

Please note: In order to accommodate those without internet access, the first part of this article can be found in the Appendix, Item 4.

Sending Peace to the Earth Relaxation/Focusing Exercise

"Sit comfortably and let yourself be still inside. . . . Be aware of how your body is feeling. . . . Relax the body and breathe in the light of peace. . . . Let the light of peace surround you . . . . Breathe out any tension . . . and breathe in the light of peace. . . . Breathe out any tension . . . and breathe in the light of peace. . . . Invite the peace to relax your muscles more. . . . This peace is quiet and safe . . . it reminds me that I value peace. . . . Let yourself be very still and think . . . I am me . . . I am naturally full of peace and love. . . . Let your body relax even more . . . and focus on surrounding yourself with the light of peace. . . . The more you concentrate on peace, the more that peace will naturally go outward to nature . . . to the mountains and streams . . . to the clouds and the ocean . . . to the dolphins and the whales . . . to the birds . . . to the animals large and small. . . . Concentrate on peace and see that peace flowing outward to our planet . . . to the rivers and ocean . . . to the trees and the meadows . . . to the mountains and the sky. . . . I am full of peace. . . . I am one who is acting to help our Earth be healthy again. . . . This will happen in time. . . . Our planet will be well. . . . I picture the light of peace all around the Earth . . . and our beautiful oceans being healthy again . . . our beautiful Earth being healthy again. . . .

Feeling relaxed and peaceful . . . begin to be aware of where you are sitting and bring your attention back to this room."

SIMPLICITY AND CARING
FOR THE EARTH AND HER OCEANS LESSON 5
What is causing climate change?

Begin with a song with lyrics about nature.

Ask how they are and if they have been thinking about the last lesson. Allow them time to share their thoughts. Listen and acknowledge.

Lesson Content

Inform: In our last lesson we looked at the effects of climate change, the Paris Agreement and subsequent UN Climate Action Summits. The Paris Climate Change Agreement set the goal of "holding the increase in the global average temperature to well below 2°C (3.6°F) above pre-industrial levels and pursuing efforts to limit the temperature increase to 1.5°C (2.7°F). ... Human activities have already warmed the planet about 1°C (1.8°F) since the pre-industrial era"[4], that is the latter half of the 19th century. "At the current rate of warming, Earth would reach the 1.5°C threshold between 2030 and 2052."

"Limiting warming to 1.5°C is not easy and requires drastic changes to our energy, transportation, food, and building systems. Net CO_2 (carbon dioxide) emissions need to drop 45 percent from their 2010 levels by 2030, and reach net-zero by 2050 (meaning that any remaining CO_2 emissions would need to be offset by removing carbon dioxide from the atmosphere).

Meeting this goal involves a large jump in renewables for the global energy supply, providing 70-85 percent of electricity use by 2050." ... It is also important to remove some "CO_2 from the atmosphere." (The remainder of this article from Climate Central is in the Appendix, Item 3.)

Say, "So let's look at how we humans contribute to the warming of the planet. The warming of the planet is called the greenhouse effect."

➢ Ask one of the students to read the following aloud to the group as you list the things that are causing global warming.

---

[4] Climate Central, April 2019

How do humans contribute to the Greenhouse Effect?

Source: West, Larry. *What is the Greenhouse Effect?* May 11, 2018. ThoughtCo. https://www.thoughtco.com/what-is-the-greenhouse-effect-1203853

"While the greenhouse effect is an essential environmental prerequisite for life on Earth, there really can be too much of a good thing.

- The problems begin when human activities distort and accelerate the natural process by creating *more* greenhouse gases in the atmosphere than are necessary to warm the planet to an ideal temperature.

- Burning natural gas, coal and oil — including gasoline for automobile engines — raises the level of carbon dioxide in the atmosphere.

- Some farming practices and land-use changes increase the levels of methane and nitrous oxide.

- Many factories produce long-lasting industrial gases that do not occur naturally, yet contribute significantly to the enhanced greenhouse effect and "global warming" that is currently under way.

- Deforestation also contributes to global warming. Trees use carbon dioxide and give off oxygen in its place, which helps to create the optimal balance of gases in the atmosphere. As more forests are logged for timber or cut down to make way for farming, however, there are fewer trees to perform this critical function."

➢ Ask another student to read the following aloud to the group as you continue to list the things that are causing global warming. Perhaps ask another student to help you mind map in order to keep up with the material being read.

What are the main man-made greenhouse gases?

Source: https://www.theguardian.com/environment/2011/feb/04/man-made-greenhouse-gases

"The strength of the Earth's greenhouse effect is determined by the concentration in the atmosphere of a handful of greenhouse gases. The one that causes the most warming overall is water vapour – though human activity affects its level in the atmosphere indirectly rather than directly.

The greenhouse gases that humans do emit directly in significant quantities are:
• **Carbon dioxide** (CO_2). Accounts for around three-quarters of the warming impact of current human greenhouse-gas emissions. The key source of CO_2 is the burning of fossil fuels such as coal, oil and gas, though deforestation is also a very significant contributor.

• **Methane** (CH4). Accounts for around 14% of the impact of current human greenhouse-gas emissions. Key sources include agriculture (especially livestock and rice fields), fossil fuel extraction and the decay of organic waste in landfill sites. Methane doesn't persist in the atmosphere as long as CO2, though its warming effect is much more potent for each gram of gas released.

• **Nitrous oxide** (N2O). Accounts for around 8% of the warming impact of current human greenhouse-gas emissions. Key sources include agriculture (especially nitrogen-fertilised soils and livestock waste) and industrial processes. Nitrous oxide is even more potent per gram than methane.

• **Fluorinated gases** ("F gases"). Account for around 1% of the warming impact of current human greenhouse-gas emissions. Key sources are industrial processes. F-gases are even more potent per gram than nitrous oxide.

Human activity also changes the planet's temperature in other ways. For example, vapour trails from planes, soot from fires and tropospheric ozone created indirectly by local pollution all tend to increase warming. On the other hand, aerosol particles produced by some vehicles and industrial processes tend to bounce sunlight away from the earth, temporarily counteracting some of the warming caused by man-made greenhouse gases.

Discuss/Share

Share: "This list on the board is the things that are causing the warming of our Earth's atmosphere. It is the beginning of a list of the things that we can impact. Each one of us has an impact on the environment; we can make a difference. We will be adding to this list in the next couple of weeks."

Ask:

• Discussion? Does anyone have a question about any of this?

• Is there anything you would like to add?

➢ Say, "Let's pick areas to explore in terms of the greenhouse gases that humans emit directly in significant quantities. Let's start with carbon dioxide (CO2). This accounts for about 'three-quarters of the warming impact of current human greenhouse-gas emissions. The key source of CO2 is the burning of fossil fuels such as coal, oil and gas.' Deforestation is also a very significant contributor.'"

Activity — Decreasing CO2 Emissions

Step 1. Inform the students that you will be asking them to work as small groups to discuss ways to reduce CO2 emissions. One way to decrease the use of coal, oil and gas is to use renewable energy sources.

Share the following news: As of April 2019, a third of global power capacity was based on renewable energy, a huge increase over ten years before.

Source: UN Climate Change News, 3 April 2019. https://unfccc.int/news/ renewable-energy-accounts-for-third-of-global-power-capacity-irena

"The decade-long trend of strong growth in renewable energy capacity continued in 2018 with global additions of 171 gigawatts (GW), according to new data released by the International Renewable Energy Agency (IRENA). The annual increase of 7.9 per cent was bolstered by new additions from solar and wind energy, which accounted for 84 per cent of the growth. A third of global power capacity is now based on renewable energy.

Say, "We still have a long way to go, but we are moving in the right direction."

Step 2. Divide students into small working groups. Ask them to discuss/research:
- current renewable energy industry methods being used to decrease the use of coal, oil and gas
- things people can do in their daily lives to decrease use of coal, oil and gas. Perhaps research the decrease in emissions if using a bicycle versus a car fueled by gasoline; how can we organize our lives to use less energy
- things people can do to decrease deforestation
- planting trees as something people and communities can do to combat climate change

Step 3. Ask each group to prepare a presentation to the class. These can be given during the next lesson.

Close with the Sending Peace to the Earth relaxation/focusing exercise.

SIMPLICITY AND CARING
FOR THE EARTH AND HER OCEANS LESSON 6
Decreasing Carbon Dioxide Emissions

Begin with a song with lyrics about nature.

Ask how they are and if they have been thinking about the last lesson. Allow them time to share their thoughts. Listen and acknowledge.

Activity

Step 1. Allow the small groups to prepare for their presentations.

Step 2. Invite each small group to present. As they present, create a list titled What We Can Do Daily on a large piece of paper or on the board of things people can do to decrease carbon dioxide emissions. After the first group, only list new actions. Keep that list in a prominent place. Lead the applause after each presentation.

Step 3. Ask them to think about increasing awareness of this challenge. Is everyone aware of the causes of climate change, the importance of decreasing emissions and what practical things they can do to help in this important task?

Step 4. Invite the small groups to create a song, poster, slogan or campaign to raise awareness.

Step 5. Invite them to share their creation with the entire group.

If there is time, close with a relaxation/focusing exercise of their choice.

SIMIIPLICITY AND CARING

FOR THE EARTH AND HER OCEANS LESSON 7

Deforestation and the Exchange Between Trees and Humans

Begin with a song with lyrics about nature.

Ask how they are and if they have been thinking about the last lesson. Allow them time to share their thoughts. Listen and acknowledge.

Ask:

- Are there any other practical things you have thought of that each of us could do to decrease carbon emissions? If so, add it to the viewable What We Can Do Daily list created during the previous lesson. (A sample What We Can Do Daily List is in the Appendix, Item 5.)

- How about turning off the television or putting on sleep a computer or tablet when not using it? Each one can do that.

Lesson Content

Source: National Geographic. https://www.nationalgeographic.com /environment/global-warming/deforestation/

Climate 101: Deforestation

By Christina Nunez, published 7 February 2019

"As the world seeks to slow the pace of climate change, preserve wildlife, and support billions of people, trees inevitably hold a major part of the answer. Yet the mass destruction of trees—deforestation—continues, sacrificing the long-term benefits of standing trees for short-term gain.

Forests still cover about 30 percent of the world's land area, but they are disappearing at an alarming rate. Between 1990 and 2016, the world lost 502,000 square miles (1.3 million square kilometers) of forest, according to the World Bank—an area larger than South Africa. Since humans started cutting down forests, 46 percent of trees have been felled, according to a 2015 study in the journal Nature. About 17 percent of the Amazonian rainforest has been destroyed over the past 50 years, and losses recently have been on the rise.

We need trees for a variety of reasons, not least of which is that they absorb not only the carbon dioxide that we exhale, but also the heat-trapping greenhouse gases that human activities emit. As those gases enter the atmosphere, global warming increases, a trend scientists now prefer to call climate change. Tropical tree cover alone can provide 23 percent of the climate mitigation needed over the next decade to meet goals set in the Paris Agreement in 2015, according to one estimate.

Causes of deforestation

Farming, grazing of livestock, mining, and drilling combined account for more than half of all deforestation. Forestry practices, wildfires and, in small part, urbanization account for the rest. In Malaysia and Indonesia, forests are cut down to make way for producing palm oil, which can be found in everything from shampoo to saltines. In the Amazon, cattle ranching and farms—particularly soy plantations—are key culprits.

Logging operations, which provide the world's wood and paper products, also fell countless trees each year. Loggers, some of them acting illegally, also build roads to access more and more remote forests—which leads to further deforestation. Forests are also cut as a result of growing urban sprawl as land is developed for homes.

Not all deforestation is intentional. Some is caused by a combination of human and natural factors like wildfires and overgrazing, which may prevent the growth of young trees.

Why it matters and what can be done

Deforestation affects the people and animals where trees are cut, as well as the wider world. Some 250 million people living in forest and savannah areas depend on them for subsistence and income—many of them among the world's rural poor. Eighty percent of Earth's land animals and plants live in forests, and deforestation threatens species including the orangutan, Sumatran tiger, and many species of birds. Removing trees deprives the forest of portions of its canopy, which blocks the sun's rays during the day and retains heat at night. That disruption leads to more extreme temperature swings that can be harmful to plants and animals.

Yet the effects of deforestation reach much farther. The South American rainforest, for example, influences regional and perhaps even global water cycles, and it's key to the water supply in Brazilian cities and neighboring countries. The Amazon actually helps furnish water to some of the soy farmers and beef ranchers who are clearing the forest. The loss of clean water and biodiversity from all forests could have many other effects we can't foresee, touching even your morning cup of coffee.

In terms of climate change, cutting trees both adds carbon dioxide to the air and removes the ability to absorb existing carbon dioxide. If tropical deforestation were a country, according to the World Resources Institute, it would rank third in carbon dioxide-equivalent emissions, behind China and the U.S.

The numbers are grim, but many conservationists see reasons for hope. A movement is under way to preserve existing forest ecosystems and restore lost tree cover. Organizations and activists are working to fight illegal mining and logging—National Geographic Explorer Topher White, for example, has come up with a way to use recycled cell phones to monitor for chainsaws. In Tanzania, the residents of Kokota have planted more than 2 million trees on their small island over a decade, aiming to repair previous damage. And in Brazil, conservationists are rallying in the face of ominous signals that the government may roll back forest protections.

For consumers, it makes sense to examine the products and meats you buy, looking for sustainably produced sources when you can."

Discuss/Share

Ask:

- Would anyone like to share their response to the article?
- Any other responses or questions?
- Trees benefit us by taking in the carbon dioxide we exhale and producing oxygen. How else do trees benefit us?
- Do you have a favorite tree? Why do you love that tree?

⭐ The United Nations Environmental Protection Agency has a project asking people to plant one tree per person to help offset our carbon footprint. There was a one billion tree project in China and they achieved their goal of planting one billion trees.

- Would you like to plant some trees as a class project?

➤ If the response is yes, discuss the practicalities for your situation and make a plan. *Consider:*
Would you like to do something schoolwide/university-wide or in cooperation with your town/city?
Or, would you like to plant more trees at your home or in a deforested area?
What trees would most benefit your area and the people in it?

Activity

Ask each student to write a message to the world from a tree or an animal in a forest. It can be a simple message or it can take the form of a poem or a song. Allow those who wish to share their message, poem or song to do so. If some have created songs, sing them as a group. If there is time, allow the students to write a response back to the tree — and share those.

Close with playing music with the sounds of nature and invite the young adults to share a line from their poem or song.

SIMIIPLICITY AND CARING

FOR THE EARTH AND HER OCEANS LESSON 8

Plastic, Toxic Gyres and the Effect on Marine Life

Begin with a song with lyrics about nature.

Ask how they are and if they have been thinking about the last lesson. Allow them time to share their thoughts and comment about the tree planting plan, if it's on. Listen and acknowledge.

Lesson Content

Inform: Eight to ten percent of the total oil supply goes to making plastic, adding significantly to the carbon dioxide in the atmosphere. However, plastic is also causing other problems.

- ➤ If students have the ability to do internet research in the classroom, allow them to do so, and then invite them to share in small groups. Or, share with them the following information.

The processing of 17 million barrels of oil for one country to make bottles of water produced more than 2.5 million tons of carbon dioxide. It took three liters of water to produce one liter of bottled water.[5]

"The manufacture of one pound of PET (polyethylene terephthalate) plastic can produce up to three pounds of carbon dioxide. . . . The manufacture of plastic resins accounts for the highest percentage of a plastic bottle's carbon footprint. During processing, hydrocarbons in petroleum and natural gas are heated to extremely high temperatures to break down large hydrocarbon molecules into smaller ones." Processing plastic resins and transporting plastic bottles contribute to a bottle's carbon footprint in a major way. Estimates show that one 500-milliliter (0.53 quarts) plastic bottle of water has a total carbon footprint equal to 82.8 grams (about 3 ounces) of carbon dioxide.[6]

Plastic Bags in Our Oceans[7]

"Plastic bags in our oceans are a source of dioxin and other pollutants that are changing marine habitats and polluting our food chain. . . .

Thousands of marine animals choke and die from ingesting this plastic, and many more are being slowly poisoned by the dioxin and other pollutants introduced by this mass of plastic. Dioxin is an endocrine disrupter, a so-called gender-bender pollutant because it causes gender mutations in fish and land animals that eat fish, like sea bass, seals, and even polar bears.

The plastic in our oceans affects us all. It enters our food chain. It contributes to extinction. It pollutes the very water that replenishes our planet."

Ocean Gyres

Source: http://5gyres.org

"Our oceans are dynamic systems, made up of complex networks of currents that circulate water around the world. Large systems of these currents, coupled with wind and the earth's rotation, create "gyres", massive, slow rotating whirlpools. There are five major gyres in the oceans of the world in which plastic trash has accumulated."

---

[5] https://pacinst.org/publication/bottled-water-and-energy-a-fact-sheet/

[6] https://sciencing.com/carbon-footprint-plastic-bottle-12307187.html

[7] https://1bagatatime.com/learn/plastic-bags-oceans/

Plastic Pollution Affects Sea Life Throughout the Ocean

Source: https://www.pewtrusts.org/en/research-and
analysis/articles/2018/09/24/plastic-pollution-affects-sea-life-throughout-the-ocean

"According to the United Nations, at least 800 species worldwide are affected by marine debris, and as much as 80 percent of that litter is plastic. It is estimated that up to 13 million metric tons of plastic ends up in the ocean each year—the equivalent of a rubbish or garbage truck load's worth every minute. Fish, seabirds, sea turtles, and marine mammals can become entangled in or ingest plastic debris, causing suffocation, starvation, and drowning. Humans are not immune to this threat: While plastics are estimated to take up to hundreds of years to fully decompose, some of them break down much quicker into tiny particles, which in turn end up in the seafood we eat."

> ➤ Please share the following story, taken from LVE's *Green Values Club* book, Chapter Three. In Chapter Two, Katie and George have found and caught an injured seagull at the beach in the previous chapter. Katie is George's older sister.

Share a Story: Toxic Plastic Soup

Katie and George took turns carrying the gull home after they tied the dinghy next to Papa's boat.

"He's heavier than he looks," panted George.

"I'll take him for a while," Katie replied, holding out her arms for the gull.

Papa and Mama were at the kitchen table when they got home. "Still hungry?" asked Papa. "You both did a lot this morning."

George and Katie told their story as they sat at the table while Papa poured some yummy smelling soup into two bowls.

Mama had taken the gull into her lap and was gently examining its wing. "He's had a rough time with that plastic bag, it looks like. Besides being underweight, it looks like he has a broken wing."

Mama soon had gauze tape wrapped around the gull to hold the broken wing still. "He should be almost as good as new in two or three weeks, unless he's been eating plastic," she said. "George, can you find a big box for him?"

"The beach was full of trash today," said Katie, "more than I've ever seen. Plastic caps and bottles, plastic cups and bags, food wrappers, Styrofoam cups, soda cans — it was terrible."

Papa frowned. "People!" He said it like a swear word.

"Papa, you sound more upset than usual about the trash," said George, bringing in a big cardboard box.

"Yeah, I am," said Papa. "Here, let me give you a hand." He grabbed a knife and helped George cut the top of the cardboard box for the gull.

"I've known for years that sea birds, dolphins, whales, seals, sea turtles and many marine animals get caught in nets, fishing wire and human trash, but I just learned last week that *over 60 percent* of marine mammals and seabirds get entangled in human trash or eat marine debris. When they eat plastic trash it causes internal injury, intestinal blockage and starvation. I had no idea the percentage of animals being hurt was that high."

"And the gyres in the ocean are growing," said Mama softly. "There are now five huge gyres in different parts of the world where the plastic trash is accumulating. The plastic breaks down into small pieces over time and the animals are mistaking it for food and eating it."

Papa and George had finished cutting off the top of the box. The family went outside with the box, Katie cradling the gull. The gull seemed to know it was being cared for. It had stopped squawking when Mama immobilized his broken wing. It was bright and beautiful outside, with a soft breeze. The trees gave some needed shade to the patio.

"You're going to be just fine," said Katie as she and George petted the gull. Katie brought some food for the gull and George brought some water. They were happy to see the gull eating. They arranged the box so the gull was safe, putting a heavy grill over the box and anchoring it with four stones so a cat couldn't get him.

"What can we do about it?" Katie asked.

"About what?" said Mama.

"About the animals getting all entangled and the gyres."

Papa and Mama looked at her and then at each other.

"You know, Katie, you and George are terrific about not trashing our world, and your Papa and I shop carefully, but I think it's time to think more and do more and spread the word. Our Earth, our ocean, is in trouble."

"I want to help," said George.

"Great," Mama smiled. "I think not being a litterbug is important and our family never uses Styrofoam which is full of toxins, but it's time to do much more than that. We need to not buy things that harm the Earth. What's creating the gyres in the ocean is plastic. Some of them are thousands of miles by thousands of miles — it's like toxic plastic soup! The North Pacific Gyre is twice the size of the United States."

"How about we don't buy plastic?" asked George.

"Well, not buying any plastic is not practical," said Mama slowly. "A lot of things are made of hard plastic, like computer keyboards, games and certain car parts. We can recycle those things when they get old — and buy fewer things. It's mostly the one-use disposal plastic that is the problem. So not buying that is a great idea. If we really try, we could probably cut buying one-use disposable plastic things by at least 90%."

"Do you mean like plastic cups, plastic bags and water in plastic bottles?" asked Katie.

"Exactly," said Mama.

"That's going to be a little hard," said George. "Does that mean no sodas in plastic bottles?"

"Yes. Can you do that?" asked Papa with a questioning look.

George winched. "Maybe for the gulls and the seals and the dolphins I could."

"And we could bring our own cloth shopping bags to the store," said Katie. "We could use a glass bottle or metal bottle when we want to bring water somewhere and we could use it over and over again."

"Terrific idea," said Mama. "And I could shop locally at Farmers Markets and try to not buy food wrapped in plastic. And we can wash our sandwich bags and reuse them, or use waxed paper or banana leaves."

"Your mother and I have been talking about this a lot the last few days," said Papa. "We're going to see if the city council will ban plastic bags. Would you like to come to the city council meeting with us?"

"Maybe some of our friends could come too," said Katie.

"Wow," said George, his face lighting up, "what if everyone did this? Maybe we could stop the gyres growing. Toxic plastic soup does not sound good for animals or the ocean. What do you think Mr. Gull?" he asked, looking at the seagull.

Did the seagull just nod in approval?

Ask:
- What values did you perceive in the story?
- Which of the ideas in the story about not contributing to plastic waste would work in your life?
- Do you have other ideas about not contributing to plastic waste?

Lesson Content

Please share the following content with students.

Source: http://5gyres.org

"Just a generation ago, we packaged our products in reusable or recyclable materials — glass, metals, and paper, and designed products that would last. Today, our landfills and beaches are awash in plastic packaging, and expendable products that have no value at the end of their short lifecycle.

The short-term convenience of using and throwing away plastic products carries a very inconvenient long-term truth. These plastic water bottles, cups, utensils, electronics, toys, and gadgets we dispose of daily are rarely recycled in a closed loop. We currently recover only 5% of the plastics we produce. What happens to the rest of it? Roughly 50% is buried in landfills, some is remade into durable goods, and much of it remains "unaccounted for", lost in the environment where it ultimately washes out to sea.

In the ocean, some of ... plastics ... and foamed plastics float on the oceans' surface. Sunlight and wave action cause these floating plastics to fragment, breaking into increasingly smaller particles, but never completely disappearing— at least on any documented time scale. This plastic pollution is becoming a hazard for marine wildlife, and ultimately for us.

The North Pacific Gyre, the most heavily researched for plastic pollution, spans an area roughly twice the size of the United States — though it is a fluid system, shifting seasonally in size and shape. Designed to last, plastic trash in the gyre will remain for decades or longer, being pushed gently in a slow, clockwise spiral towards the center. Most of the research on plastic trash circulating in oceanic gyres has focused on the North Pacific, but there are 5 major oceanic gyres worldwide, with several smaller gyres in Alaska and Antarctica.

We must demand zero tolerance for plastic pollution. Reducing our consumption and production of plastic waste, and choosing cost-effective alternatives will go a long way towards protecting our seas — and ultimately ourselves."

Ask:
- Does anyone want to share their response to this information?
- Can you think of other ideas to prevent plastic becoming trash in fields and rivers?
- Can you think of other ideas to help not contribute to plastic waste?
- It's hard to do some of these things sometimes. What thought would encourage you to commit to not using single-use plastic items?

Activity

Step 1. Show the students pictures of the gyres. There are many websites on this subject.

Step 2. If there is time, allow the young adults to divide into small groups to further research this topic, such as the effects of Styrofoam and how plastic particles in the ocean "act as sponges for waterborne contaminants such as PCBs, DDT and other pesticides, PAHs and many hydrocarbons washed through our watersheds." (Same as source cited above.)

Step 3. Invite each small group to create a poster with their message.

Step 4. Invite each group to display their poster. They may wish to display their posters around the class and school, and post pictures of their posters and messages on social media sites.

Close with the Sending Peace to the Earth relaxation/focusing exercise. Perhaps add a line or two more about the ocean and marine animals and seabirds.

SIMPLICITY AND CARING

FOR THE EARTH AND HER OCEANS LESSON 9

Nitrous Oxide Emissions and the Ocean's Dead Zones

Begin with a song with lyrics about nature.

Ask how they are and if they have been thinking about the last lesson. Allow them time to share their thoughts. Listen and acknowledge.

Lesson Content

Share: "We learned in prior lessons that . . .

Nitrous oxide (N_2O). Accounts for around 8% of the warming impact of current human greenhouse-gas emissions. Key sources include agriculture (especially nitrogen-fertilized soils and livestock waste) and industrial processes. Nitrous oxide is even more potent per gram than methane."

Please read the abbreviated version of Chapter Four of the *Green Values Club* below.

Share a Story: We Can Make a Difference

Katie talked to some of her friends at school on Monday. They were amazed to hear about how she and George helped their father cut the netting off the trapped whale, rescued the seagull with the broken wing, and totally didn't know about the gyres.

"Why don't you talk to the teacher?" asked Carol. "Let's see if she'll let you tell the class about the gyres and the animals that die because they eat plastic. Maybe we can all get involved in helping."

"You really think everyone will want to?" asked Katie.

"Well maybe not everyone," said Kinesha, "but kids our age have really good hearts. We care about our planet — and our animal friends."

The girls talked to their science teacher at break and she was delighted. "Yes," Ms. Bennett said. "Katie, it would be great to have you share your story, and then let's see what ideas everyone comes up with. Learning about things is good, but doing something for our Earth is proof that we care."

Katie shared her story about the whale, the seagull and learning about the gyres with the whole class. She was a little nervous, and kept clearing her throat. She shared the ideas she and her family had come up with about reducing their use of one-use disposal plastic by 90 percent. Katie was amazed at the interest and the willingness of most of the students to commit to using less plastic.

"No more plastic bottles for me," offered Dana.

"My aunt brings her own cup when she travels on planes," offered Ta.

"No more plastic cups or straws when I'm out," said Maria, "I can ask for a real cup or bring my own."

"Great ideas," said Todd. "If it's going to help, I'm willing to not buy plastic bottles of stuff. But, what if it's really, really hot and I really want a soda? What if I buy it in a can?"

"Well, using an aluminum can is taking something you don't need from the Earth," said Ms. Bennett, "but IF you recycle it's not so bad. It's much better than using plastic."

"Well, I don't know," said a girl named Pam in a doubting voice, "why should we even try? If just a few of us do this, it's not going to help. We can't affect thousands of square miles of toxic plastic soup."

"Think of the one whale and the one seagull," said Katie, all of the sudden feeling confident. "It was a few people that made a difference for them. Small groups of people can make a difference — and imagine what would happen if kids all over the world did this. Some adults are really into this already. What if all the kids got all their parents to help?"

Katie shared her parents' idea about going to city council to ask for a ban on using plastic bags and plastic straws in the city. "I asked if I could invite some friends to go with us. Would anyone like to help?"

"Me," "me," "me" was heard all around the room.

Ms. Bennett divided them into three action groups on Friday. One group was going to make posters to support the ban on plastic bags and straws and another group was going to make up banners with slogans on respect for the ocean and the Earth by reducing the use of disposable plastic. The third group was going to create a petition to the school superintendent to ban all Styrofoam and reduce the use of plastic.

George and Katie talked on the way home. Katie told all him all about Ms. Bennett's science class on the environment.

"She told us," said Katie, "that there are dead zones in the ocean where there is little or no oxygen due to fertilizer-run-off and nitrogen pollution. She said that there are 405 reported dead zones and that they are doubling every ten years!"

"That's terrible," said George. "So what happens in these dead zones?" asked George. "There isn't enough oxygen for most fish to live?"

"Good thinking," said Katie. "Unfortunately, the fertilizer-run-off and nitrogen pollution and pesticides kill the kelp. She showed us some pictures of these really cool kelp forests. They are so beautiful. The kelp forests provide food and shelter to thousands of species — and 50 percent of the world's oxygen! Ms. Bennett said it's just as important to keep the kelp forests healthy as it is to keep the rain forests healthy!"

"So how do we stop the fertilizer-run-off and nitrogen pollution?" asked George.

"George, that's a really great question. We didn't think to ask it," said Katie. "Let's ask Mama and Papa when we get home."

Katie's mind flashed back. What had Ms. Bennett said?

"The chemical fertilizers and pesticides pollute the rivers and ocean," Ms. Bennett had said. "Unfortunately, this can also impact the ground water and negatively affect the quality of the soil. Food grown with pesticides has been shown to have harmful effects on humans, contributing to many different kinds of disease."

Ms. Bennett had assigned different groups to research specific components of fertilizers and pesticides. Tanya was part of the group Katie was in. "Wow," Tanya had whispered to Katie, "no wonder we have dead zones in the ocean! Gyres and dead zones. We humans are not taking good care of our world."

Ms. Bennett overheard, "You're right, Tanya," she smiled. "It's important to take care of our world."

Lesson Content

Source: The following excerpts were taken from the website of One World One Ocean.

> **The ocean is in trouble.**
> **90% of the big fish are gone.** Tuna, swordfish, halibut, cod, and flounder populations have been devastated by overfishing. Many of the fish caught today never even have the chance to reproduce.

"There are a reported 405 ocean 'dead zones' — areas where there is little to no oxygen due to fertilizer run-off and nitrogen pollution. Dead zones are doubling every ten years.

Our oceans account for 71% of the planet, but less than 2% of our oceans are protected. We have protections in place for nearly 12% of all land (through areas like national parks).

The ocean is at a tipping point. Oceanographer Sylvia Earle says human actions over the next 10 years will determine the state of the ocean for the next 10,000 years."

Lesson Content

Please read, or have one of the students read, the following information.
Source: Dolphin Research Center.

"Toxins enter the marine environment through land-based runoff and air pollution as well as ocean dumping. Things we use every day, like automobiles, air conditioners, and household products, create many toxins. Researchers routinely find high levels of toxins in the blubber of stranded marine mammals.
For years we dumped heavy metals and organic pollutants into our oceans thinking it was a resource so vast it could absorb any and all materials. It now seems that the oceans are finally becoming saturated. The evidence is in the marine life itself. Fish, turtles, and, most recently, dolphins are now growing cancerous tumors. There is also evidence that pollution in our oceans is weakening the immune systems of marine mammals.

Polychlorinated biphenyls (PCBs), which are linked to immune system suppression and reproductive failure, exist in extremely high levels in the blubber of dead dolphins and whales in many parts of the world. PCBs are a form of industrial waste.

Sewage and runoff from excess fertilizer feeds the growth of algae, which not only produce toxins, but also rob the water of huge amounts of oxygen needed by other forms of aquatic life to survive. Anything that upsets the delicate balance of the natural food web can ultimately destroy those species at the top: dolphins, whales, and humans.

Certain chemicals such as DDT and PCBs disrupt biological processes and cause widespread sterility, cancers and genetic abnormalities in populations of land animals."

Discuss/Share

Invite the students to share their reactions to the given information, acknowledging their concerns and answering any questions.

Ask:

- Have you ever seen green algae growing on rocks near the ocean's coast? (That is actually algae growing as a result of fertilizer contamination and is an indicator that the ocean in that area is polluted.)

Activity

Step 1. Ask the young adults form small groups and think about possible solutions. They may wish to do some further research.

Step 2. Ask each group to share their discussion and thoughts about possible solutions. Begin a Possible Actions list as they report. Is there anything they can do now?

End with the relaxation/focusing exercise, Sending Peace to the Earth.

SIMPLICITY AND CARING

FOR THE EARTH AND HER OCEANS LESSON 10

Methane Emissions and Diet

Begin with a song with lyrics about nature.

Ask how they are and if they have been thinking about the last lesson. Allow them time to share their thoughts. Listen and acknowledge.

Lesson Content

Share: "We learned a couple of lessons back that:

Methane (CH4). Accounts for around 14% of the impact of current human greenhouse-gas emissions. Key sources include agriculture (especially livestock and rice fields), fossil fuel extraction and the decay of organic waste in landfill sites.

Methane doesn't persist in the atmosphere as long as CO2, though its warming effect is much more potent for each gram of gas released."

Inform the class that you are going to share an excerpt from another chapter of the *Green Values Club*.

Share a Story: An Organic Garden

Katie announced at dinner one night, "I've decided on my answer to Ms. Bennett's homework question about one thing we can do that will most benefit the planet."

"What's that?" asked Mama.

"Be a vegetarian that eats organic food," said Katie.

"How would that help?" asked George looking puzzled.

"Well," said Katie enthusiastically, "if everyone was a vegetarian then people wouldn't fish and we wouldn't be overfishing and killing millions of fish, and if we all ate organic food then we wouldn't be poisoning the ocean and creating dead zones and the oceans would have healthy kelp forests and enough oxygen for a healthy ocean and enough fish again for the whales, and then the whales and dolphins wouldn't be getting trapped in nets because no one would be using nets!"

"You've really been thinking about this," said Papa, looking a little surprised.

"And," said Katie with a big smile, "that's not all. If everyone was a vegetarian, then we wouldn't be deforesting the Amazon because of the production of cattle and the demand for meat and the output of greenhouse gasses would be less so the whole planet would be healthier."

"Good reasoning," said Mama.

"But you're not really going to do it are you?" asked George.

"Do what?" asked Katie.

"Be a vegetarian."

"Well," said Katie, with a pause and a pleading look at her parents, "I was thinking that maybe I can't be a vegetarian that eats *only* organic food, but I could be a vegetarian that eats as much organic food as we can get." She took a deep breath as she looked at Mama and Papa. "I would really like to try it. Can I please? I really do think it would help our planet."

Mama looked at Katie, and then at Papa. "Luke?"

Papa looked at Mama. "It's okay with me. She has some great reasons. Is it okay with you?"

"Oh Katie," Mama said a tiny worried look. "You would have to promise me that you would eat healthy."

"The World Health Organization says it's the healthiest diet for human beings," said Katie.

"*If* you eat healthy," said Mama firmly. "Promise?"

"Yes."

"Okay. Then it is okay with me," Mama said.

Katie sprang up and gave Mama and then Papa a big hug.

"I am proud that you've really thought about it and want to help our planet," said Mama.

"Is it okay if I'm a vegetarian with her for two months and see if it works for me?" Papa asked Mama with a quizzical look.

Mama just laughed as she looked at her husband. Then she looked at her son with a questioning look. "George?"

"Not me," cringed George. "It wasn't my homework!"

"Okay," laughed Mama. "Two veggies and two non-veggies. But if you two don't eat healthy, I'm changing my mind!"

Discuss

- What do you think the best human diet would be to help our Earth and the ocean?

Activity

Divide the young adults into two or four groups, as you wish, and study the following.

Group One: The impact of the production of cattle, chickens and other animals in response to the demand for meat and the relationship of this to climate change. Include the output of greenhouse gasses and deforestation as a result of cattle production.

Group Two: Study the effect of different diets on your carbon footprint: meat-based diet, vegetarian diet, vegan diet.

Group Three: Study the effect of nitrogen-based fertilizers versus organic fertilizers on the Earth and her rivers and oceans. They may wish to create a mind map or a flow chart of the effects. They could include the benefits or harmful effects of non-organic versus organic food on the human body.

Invite each group to share their findings.

Close with a relaxation/focusing exercise of your or their choice.

SIMPLICITY AND CARING

FOR THE EARTH AND HER OCEANS LESSON 11

Reducing Your Carbon Footprint

Play a song with lyrics about nature.

Lesson Content

To reduce your **carbon footprint** means you are reducing your negative effect on the Earth. While technically a carbon footprint means the sum of all emissions of carbon dioxide that humans create in the use of products, the real intent is to reduce the sum of all emissions of greenhouse gases. In caring for the Earth and her oceans, we can not only decrease our use of products that create greenhouse gas emissions but we can offset our carbon footprint by doing something "green" to negate the effect of the emissions.

Discuss/Share

Ask:

- What would happen if everyone on Earth reduced their carbon footprint to zero by both reducing their use of products that create greenhouse gas emissions and doing something green?
- What are the things you can do to reduce your carbon footprint?

Activity Options

Option One: Ask the students to draw a large footprint on a piece of paper. Inside the footprint they are to write all the things that contribute to their carbon footprint. Ask them what things they think they can do to reduce their carbon footprint. For example, they can walk or bicycle more or not buy so many material things. They can repair or recycle their toys and other material things. They can also reduce their footprint by planting a tree or _____? Ask them to make another picture with another footprint that is smaller, writing all the things they can do to make that happen.

Option Two: Each individual could calculate his or her carbon footprint using one of the internet carbon footprint calculators. Do this for one year ago, and what it will be in one month.

Option Three: Divide the class into groups to calculate the percentage of reductions different changes would make. Make a graph or a poster with a footprint showing the different reductions. What offsetting changes will change your footprint from black into green? Invite them to present their poster to the entire group.

Close with the Sending Peace to the Earth Relaxation/Focusing exercise.

Thinking Homework: I would like all of you to think of one thing you could do that would make a positive difference for the Earth and her oceans — and the amazing things that would happen if everyone on Earth did that one thing. Tell them you know they will do many things to reduce their carbon footprint, but that you want them to think about some of the most important things humans can do.

SIMPLICITY AND CARING
FOR THE EARTH AND HER OCEANS LESSON 12
Systems Thinking — One amazingly helpful thing to do . . .

Play a song with lyrics about nature.

Share

- Please tell me about your thinking homework. What one thing you could do that would make a positive difference for the Earth and her oceans — and what amazing things would happen if everyone on Earth did that one thing?

- ➤ I'm going to ask you to put your idea in a circle in the middle of a piece of paper and mind map all the effects if everyone in the world were to do that thing.

    Examples:
    - ❖ What would be the many benefits of solar and wind power? What changes would be made in terms of cleaner air, the savings of not moving entire island-based communities, and health benefits with less lead poisoning near freeways?
    - ❖ If you chose picking up trash, do you want to define trash as anything harmful to humans or animals, such as land mines? What else would be affected by that?
    - ❖ Or, do you think organic farming might make an amazing impact on the land and the ocean?
    - ❖ If you were to choose being vegetarian, what would the many effect be? What would be the impact on biodiversity? How would it positively impact the migration of different species?
    - ❖ Or, how would the practice of one value effect our Earth and her oceans and all humans and animals?

Activity Options

Option One: Ask the students to mind map their idea individually.

Option Two: Invite the class to select different ideas that they feel would be amazingly helpful and form small interest groups to mind map that action and its effects. Invite each group to share their mind maps.

Close with the relaxation/focusing exercise, Sending Peace to the Earth.

SIMPLICITY AND CARING
FOR THE EARTH AND HER OCEANS LESSON 13
Choosing and Carrying Out an Ecological Project

Play a song with lyrics about nature.

Choosing an Ecological Project

Step 1. Ask the students if they would like to do an ecological project to benefit the school, organization or community — and if so, what they would like to do.

Step 2. Present some of the ideas below that you think might be pertinent to the students' areas of interest or important for the community. Or, they may have other ideas.

❖ *Agriculture:* Is there a space to have an organic garden in your location? Are there others interested in the school? Could some of the fresh produce be served for lunch? What organic fertilizers are available which could replace chemical fertilizers and pesticides? What changes occur in the soil when organic fertilizers are used? What challenges are there? Why do organic vegetables have greater nutritional value?

❖ *Energy:* Learn more about solar power, wind power or other renewal sources of energy. Is it possible for the school to actually save money by converting to solar? Perhaps making solar cookers would be of benefit in your community. Are there homes that do not have ovens? They might wish to study the new technology that converts plastic back into petroleum.

❖ *Forestry:* What about organizing planting of trees in the community with the help of businesses? What trees would be most beneficial in your area? They might wish to study what types of trees can grow well when there is pollution if they are to plant in an area with heavy air pollution. What density of trees would compensate most for the poor air quality? Maybe the city would allow them to create a natural garden in a vacant lot. Perhaps they can inspire businesses to donate trees so the city can become more beautiful — and healthy. Or, perhaps it would be beneficial to plant fruit trees.

❖ *Increasing Environmental Awareness:* Spread the word about the importance of reducing our carbon footprint and sensible, constructive ways to achieve such. Perhaps share your mind maps of "one amazingly helpful thing to do" for our Earth and her oceans on social media or video your presentations. Begin planning skits/dramas and artistic presentation about conservation (lesson 16) to the wider community. Students may also wish to take and ask others to take a test to see how green they are. Perhaps include this in your skits/drama. Post your skits on line and let us know at www.livingvalues.net! Make up respect-for-the-Earth slogans and post them at school and at other appropriate locales in the community as well as on social media. Or . . . ? Your generation is tops at spreading the word — thank you for your help in caring for our Earth and her oceans, and its humans and animals.

❖ *Recycling/Consumption:* What about a project to recycle in order to reduce the need for buying new things? Perhaps some students would like to organize a drive to clean and repair older things rather than buying new things, such as bicycles. The students could do this for themselves and their families or donate needed things and toys to homeless shelters.

❖ *Preventing Trash and Toxic Plastic Soup Build-up:* What about keeping the shore of the ocean or a lake or a local river or waterway clean of trash? Perhaps combine beach or river clean-ups with an awareness campaign about the gyres of toxic plastic soup. Has your city banned plastic bags yet? Has the city asked local organizations and restaurants to stop using Styrofoam?

❖ *Helping Whales and Dolphins:* Research solutions to stop harming whales and dolphins. For example, "backing down" nets so dolphins can swim over the top, using advanced technology "pingers" so dolphins and whales are warned away from the nets, and providing human monitors on each boat to make sure that no dolphins are hauled up in the nets. Are these reasonable solutions being used in your area?

❖ *Water:* What is the quality of water in the river or ocean? How is it tested? Do all people in your area have clean drinking water? What are simple methods to purify water? Is there an ocean dead zone in your area? What can be done to help the ocean be healthy again in that zone? Are there marine protection zones in your area?

❖ *Environmental Needs in the Community:* What are the Earth's needs in your community? If rubbish or waste are affecting the clean water supply, address those issues. Some students may want to research local usage of pesticides and natural and less expensive alternatives that do not pollute the Earth or its inhabitants. Get involved in creating organic gardens or change an empty space with rubbish into a garden or park. If a nearby river is being polluted, students can investigate alternative methods for the polluters to dispose of their waste safely and effectively. Thoroughly research the topic, plan a formal presentation, and then as a team discuss how you can present it to the polluting farm or company with your best "people skills."

Step 3. Allow the students to create a number of project ideas and then select several that create the greatest interest. Do they wish to all do the same project as a class, or would they like to form groups and take on different projects?

Step 4. Students could choose to do a project for a week or two, or do a semester long service-learning project. Each group may wish to study further before creating a plan/proposal. Please allow them time to study and develop their plan. They may need a week or more. Please help them during this lesson and the next to make their plans practical, so it is possible for them to achieve their goal.

End each lesson with the relaxation/focusing exercise, Sending Peace to the Earth. The students may wish to add a few more lines. Or, they may wish to create their own relaxation exercise.

SIMPLICITY AND CARING
FOR THE EARTH AND HER OCEANS LESSON 14
Messages from the Media

Begin with a song.
Ask the students about their environmental project.

Lesson Content

Please share the following points, discussing them with students as appropriate.

- Appreciating the beauty of nature and the Earth sometimes allows us to appreciate the natural beauty of the self more.
- The more we appreciate natural beauty, the less we are fooled into thinking we have to own certain things or look a certain way to feel good about ourselves or be accepted by others.

- In order to sell things, businesses hire advertising firms to create impressive advertisements so people buy their products. Sometimes they imply you will be more attractive or "cool" if you use their product or own what they are selling.

- These advertisements fool people into thinking they need these things to be okay and for other people to consider them okay.

- When people hear many messages like that, they often forget about the importance of inner beauty. These messages do not encourage people to respect the Earth or the inner self.

- The self knows there is natural beauty inside. When we keep that awareness in mind, we can be content about our own value, enjoy others for who they are, and give happiness. Simplicity is being natural. Simplicity is beautiful.

Activity

Invite the students to do the following.

❖ Brainstorm messages from the mass media and advertisements. List those on the board.

❖ Choose one of the messages and discuss.

• Ask: Is this message true?

❖ Make another list of thoughts they think are closer to nature and natural beauty.

Select another message or two and do the same. Ask them to bring in examples of ads for the next lesson.

Discuss/Share

Invite the students to divide into groups of four to six to discuss one or two of the reflection points in regard to the messages from advertisers and peer pressure.

♦ Simplicity asks whether we are being induced to purchase unnecessary products. Psychological enticements create artificial needs. Desires stimulated by wanting unnecessary things result in value clashes complicated by greed, fear, peer pressure, and a false sense of identity. Once fulfillment of basic necessities allows for a comfortable lifestyle, extremes and excesses invite overindulgence and waste.

♦ Simplicity avoids waste, teaches economy, avoids value clashes complicated by greed, fear, peer pressure, and a false sense of identity.

♦ Simplicity helps create sustainable development.

♦ Simplicity is the precursor to sustainable development. Simplicity teaches us economy — how to use our resources with the needs of future generations in mind.

♦ Simplicity calls upon people to rethink their values.

Invite each group to share.

End with a song, dance simplicity or enjoy a relaxation/focusing exercise of their choice.

Homework: For one week, ask everyone to experiment with simplicity by wearing simple clothes to school or when out with friends. Suggest that rather than being so conscious of how they look, that they keep in mind that simplicity is beautiful and that is being natural.

SIMPLICITY AND CARING
FOR THE EARTH AND HER OCEANS LESSON 15
More Ads

Begin with a song.

If they took up the last lesson's homework, ask for their feelings and reactions.

Ask the students about their environmental project.

Activity

Ask the students to share ads and other messages they have brought in.

For each ad, ask them what the message is, and if the message is true.

Also question:

• What is the advertiser valuing?

• Are there some ads that have beneficial messages? Which do and which don't?

Share: "Sometimes there are high prices to the Earth for the things manufacturers want us to buy. A short video from the World Economic Forum states:

Here are 7 astonishing facts on how our culture of fast fashion harms the environment.

1. The fashion industry causes 10% of all greenhouse gas emissions. Producing more emissions than all international flights and shipping combined.

2. Every second, one garage truck of textiles is burned or sent to landfills. And three in five items bought are thrown away in a year.

3. Washing one synthetic garment releases about 2,000 plastic microfibers which enter the ocean and the food chain.

4. It takes 2,700 liters of water to make a cotton shirt. That's what one person drinks in 2.5 years.

5. Making and washing one pair of jeans emits the same CO_2 as driving 69 miles.

6. 120 million trees are cut down every year to make clothes. And 30% of the rayon and viscose used in fashion comes from endangered and ancient forests.

7. Up to 16% of the world's pesticides are used in cotton farming every year. The chemicals degrade soil and pollute water as well as poisoning cotton pickers.

You can help reduce the impact of fashion by buying fewer clothes, choosing natural fibers, and recycling what you discard.

- Will you change your wardrobe to help the environment?"

➢ Invite their reaction. (Is there a possibility of not only buying less but recycling and reusing within the school or neighborhood?)

➢ Ask them to generate messages they believe in.

Discuss/Share

Divide the class into small groups and ask them to discuss one or more of the following reflection points.

Ask each group to summarize their discussion by creating a new reflection point or creating a slogan to display.

♦ Simplicity teaches us economy — how to use our resources keeping future generations in mind.

♦ Simplicity is appreciating inner beauty and recognizing the value of all actors, even the poorest and worst off.

♦ Simplicity helps decrease the gap between "the haves" and "the have nots" by demonstrating the logic of true economics: to earn, save, invest, and share the sacrifices and the prosperity so that there can be a better quality of life for all people regardless of where they were born.

Close with a relaxation/focusing exercise of their choice.

SIMPLICITY AND CARING

FOR THE EARTH AND HER OCEANS LESSON 16

Which Sustainable Development Goals are we making progress on?

Play a song with lyrics about nature, a better world or healing the world.

Lesson Content

| Goal 1: No Poverty |
| Goal 2: Zero Hunger |
| Goal 3: Good Health and Well-being |
| Goal 4: Quality Education |
| Goal 5: Gender Equality |
| Goal 6: Clean Water and Sanitation |
| Goal 7: Affordable and Clean Energy |
| Goal 8: Decent Work and Economic Growth |
| Goal 9: Industry, Innovation and Infrastructure |
| Goal 10: Reduced Inequality |
| Goal 11: Sustainable Cities and Communities |
| Goal 12: Responsible Consumption and Production |
| Goal 13: Climate Action |
| Goal 14: Life Below Water |
| Goal 15: Life on Land |
| Goal 16: Peace and Justice Strong Institutions |
| Goal 17: Partnerships to achieve the Goal |

Activity

Step 1. Look at the list of 17 Sustainable Development Goals. Go down the list, asking the class which goals they feel they are making progress on. They can evaluate this in terms of their own personal efforts and/or their effort as a class. Mark the goals with a plus mark if they affirm progress

Step 2. Make Simplicity and Caring for the Earth and Her Oceans "Leaves" in an aqua for each one of the SDGs upon which their group is focused, writing specific ways that value is affecting the SDGs. Ask them to be specific about the ways they are making progress on each goal either as individuals or as a class. For example, the relaxation/focusing exercises may be contributing to their wellbeing. Many of the actions they may have taken during this unit could be listed under Climate Action.

Step 3. Invite them to attach their Simplicity and Caring for the Earth Leaves on the class artistic presentation of the SDGs.

Step 4. Ask the students to look at each SDG on the class artistic representation and reflect on the possibility of making further progress on any one of these. Discuss specific options. Don't feel like you need to do them all, but begin with verbalizing possibilities.

Examples:

❖ Is the quality of water good at your school? Research simple ways to make it better if it is not. A temporary method of putting water in glass bottles in the sunlight is one method to purify water and would help physical health. However, if the water quality is not good, research what is causing it to be of poor quality locally. What can be done about that? Is there a group of students in your class or school that would like to investigate or act to promote positive action?

❖ Are you helping Life Below Water with reduced use of plastic and chemical fertilizer run-off by using only organic foods?

❖ Can your physical facility use clean energy or reduce energy use of fossil fuels?

❖ Is there a school pantry or access to food for those who do not have sufficient or healthy food?

❖ Would you like to create an organic garden and use that food to help students or families who are hungry?

Step 5. Ask the class if they would like to put into action any of the possibilities they discussed. See what is practical, sensible and possible. Perhaps they would like to form several action groups.

Step 6. Invite the action groups to meet and form a plan.

Step 7. Invite each group to present their ideas.

Step 8. Congratulate them all for the progress they are making for a better world for all and put on some music to dance, inviting them to make movements they would feel if they were the Earth and knew the people of the Earth cared and were working to make her heathy again.

End with breathing with the Earth for two minutes in silence.

SIMPLICITY AND CARING

FOR THE EARTH AND HER OCEANS LESSON 17

An Artistic Creation and Presentation for Our Earth and Her Oceans

Play a song with lyrics about nature.

Reflect

Invite the young adults to reflect for a moment on the most important things they learned during this simplicity and caring for the Earth and her oceans unit. Ask them to write down two of these.

Creative Expression

Step 1. Invite the students to form groups and create songs, poems, dramas/skits about the Earth and her ocean, highlighting some of the things they think are most important.

Step 2. Give them time to perform. Enjoy.

Step 3. Think about sharing their creations at another time, perhaps with another class, at a special assembly, at another school with younger students, or at a community gathering. Perhaps post some of the creations on social media.

Additional Lessons for Another Year

SIMPLICITY AND CARING
FOR THE EARTH AND HER OCEANS LESSON 17
The Simplicity of Nature

Begin with a song with lyrics about nature.

Lesson Content

Read the following poem by Adelia Prado.

> ### Anímico
> A new tree was born in my garden,
> Which gives a yellow flower,
> Every morning I go there to hear the sounds,
> Of the insect tapping and its party.
> There are all kinds of sounds,
> The indelicate, the refined, the learner's and the master's,
> Sounds like feet, wings, mouths, beaks and of pollen dust,
> In front of the heat of the sun.
> It seems that the little tree is having a chat.

Discuss/Share

Ask:

- How does the author describe the simplicity of nature?
- What helps you tune into the beauty of nature?
- What values can we learn from nature?

Activity

Step 1. If there is a garden or a small forest near the school, organize a short visit. Give the students the opportunity to practice silent observation. Allow them some time to sit silently and write some of their observations or begin to write a poem.

If this is not possible, do the Imagining a Peaceful World visualization from Lesson 3 of the Peace I values unit in this book. Please adapt it, including more nature images.

Step 2. Afterwards, divide the class into several groups.

Step 3. Ask them to read the same poem again and then create a collective poem about different experiences with nature. Allow them to write individual poems also, if they wish to do so.

Step 4. Finish the activity by asking the students to share their experiences and poems. The poems can be displayed in the classroom or in another area of the school.

— Contributed by Paulo Barros, Brazil

SIMPLICITY AND CARING

FOR THE EARTH AND HER OCEANS LESSON 18

Stories and Interviews

Begin with a song.

Read a story about the theme of simplicity.

Discuss the Reflection Points:

♦ Simplicity is being natural.

♦ Simplicity is staying in the present and not making things complicated.

♦ Simplicity is giving patience, friendship, and encouragement.

♦ Simplicity is appreciating the small things in life.

Activity Options

Write a short personal essay or poem on one of the above Reflection Points.

Divide the students into small groups and ask them to make up a song. Allow them to share their song to the class.

Homework: Interview important people in your life about the simple things in their life that are most important.

SIMPLICITY AND CARING

FOR THE EARTH AND HER OCEANS LESSON 19

Simplicity Skits

Begin with a song.

Discuss/Share

Ask the young adults to share about the interviews they did as homework from the prior lesson. When several have shared, ask them which values are inherent in the simple things people felt were important.

Activity

Form small groups and invite them to make up a skit on making life simple. (Do they want to include the complexity of worry in their skit?)

Allow each group to present their skit to the class.

Close with a song or a relaxation/focusing exercise.

SIMPLICITY AND CARING

FOR THE EARTH AND HER OCEANS LESSON 20

Environmental History

Begin the activity with a song or music related to nature.

Lesson Content

Knowing and appreciating the history of individuals and organizations that have developed activities in favor of the environment leads us to develop a deeper social and environmental commitment and practice our love and respect for nature with greater intensity. Environmental issues directly affect the quality of life of society and contain facts and problems that can be analyzed through their history.

Discuss

Invite the students to comment on the following quotes.

- The use, on a wide and growing scale, of natural resources by industrial society has caused social and environmental imbalances that have made up the international political agenda in recent decades. —*Paulo Henrique Martinez*

- We're consuming 20% more than the earth can sustain. And more than that: if the entire population of the world consumed like North Americans and Europeans, who have the highest rates of consumption, today, we would need four planet Earths. —*Hélio Mattar*

- High levels of obesity and personal debt, less free time and a more damaged environment are all signs that excessive consumption is diminishing the quality of life for many people. —*State of the World 2004, Worldwatch Institute.*

Activity

Ask students to research the history of the commitment to the environment of people, communities, governmental and non-governmental organizations in their community, country and in the world. Some examples of wonderful projects are:

- ❖ Chico Mendes in favor of forest peoples in the state of Acre, Brazil;
- ❖ Wangari Muta Maathai, a Kenyan environmentalist awarded the Nobel Peace Prize in 2004 for recognition of her work in support of sustainable development, democracy and respect for human rights and peace in both Kenya and throughout Africa;
- ❖ Organizations such as Greenpeace and WWF and others known in their own country; and
- ❖ United Nations conferences on the environment.

Their research can be presented in the form of panels, exhibitions, videos, skits and sketches, etc. at a fair in the school or in a nearby square or public space.

– Contributed by Paulo Barros, Brazil

SIMPLICITY AND CARING
FOR THE EARTH AND HER OCEANS LESSON 21
Sustainable Consumption

Play a song with lyrics about nature.

Talk about organizations that work with sustainable development in your country and overseas, regarding organic agriculture, vegetable gardens, animal rights, alternative energy sources and so on.

Lesson Content

Kelma de Matos and Miguel Angel Bordas wrote the following in one of their books about the environment and sustainability.

"Media stimulates a consuming society and does not consider the consequences for future generations, and the planet as a whole. The fact that products do not last long makes them obsolete much faster, and creates the need for a consuming way of life that disregards the preservation of our planet. We live in a disposable society and we must follow the trends, otherwise we are out.

On the one hand, consuming is necessary for living but could be done in a sustainable and conscious way. On the other hand, aggressiveness is present and contributes with showing off, social injustice and conflicts. These external factors have an effect on our bodies and in our lives as a whole and can affect us negatively because we are part of the environment. "

Discuss/Explore

Ask:

- The media entices people to want certain things. Can you give me some examples from the advertisements you see?
- What do you think the consequences for future generations and the planet as a whole would be if people continue to disregard conservation and engage in excess consuming?
- What pressures do some young people experience from their peers when they do not follow the fashion promoted by the media?
- What could a person do to resist this type of pressure?
- What values or qualities would help you resist this type of peer pressure?

Say, "Let's make a list of what the media promotes and another list of what you need."

Invite students to create two lists on the board or flipchart. Then ask:

- What kind of respect would you need inside to live with only the list of needs?
- What values would you need to be able to live only with this list of needs?
- How could teens help promote a culture of conservation?

Invite students to make comments about the following quotes.

- ◆ The environment is inside our bodies and the health of the environment affects our physical, emotional and mental health. — *Maurício Andrés Ribeiro*
- ◆ There is enough in the world for human needs, but there is not enough for human greed. — *Mahatma Gandhi*
- ◆ How can we use our love for the environment and the world to help us assess our wants versus our needs?" *Living Values Activities for Young Adults*
- ◆ There is a sustainable bond among youngsters and the environment. — *Mateus Fernandes*

Activity

Ask the students to form groups of four or five to think about Kelma de Matos and Miguel Angel Bordas's thoughts: "Young people, regardless of social groups, are driven to unstoppable consumption by the media so they can fit in a mold and be recognized as successful citizens, and even experience the feeling of not being excluded from a society that excludes the overwhelming majority most of the time."

After the discussion, ask each group to think about creating a project for sustainable consumption at school, taking into consideration books, food, water and so forth.

Finish the task by having each group present their ideas. The class as a whole can then select two or three ideas that they feel they can all carry out. If they would like the entire school to be involved, or need to obtain cooperation from the administration, they can create an essay and present their proposal to the school.

— Contributed by Paulo Barros, Brazil

SIMPLICITY AND CARING
FOR THE EARTH AND HER OCEANS LESSON 22
Ethics and the Environment

Play a song with lyrics about nature. Ask how they are and if they have been thinking about the last lesson. Allow them time to share their thoughts and any related actions. Listen and acknowledge.

Lesson Content

Many feel that environmental education only concerns ecology. Is that true? Are there also social, economic, cultural and ethical aspects to consider? It can be said that the exploitation of the Earth is related to humanity's social problems, that is, the exploitation of some by others. The exploitation of the planet's natural resources has been driven by man's greed. This has had disastrous consequences for the environment as well as poorly treated laborers. These attitudes are the cause of different forms of exclusion and conflicts which affect our whole world.

Marcos Reigota, in his book *What is environmental education?* (original in Portuguese: *O que é educação ambiental*), argues that "ethics has a fundamentally important role in environmental education" for it is "imbued with the ideal of radically changing the relationships that we know today, whether between mankind itself or between mankind and nature."

In the book *Eco-pedagogy and Planetary Citizenship* (original in Portuguese: *Ecopedagogia e Cidadania Planetária*), Francisco Gutiérrez and Cruz Prado propose exploring the relationship between valuing our planet and each other.

Activity

Ask students to discuss these questions in small groups and then present their findings to the larger group.

- ◆ Environmental education proposes a just, equitable and peaceful world.
- It is impossible to create a sustainable society while there is social injustice, religious intolerance and racism?
- Do you believe ecology is promoting new values? If so, list some of them.
- What would society be like if solidarity, gender equality, kindness, and positive and harmonious life skills were valued?
- What values support both the health of the Earth and Society?
- In your involvement in caring for the Earth are there signs of change in your everyday family, institutional and social life?

— Contributed by Paulo Barros

Close with the relaxation/focusing exercise, Sending Peace to the Earth.

SIMPLICITY AND CARING
FOR THE EARTH AND HER OCEANS LESSON 23
Greed versus Simplicity as We Use the Earth's Resources

Begin with a song.

Discuss/Share

Read aloud and then discuss the following paragraph, taken from *Living Values: A Guidebook*.

> "The ethic of simplicity is the precursor to sustainable development. Simplicity teaches economy. It teaches investment by example to those clear and honest about their needs and who live accordingly. Simplicity is the conscience which calls upon people to rethink their values. Simplicity asks whether we are being induced to purchase unnecessary products. Psychological enticements create artificial needs. Desires stimulated by wanting unnecessary things result in value clashes complicated by greed, fear, peer pressure, and a false sense of identity. Once fulfillment of basic necessities allows for a comfortable lifestyle, extremes and excesses invite overindulgence and waste. While that approach can be defended as a means to build certain economies, it should not be used at the expense of pushing other economies into dire poverty. It should not be that imposed sacrifice of some brings great affluence to others. That is not a principle but an injustice."

Ask:

- What is the role of greed with overindulgence and waste?
- How does the value of simplicity help us avoid waste?
- What are the consequences for the environment when overindulgence and waste continue over time?
- What happens when we care for the Earth and her oceans?
- How can we use our love for the environment and the world to help us assess our wants versus our needs?

Activity

Step 1. Ask the young adults to reflect on their personal situation. Ask them to pretend that they have a wonderful position in the government or a company in twenty years. "You also have a terrific salary and an opportunity for more money on the side. What advice can you give yourself for the future? What suggestions would you like to make to improve the environment?"

Step 2. Invite them to write a letter to themselves for the future, and confirm their individual commitment for the health of the environment now.

Step 3. Invite the students to read one sentence from his or her letter to the self. Close with a relaxation/focusing exercise of their choice.

SIMPLICITY AND CARING

FOR THE EARTH AND HER OCEANS LESSON 24

One Amazingly Helpful Thing I Can Do — and its Contrast

Play a song with lyrics about nature.

Discuss/Share

Share with the young adults: "This is now your third year (put in the appropriate number of years) working with Caring for the Earth and Her Oceans. In the first year, there was a lesson in which you were asked to think about one thing you could do that would make a positive difference for the Earth and her oceans — and what amazing things would happen if everyone on Earth did that one thing. I would like you to think about that again.

Ask:

- Two years after that lesson, what do you think now is the most amazingly helpful thing one could do to help the planet — and what would happen if everyone on Earth did that?

239

- If you could get everyone to do three things to help our planet and all its inhabitants, both humans and animals, what would you suggest?
- Has everyone shared their suggestions? Please do.

Activity

Step 1. Invite the students to form interest groups, based on the suggestions they have made.

Step 2. Provide them with large pieces of paper and ask them to mind map their ideas, placing their positive suggestions on the one side of the circle in the middle and its opposite on the other side of the circle in the middle. They may choose only one suggestion and its opposite or up to three. They are to create a mind map of all the consequences and ramifications of doing the positive action and its opposite negative action if everyone on the planet did that. This is likely to take the rest of your time together.

Close with the Sending Peace to the Earth relaxation/focusing exercise.

SIMPLICITY AND CARING

FOR THE EARTH AND HER OCEANS LESSON 25

Continuing Lesson 24 . . .

Begin with a song and ask them how they are doing.

Discuss/Share

Ask the following questions, or other questions appropriate to the discussion.

- In regard to the last lesson's mind map that you created, are you doing what you suggested that others do? (If yes: Great!)
- If no, ask: What makes it hard to do?
- What thought would help you counteract that?
- Has anyone else felt that way?
- What do you think about that helps you do it?
- Are there other practical things that would help you do it?
- If we want others to do what we suggest, we have to be examples. I want you to think about what helps you be committed to carrying out these actions and create a campaign to get others thinking about doing this too.

Activity

Step 1. Instruct the young adults to form the same groups as in the previous lesson, look at the mind map they created together, and think about a way to convey their message to others.

Step 2. Invite them to work out a plan to convey their message. Ask them: What medium would they use? Would this involve creating a video, doing rallies, creating skits or songs, writing letters or visiting legislators or local officials? Would it involve teaching younger students something or creating a model program to invite others to? Would it involve teaching organic gardening to the community? Would it involve helping people become vegan to help free land so that biodiversity of plants and animals can flourish?

Step 3. Ask each group to present their mind map and action plan to the entire class.

Step 4. Ask the class if they would like to choose just one action plan to work on together, or if they would like to carry out some of their ideas as a smaller group. Discuss it as needed.

Close with a relaxation/focusing exercise of their choice.

Follow up: In subsequent lessons serve as a resource to help them make their plan a reality.

Simplicity and Caring for Our Earth and Her Oceans Activities in Subject Areas

Language/Literature

Write one Reflection Point on the board every day. Ask students to think about it briefly, then discuss it for a few minutes. Create your own Reflection Points.

Read stories or works on simplicity and ask students to write an essay, linking the story's message with one or more Reflection Points.

Read books by famous naturalists. Go for nature walks and experiment seeing the natural world through their eyes.

Read poetry about nature.

Observe the simple things: the light on the leaf, a tree, a small flower, a bird, or whatever element of nature you notice. Lie under a tree and watch the leaves. For a few minutes, simply be in the space of an observer, free from desires. Then, write a poem as though it were from part of nature.

Experiencing Nature

Plan a venture to a natural wonder near the school. Spend a day there, half in nature study and half in silence. Invite a naturalist, aborigine, or someone from a native culture to teach you about plants of the area. Perhaps someone from a native culture can teach you from their wisdom. Write about your experience.

History/Social Studies

Discuss the following Reflection Point in relationship to the cultures and/or historical period the class has been studying in the last few months or semester.

- ◆ Simplicity helps decrease the gap between "the haves" and "the have nots" by demonstrating the logic of true economics: to earn, save, invest, and share the sacrifices and the prosperity so that there can be a better quality of life for all people regardless of where they were born.
- • How has the value of simplicity or its lack been demonstrated, and with what consequences?

Science

Study solar power, a simple alternative for dwindling nonrenewable energy sources. How can solar power be used in your local setting?

Study a local environmental problem that was identified during the Simplicity Lessons. Research options and select those that are most natural and environmentally friendly.

What inventions are helping clean up the toxic plastic soup of the ocean's gyres?

Some landfill companies are drilling into the trash to extract methane gas and use it to generate electricity. In some areas this supplies more than half of an area's electricity. Study this. Is this being done in your country?

Study ozone depletion through human production of CFCs and related halocarbon gases and its relationship to cancer, mutation and decreasing crop yields.

Economics

Cost It Out

Step 1. Consider some of the concepts stated in the above Science section and/or ask students to state some of their ecological concerns.

Step 2. Ask them to form small groups and create a simple and effective environmental project and "cost it out". For example, they could think about solar heating systems in the homes if you are in a warm climate. What is the cost of that over 10 years versus the cost of the heating system in existence? If deforestation is occurring in your country, would simple solar stoves be better than using wood for fires?

Step 3. Make a plan. Include in the plan, for instance, the benefits of planting trees throughout the country over a five-year period. Note how it would save by reducing erosion, etc.

Step 4. Invite them to share their ideas.

Think of a project for your country that would be simple, economical, and good for all children and/or people. "Cost it out." Share your ideas with the class.

Mathematics

Simplifying Rational Expression

Start with the statement: Numbers can take different forms. For example, $4/5^{th}$ can be expressed as $8/10^{th}$; 15 can be expressed as $-1 + 16$, etc.

Ask:

- Can people like numbers take many different forms? Let the students cite examples. For example:

    People are like numbers because a person can have different names, positions, and characteristics.

    A person can be positive or negative.

Discuss the Simplicity Reflection Points:

- Simplicity is finding one's original value and identifying with it.
- Simplicity is beautiful. Simplicity is being happy and peaceful.

Ask:

- Of the different forms that a person takes, which is the most comfortable or natural? Why?
- What are the personal benefits?
- What are the benefits for others?

— Contributed by Vicky Calicdan

Art

Explore works of art, historical pictures, or magazines for examples of simplicity versus something gaudily or excessively adorned. What famous artists were recognized for their simplistic style? Make a collage or picture of your own allowing simplicity to inspire your work.

Collect a few leaves and items from nature and make an artistic creation.

Draw simplicity, using only two colors.

A Still Life: Ask the students to set up a still life which expresses simplicity. It could be a small table with a vase of flowers against a white wall, or something else that is easily obtainable. Let them experiment with light falling on the objects. Allow them to draw or paint the still life using only a few colors.

— Contributed by Eleanor Viegas

Dress simply tomorrow.

Create a cartoon or a story on respect for the environment. Share your creations.

— Contributed by Marcia Maria Lins de Medeiros

Music

Use native instruments to play music. Study the compositions. Are they closer to the rhythms of nature than many current compositions?

Make your own native instruments.

Home Economics

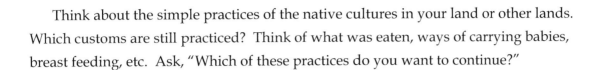

Think about the simple practices of the native cultures in your land or other lands. Which customs are still practiced? Think of what was eaten, ways of carrying babies, breast feeding, etc. Ask, "Which of these practices do you want to continue?"

Physical Education/Dance

Dance simplicity.

Experiment with keeping your mind simple when you dance and play sports. Keep your mind in the moment. How does this effect your game? Do you enjoy the game more?

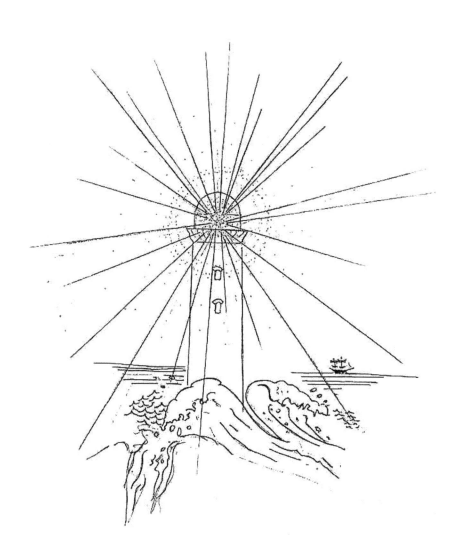

HONESTY

UNIT SIX: HONESTY

Honesty Lessons

The importance of honesty and integrity is becoming ever more apparent as dishonesty, fraud and corruption grow in many lands across the world. This unit brings forth the building of trust and good relationships through honesty, and contrasts the effects of honesty and dishonesty in individuals, friends and families, as well as the effects of dishonesty and corruption in business, society and the world. The lessons offer educators activities to go as deep into the subject as they wish, in accordance with the age and interest of their students. Thank you for your willingness to help students understand the impoverishment that dishonesty brings, and the beauty and benefit for all inherent in honesty and fairness.

Continue to play a song daily. Do one of the Relaxation/Focusing Exercises every day or every several days, as suitable for your group. Young adults often enjoy making up their own exercises.

Honesty Reflection Points

- ◆ Honesty is telling the truth.
- ◆ Integrity is part of honesty, it means doing what is right.
- ◆ Integrity is part of honesty, it means being fair.
- ◆ Integrity is part of honesty, it means keeping your word, keeping your promises.
- ◆ Integrity is part of honesty, it means being true to yourself and your values.
- ◆ When I am honest, I feel clear inside.
- ◆ A person who is honest and true is worthy of trust.
- ◆ Honesty and kindness build trust.
- ◆ Honest thoughts, words, and actions create harmony.
- ◆ There is a deep relationship between honesty and friendship.
- ◆ Honesty means there are no contradictions or discrepancies in thoughts, words, or actions.

♦ Honesty is the awareness of what is right and appropriate in one's role, one's behavior, and one's relationships.

♦ With honesty, there is no hypocrisy or artificiality which create confusion and mistrust in the minds and lives of others.

♦ Honesty makes for a life of integrity because the inner and outer selves are a mirror image.

♦ Honesty allows me to be free of worries.

♦ When I am honest, I can learn and help others learn to be giving.

♦ Greed is usually at the root of corruption.

♦ There is enough for man's need, but not enough for man's greed.

♦ When we are aware we are interconnected, we recognize the importance of honesty.

♦ Honesty is to use well what has been entrusted to you.

♦ To be honest to one's real self and to the purpose of a task earns trust and inspires faith in others.

HONESTY LESSON 1
Mind Mapping Honesty and Dishonesty

Begin with a song.

Discuss/Share

Inform: Let them know that the new value unit is on honesty. A really honest person is automatically considered to have a value called integrity. Integrity is part of honesty, it means doing what is right, doing what is fair.

Discuss the following Reflection Points:

♦ Integrity is part of honesty, it means doing what is right.

♦ Integrity is part of honesty, it means being fair.

♦ Integrity is part of honesty, it means keeping your word, keeping your promises.

♦ Integrity is part of honesty, it means being true to yourself and your values.

Say, "Some of the people in the world have integrity and others are dishonest. Someone can be honest most of the time, but occasionally tell little lies. Some people are dishonest and lie whenever they find it convenient. But when people are so dishonest that they try to cheat others, they are being fraudulent or corrupt.

Honesty may not sound like an important value, but the ramifications of honesty versus corruption are immense."

Activity

"Let's explore the differences between a world with all honest people, people of integrity, and a world with many dishonest and corrupt people through mind mapping."

Mind Map: Begin by drawing a large circle on a white board, putting Honesty on the right side and Dishonesty/Corruption on the left side. Start with a branch for Self on the Honesty side of the circle, asking them what happens when there is Honesty in the Self and writing in brief their responses. Then ask them what happens when there is a lack of honesty in the Self. The students are to supply all the answers. Also do branches for Families and Friends, Business, Society, Education and Government.

Share and discuss the Reflection Points:

- ◆ Greed is usually at the root of corruption.
- ◆ There is enough for man's need, but not enough for man's greed.
- ◆ When we are aware we are interconnected, we recognize the importance of honesty.

Creative Activity

Divide the students into groups of six or seven. Ask each group to create a song or poem about honesty versus dishonesty/corruption. It could be a rap song. Allow them to perform their creation for the group.

Homework: Ask students to start collecting stories on honesty and corruption from the news or from history.

HONESTY LESSON 2

People of Integrity

Begin with a song.

Discuss/Share

- ◆ Honest thoughts, words, and actions create harmony.
- ◆ Integrity is part of honesty, it means doing what is right.
- ◆ Integrity is part of honesty, it means being true to yourself and your values.
- ◆ When I am honest, I can learn and help others learn to be giving.

Share a Story

Share a story from an autobiography of a woman or man of integrity in your own country and how they make a positive difference, or select a folk tale or another work on honesty. Or, invite the students to find stories of people of integrity and share them.

Ask:

- What was inspiring about the story?
- What do you feel are the current needs for honesty and integrity in today's world?

Movement Activity

Play some music and invite the students to dance dishonesty. After two or three minutes, ask them to dance honesty. Allow them to dance honesty for twice as long as dishonesty.

You may wish to ask them to share about the difference in their feelings, in themselves and about the interaction with others during the dance.

Close with a relaxation/focusing exercise of their choice.

HONESTY LESSON 3

Current News and Stories of Honesty and Dishonesty

Begin with a song.

Activity

Step 1. Ask students to share current news and stories of honesty they have been collecting. As each story is shared, ask them who benefited from the honesty.

Step 2. Discuss the following Reflection Points:

- ◆ Honest thoughts, words, and actions create harmony.
- ◆ An honest person knows that we are all interconnected.

Step 3. Ask students to share current news and stories of dishonesty they have been collecting. Or, discuss past examples of corruption. For example, in one country there was a case in which more than twenty children died in a fire because of inferior housing at a camp. The owners had received money to build proper housing, but did not use it for that purpose. Some of the money they pocketed was then used to bribe others to not report what they had done. The situation in Sudan is tragic, with food aid being stolen and consequent starvation.

Step 4. Divide students in groups of six to eight and ask them to make up skits/dramas portraying the themes of honesty and dishonesty. The students can take the context from stories they have collected, a current conflict in the world, or a theme from a social studies unit.

Step 5. Invite each group to perform their skit. After each skit/sketch is performed, ask:

- What was the effect on the people who were cheated?
- What was the effect of the dishonesty on these people's lives — short term and long term?
- If you could, what would you like to tell the corrupt person?

Step 6. Ask the small groups to pretend they had a magic wand and could change the heart of the person from small to big, that is, from selfish and greedy to kind and benevolent. Do the skit/sketch one more time, but tell the corrupt person what you want them to know, wave your magic wand and play out what happens as a result.

Close with a relaxation/focusing exercise.

HONESTY LESSON 4
Corruption versus Fairness

Begin with a song.

Discuss/Share

Explore the concept of greed and corruption. Possible questions:

- Why do you think people become corrupt and greedy?
- What do they want? What might be under that want?
- What do they want for their family?
- Do they want happiness and security?
- Does being corrupt generate happiness or security in the long run?
- What do you think corrupt people worry about?
- Would everyone in the country benefit if everyone were honest? Why or why not?
- What would happen to the safety level if everyone in the country was paid well and had fair employers?

Comment: It is reality that in situations where there is a high level of corruption there is a low level of safety. For example, in areas of high unemployment in Mexico, more people are involved in drug trafficking. Almost all people want to provide for their families. Perhaps some people could not figure out another way to provide for them and that's why they got involved in the drug trade. One nearby city with a progressive major made a very positive difference in fighting the drug trade and a high level of crime and violence simply by generating jobs. That one city has very few problems with drugs and violence compared to the surrounding towns.

Ask:

- Do you think the moral of this story could be that when people are provided fair wages that most of them will take care of their families and not engage in illegal activities?
- True, it seems that there are always a few that are looking for an easy way to make lots of money and so take to cheating others, but isn't it true that most people are good?
- Does bribery and corruption simply beget more bribery and corruption as everyone lower in the chain tries to survive?
- Could one person at the top make a difference?

Activity

Briefly research the history of Singapore and how the Lee Kuan Yew, the first Prime Ministers, worked hard to ensure there was no corruption. Explore why Denmark and New Zealand are considered to be the least corrupt countries in the world on the Corruption Perceptions Index. CPI defines corruption as "the misuse of public power for private benefit".[8]

Discuss the following Reflection Points:

- ◆ Honesty is to use well what has been entrusted to you.
- ◆ When we are aware we are interconnected, we recognize the importance of honesty.
- ◆ When I feel honest, I feel clear inside.
- ◆ When I am honest, I can learn and help others learn to be giving.

Activity

Paint greed and corruption on one side of the paper and fairness and knowing we are interconnected on the other.

Close with a relaxation/focusing exercise.

---

[8] www.transparency.org

HONESTY LESSON 5

Power, Corruption and the Effect of Honesty on Sustainable Development Goals

Begin with a song.

Discuss/Share

Share: Corruption and graft have robbed many societies of well-being and adversely effected the lives of hundreds of millions of people.

Ask:

- In history, has there been a relationship between greed, corruption, and the denial of human rights? Think of three examples. Please share a few.

Share: There is a saying, Power corrupts, and absolute power corrupts absolutely.

Ask:

- Can you think of some examples of this? What are they?
- Do you think this saying is true? Why or why not?

Think of examples in which corruption has robbed people of education, medical treatment, and even food.

- If you were elected to political office, what do you think would keep you safe from being corrupted?
- What personal understanding would help mitigate corruption by power?

Activity

Step 1. Invite the students to form the same groups they were with during the previous SDGs lessons.

Step 2. Ask them to explore the effect of honesty on the SDGs. If everyone in the world were honest, fair, not greedy and had integrity what would be positively affected? Do any more SDGs need to be added?

Step 3. Ask them to write specific ways holding the value of honesty would affect the SDGs on which their group is focused and write those on yellow Leaves. If the availability to research exists, you may wish to ask them to investigate a specific situation and how many people's wellbeing would be affected by honesty for a particular SDG — in a specific country or in the world.

Step 4. Invite them to share their Honesty Leaves with the entire group.

Step 5. Invite the groups to attach their yellow Honesty Leaves to the class artistic presentation of the SDGs.

Close with a relaxation/focusing exercise.

HONESTY LESSON 6
One Minute of Courage

Begin with a song.

Discuss/Share

Reflection Points:

♦ With honesty, there is no hypocrisy or artificiality which create confusion and mistrust in the minds and lives of others.

♦ Honesty makes for a life of integrity because the inner and outer selves are a mirror image.

➢ As the educator, if you are comfortable, share a real-life story of personal honesty or dishonesty to the students. Or, invite students to share a story.

Ask:

• Do you want your friends to be honest? Why?

• Would you want your husband or wife to be honest? Why?

• Think of a person in your life who has always kept his or her promises to you. How do you feel about that person?

• How do you feel when someone lies to you or breaks her or his promise?

• How does it feel to be dishonest, if found out? If not found out?

• When do we want to lie?

• Why do people lie?

• Are there situations in which it is okay to lie?

• When is it not okay to lie?

• Is it possible to both lie and maintain integrity? How?

• What are the consequences of dishonesty?

• When can lying hurt others, or destroy the lives of others?

Content Comment: People usually lie initially to avoid embarrassment and possible punishment for having done something wrong. When they try to cover the lie, things get very complicated because they have to remember what they said and what they did not say.

Think about how much energy it takes to cover a lie versus one minute of real courage to tell the truth. In the long run, the truth makes us feel better in our hearts and in our relationships. We become free from the worry of hiding the lie. However, some people become accustomed to lying and it destroys the trust in their relationships.

Activity

Ask the class to write a short story using a real or imaginary situation in which a person lied. Or, do the Group Story Game, going around the classroom and asking each person to add a few sentences to the tale.

Close with a relaxation/focusing exercise of their choice.

HONESTY LESSON 7
Privacy and "Busy Bodies"

Begin with a song.

Lesson Content

Inform: In Living Values Education, honesty is used as a universal value to help create a better world. It is not a mandate to share personal matters when you would rather have a little privacy or space to work things through.

Honesty is telling what is true. Honesty is being fair to others. Honesty does not mean a person must bare her/his soul to everyone, nor tell personal details to people with whom you do not wish to share.

Ask:

- What kinds of things do you think are only your business?
- Who do you not want to share that information with?
- If someone is asking about something that you do not wish to share, what can you say that is still honest? (Such as "I'd rather not share that right now.")
- Do you want your privacy even during close relationships sometimes?
- How can you communicate that in such a way that others understand?
- When do you want to share?

"There are also circumstances when people can be cruel under the guise of 'honesty'."
Ask:

- Can you think of some examples?
- What examples have you seen in social media?
- What do you think is the right thing to do instead of that?

- When is being 'too honest' not really honesty, but a lack of love and respect for another person?
- What is the balance of love and honesty?
- Is an honest heart a heart full of love?

Activity Options

Invite students to write a poem about sharing in an honest way with a friend.

Invite a few students to share their poems, if they wish to do so.

Close with some relaxation/focusing time by playing relaxation music and asking students who wish to do so to share one line from their poem that they feel is centering or grounding.

HONESTY LESSON 8

Trust

Begin with a song.

Discuss/Share

- How would you feel if your boss said she would pay you a certain amount and then paid you half of that?
- How do you feel when someone cheats you rather than keeping their word?
- Do societies run better when people keep their word?
- What about personal relationships?
- What kinds of words and actions break trust in relationships?
- How do you feel when people lie to you?
- What kinds of words and actions build trust in relationships?

Activity

Step 1. Divide students into groups of three to five to discuss the building blocks of trust. Draw a "trust wall," filling in bricks with different words or actions that build trust in relationships. What is important in the foundation?

Step 2. What are the emotional words or actions that act like boulders to break the trust wall? Perhaps a little bit of blame is like a pebble, but what is the effect of frequent blame on a relationship? What is the effect of lying? What are other pebbles or boulders?

Step 3. Invite each group to artistically present their trust wall by making a poster or drawing. Are their certain attitudes that make the wall more beautiful?

Step 4. Invite each group to share their trust wall poster or drawing. Lead the applause.

Close with a relaxation/focusing exercise of their choice.

HONESTY LESSON 9

Situation Cards

Begin with a song.

Activity

Step 1. Ask the young adults to form small groups and generate situations in which they become upset when others are not honest or trustworthy, that is, they lie, cheat or steal, or situations in which they would like to be honest but it is difficult to do so. Ask them to fill in the situation on the Situation Honesty Cards. (The cards are located on the next page. You may wish to copy them for the students to use, or they can make their own.)

Step 2. Introduce the following interpersonal skill and ask a student to model it.

Key phase: "It takes courage to apologize for not keeping a promise."

Ask:

- If someone did not keep their promise to you, what would you like her or him to say?

- If you did not keep your promise to someone, what could you say? Please start your sentence with "I" and share your feelings.

Use the previously presented communication skill of: "I feel _____ when _____ because _____." For example, "I felt badly when I was late because I let you down and I really value your friendship."

Ask:

- This is one way to handle the situation; what are other alternatives?

➢ List the alternatives and discuss together the consequences of each.

Step 3. Invite each group to act out one of the situations they have generated.

Close with a relaxation/focusing exercise of their choice.

Situation Card — Honesty

Situation:

Act out the above situation in two ways:

1. Lie about the situation and see what consequences develop.
2. Be honest about the situation and see what happens.

Ask the characters to occasionally freeze their actions, so they can tell the audience what their thoughts and fears are.

Situation Card — Honesty

Situation:

Act out the above situation in two ways:

1. Lie about the situation and see what consequences develop.
2. Be honest about the situation and see what happens.

Ask the characters to occasionally freeze their actions, so they can tell the audience what their thoughts and fears are.

HONESTY LESSON 10
Resisting Pressure

Begin with a song.

Discuss/Share

The Reflection Points:

♦ A person worthy of confidence is honest and true.

♦ To be honest to one's real self and to the purpose of a task earns trust and inspires faith in others.

Say, "Sometimes there is pressure to be dishonest, and sometimes it is difficult to resist that pressure."

➢ Ask the students to create examples of problematic situations in small groups.

Ask:

• What things can you think of that would help you resist the pressure to _____ _____. (Put in one of the examples the students gave you, it might be about lying, cheating, or stealing, etc.)

• What kinds of things could you say to yourself, or a friend, if there is a temptation to be dishonest?

• What doesn't help?

• Would it help you resist the temptation if you looked at the consequences? What could happen as a result? (Teachers might want to question further about consequences, such as the feelings or happiness over time of the one who has cheated, the effect on relationships with friends, trust and loss of trust, hurt or harm to others, belief in the self, etc.)

• What else can you think of that might help? Would anyone like to share a personal experience?

Activity

Organize students into groups of four or six to make up a Situation Card on honesty. Instruct each group to act out a situation, acting out the dishonest and honest responses, and the consequences. The "actors" may freeze the skit at times to share their thoughts in an aside to the audience.

Close with a relaxation/focusing exercise of their choice.

HONESTY LESSON 11
The Power of One

Begin with a song.

Lesson Content

Please share this following, contributed by Kurt Krueger:

In 1645, one vote gave Oliver Cromwell control of England.

In 1776, one vote gave America the English language instead of German.

In 1923, one vote gave Adolph Hitler control of the Nazi Party.

♦ How wonderful it is that nobody need wait a single moment before starting to improve the world. — *Anne Frank*

♦ A small body of determined spirits fired by an unquenchable faith in their mission can alter the course of history. — *Mohandas Gandhi*

Discuss/Share

Sometimes honesty can seem like a simple value that is not so important, but it is probably one of the most important ones in terms of affecting our lives and the lives of others. Corruption has killed many people, be it through using cheap poor-quality materials to build bridges or stealing food aid for a starving populace.

Activity

Step 1. Ask individuals or small groups of students to research stories of people of honesty and goodwill who made a difference in the lives of others. For example, some companies treat and pay their employees well and others treat them poorly and pay them poorly. They may wish to consider:

• Which companies do better in the long term?

• Which companies have more satisfied employees?

• Which companies have more loyal employees?

• What are other advantages of having honesty as an ethic in a company?

• Is there a relationship between honesty and generosity?

• What other values do honest people seem to have?

Step 2. Invite those who wish to do so to share their discoveries.

Close with a relaxation/focusing exercise.

HONESTY LESSON 12

Creating Stories to Inspire Honesty

Begin with a song.

Activity

Step 1. Invite students to imagine what the world would be like if everyone in it were honest and behaved with integrity.

Step 2. Ask:

- Can you think of a time when you really appreciated someone else's honesty?
- Can you think of a time when you were appreciated for your honesty?

Step 3. Individually or in small groups create stories or plays for younger children or their peers to inspire them to be honest and true to their values.

Step 4. Ask those who wish to do so to share their stories.

Step 5. Create slogans together in small groups.

Step 6. Would they like to create a program for younger students or their peers? They could share a couple of stories, one or two of the skits/sketches they did earlier and perhaps have everyone dance honesty. Would they like to put the slogans into artistic form and display them? Allow them to think about what they would like to do — and do it.

Close with a relaxation/focusing exercise of their choice.

Honesty Activities in Subject Areas

Language/Literature

Read autobiographies of woman and men of integrity and how they make a difference in the world.

Select folk tales, classical novels, or other works on honesty or greed and corruption. Discuss the consequences on individuals, families, and society.

Ask students to create their own fairy tales for younger children illustrating one of the Honesty Reflection Points.

On several different days, discuss one or more Reflection Points. Ask students to write a short story or short essay based on one of the Reflection Points. For example: There is a deep relationship between honesty and friendship.

Read about the ancient philosopher Epictetus and his teachings. In a novel by Tom Wolfe, "A Man in Full," Epictetus' teachings are revealed through the character of a former slave and some of Wolfe's characters learn to value personal integrity over material gain.

History/Social Studies

Skits Portraying the History of Fairness or its Lack

Ask students to make up a skit, portraying the theme of honesty and fairness versus corruption and greed. If you are working with a large group of students, divide them into smaller groups. Students could take the context from a unit they have been studying, such as a feudal lord of medieval times or a current conflict in the world. After the skits, discuss the effects economically and socially.

Ask:

- What was the effect on the people who were cheated?
- What was the effect of the dishonesty or greed on these people's lives?

Ask the actors to add how they felt from a subjective standpoint.

Science

Ethics in Science

Discuss ethical issues in science today and the effects of not being honest. For example, there have been instances of scientists falsely reporting scientific data in order to support the bias of the corporation paying for the research.

Ask:

- What do you think the code of conduct should be?
- What happens to progress in scientific research when someone misrepresents data?
- How could that negatively affect the health of consumers?
- What would you do if you were a scientist and why?
- What is the relationship between lack of honesty and integrity and self-respect?

Name and Fame

Sometimes there is lack of integrity when people are greedy for name and fame. There have been instances of scientists stealing other people's data and inventions. People often want such recognition so others will admire, respect, and even love them. They hope with name and fame — and the consequent love and respect — they will feel powerful and better about themselves.

Discuss:

- Will they really feel better inside when they get respect for something they know they cheated on and is not true?
- How would you feel if you were working on an invention and someone stole your ideas?
-

Economics

Skits

Students can make up a skit, portraying the theme of honesty and dishonesty. If you are working with a large group of students, divide them into smaller groups. They could take the context from a unit they have been studying or from a current situation in your country. For example, the skit could take place in a stockbroker's office, with investors and brokers using the Internet or other appropriate means to create a "get-rich" scheme at the expense of others.

After the skit(s), discuss the effects economically and socially.

- What was the effect on the people who were cheated?
- Is it fair for someone to misrepresent something and cheat others if the ones cheated are "dumb enough to fall for it"? Why or why not?
- What is the effect of dishonesty or greed on these people's lives?
- How would you feel if that happened to you?

Discuss:

- To be a successful businessperson, honesty is of prime importance.
- How possible is honesty in today's business world?
- What would the business world be like if everyone were honest?
- If you were going to start a business with a partner, would you want your partner to be honest? Why or why not?

Act It Out

How would you feel if you were an honest businessperson? How would you feel if you were a dishonest businessperson? Act it out.

`

Ethical Issues

Discuss ethical issues pertinent to economy. While some example issues are below, please discuss current issues relevant to the young adults and their future.

- When medical laboratories over-bill insurance companies, who reaps the profits and who eventually pays?
- When an individual has violated professional ethics and is seeking public office, should he or she be elected?
- When people claim false injuries in an auto accident or on their job, are they hurting others? Why?
- If you were the owner of the business, what would you say?
- What would you like to tell the worker who claims a false injury?

Art

Discuss ethical issues within the art community of your country.

Make up slogans about honesty or integrity, and then use them on artistic posters or banners. Place them around the school.

Create a picture expressing the feeling of honesty — a picture in which there is harmony of color and shape. Select a regional artist that shows this quality in his or her paintings, or perhaps look at the paintings of Jackson Pollack. Create your own picture using colors and abstract shapes which express harmony of feeling.

— Contributed by Eleanor Viegas

Student Council/Student Government

In high schools, set up a system whereby acts of honesty and virtue are rewarded, for example, when someone turns in an item which has been lost. The members of Student Council or Government would determine the criteria for the reward, depending, of course, on your culture. Suggestions for rewards are:

- A special telephone call or a letter from the principal or teacher.
- A "thank you" from the Student Council president.

- A certificate of honesty and virtue.
- As a student cited for honesty/virtue, your name could be placed in an Honesty/Virtue Box. Once a week or month, one name could be drawn and a special prize given. Prizes could be food items or other gifts donated by local businesses, the best seats at the soccer game, or . . . ? Use your imagination!

— Contributed by Mryna Belgrave

Home Economics

Discuss honesty within the context of home economics.

For example, ask:

- What skills do we need to ensure we are not cheated?
- What skills must we develop in order to be honest ourselves?
- Is there benefit in honesty? What is the benefit?"

Discuss the following Reflection Points:

- Honest thoughts, words, and actions create harmony.
- Honesty is to use well what has been entrusted to you.
- An honest person knows that we are all interconnected.

Discuss: How do the above points apply to life in the home? In your neighborhood? In society?

Physical Education

Discuss the ethics involved in sports today. The teacher may wish to discuss the elements of honesty and ethics most relevant to his or her students. One topic of worldwide interest is the Olympics. In the past Olympic games, steroids and body-enhancing drugs have been an ethical issue. Discuss.

Talk about current sports stories, such as the widespread drug use at the French Open Bicycle Races, to illustrate how everyone loses when there is dishonesty.

— Contributed by Irene Miller

Relate cheating to our feelings about the self.

Ask:

- How would you feel inside if you know you have won because you had an unfair advantage?
- How do you feel when you win because of your honest efforts?
- Is winning the only important thing?

HAPPINESS

UNIT SEVEN: HAPPINESS

Happiness Lessons

Thank you for being the keeper of a values-based atmosphere and providing a safe place for young people to be, share, explore and grow. Some of the lessons in this unit will be fun and others may be a little challenging; I hope you and the students will find them meaningful and productive.

The lessons on happiness in this updated version contain research on happiness, the message that their thoughts, words and actions are pivotal in creating their own happiness or sadness, social and emotion skills and the topics of the depression and social media link, drug awareness, and dealing with the feelings of sadness and hurt. As sadness is the opposite of happiness, this felt like the most appropriate place to put in this material.

There are three optional drug awareness lessons in this values unit, as some young adults experiment with drugs and alcohol as a way of hoping to experience more happiness, or as a relief from sadness and pain. As the educator, you will need to decide if this is appropriate in your situation and culture.

In addition to the three drug awareness lessons, there are 13 lessons adapted from *Living Values Activities for Drug Rehabilitation* following the Happiness Values Unit. These lessons are deliberately later in this book as it is essential to complete some of the peace, respect and love values units first of they build the understanding, attitudes and skills necessary to complete these successfully. Our experience is that this prerequisite empowers participants to co-create with you a safe accepting atmosphere in which they can be honest. As the facilitator, you will need excellent active listening and validating skills, should you decide to do the substance abuse lessons. A caring, matter of fact, firm and yet supportive nonjudgmental attitude is vital in facilitating these lessons. Shaming and blaming are not part of Living Values Education. If at all possible, please take part in an LVE Educator Workshop. Depending on your situation, you may choose to do the substance abuse lessons in place of the last unit on responsibility.

You may want the students to bring in songs that relate to the theme of happiness. Some students enjoy learning traditional songs.

Happiness Reflection Points

♦ Give happiness and take happiness.

♦ When there is love and peace inside, happiness automatically grows.

♦ When there is a feeling of hope and purpose, there is happiness.

♦ Having good wishes for everyone gives happiness inside.

♦ Happiness cannot be bought, sold, or bargained for.

♦ Happiness is earned through selfless attitudes and actions.

♦ Happiness of mind is a state of peace in which there is no upheaval or violence.

♦ Kind and constructive words create a happier world.

♦ When one is content with the self, happiness comes automatically.

♦ Happiness follows giving happiness, sorrow follows giving sorrow.

♦ Lasting happiness is a state of contentment within.

♦ When all resources are focused on socioeconomic infrastructure at the expense of the development of the character, then priorities in life are misrepresented and there is a gradual erosion of happiness.

♦ Values help people assess priorities and allow for proactive and preventive measures to take place at opportune moments.

HAPPINESS LESSON 1
Happiness

Play a song that has a happy feeling as the young adults enter.

Discuss/Share

Explore general concepts of happiness through questions and discussion:

Ask:

• Would you all like to be happy all of the time? (Usually everyone nods "yes".)

• How do people try and create happiness?

• What do you think works?

• What doesn't work?

• What gives happiness for only a little while?

• What can give contentment that lasts for a long time?

• Can we create our own happiness?

• What kinds of feelings inside do you think about when you think about happiness?

- When do you experience those?

Reflective Activity

Step 1. Play some relaxation music and tell the students you would like them to reflect on the statements you make and write down brief responses. Allow adequate time for them to respond to each item.

- Please make a list of things that give happiness. These may be physical things or nonphysical things, such as words, actions, experiences with nature, relationships with others, activities, and ways of being.
- Now reflect for a few minutes about three or four times of happiness in your life. What was going on inside and around you? (Allow five minutes.)
- What are the things that make you happy?
- Please note down by each item the qualities or values that you experience during those activities or times.

Step 2. Allow them to share their thoughts in small groups.

Step 3. Write a poem or a song about the quality or value that appears most often on your list. Allow them to choose if they wish to do this individually or in small groups.

Step 4. Invite those who wish to share their song or poem to do so, as time permits.

Note to Educator: Some students may prefer to write on sadness as a memory of loss or sorrow can occur during the reflection time. Actively listen if a student wishes to share, and then affirm the value or quality that he or she feels is most important.

HAPPINESS LESSON 2
Can we buy happiness?

Begin with a song.

Discuss/Share

Ask:

- Do you see people try to buy happiness sometimes? If yes: How do they do that?
- Do you see people trying to boost their respect by having expensive things?
- Do you try to buy happiness sometimes? How?
- Do you think you will always be happy once you get a new thing you wanted?
- How long does that happiness last?
- What values or feelings for our Earth and her oceans would help you not need to buy so much to prove your worth?

- Is happiness temporary when sought from outside sources — from wealth, material possessions, and status? Why or why not?
- How can you remain happy when you do not get something you want?
- What kinds of thoughts and actions create lasting happiness?

Reflection Points:

- ◆ Happiness cannot be bought, sold, or bargained for.
- ◆ Happiness is earned through selfless attitudes and actions.
- ◆ When one is content with the self, happiness comes automatically.

Activity

Divide the class in small groups of eight to ten and ask them to create a skit based on the discussion.

Or, do a fun values activity contributed by Roger Miles: Ask students to think about their most important value. Then invite to play with balloons: blow them up, write their most important value on their balloon and have a balloon fight, batting them around to music. When the music stops, whichever balloon they are holding or is closest is to become the value to focus on for a day.

Close with a relaxation/focusing exercise.

HAPPINESS LESSON 3

Words I Want to Hear

Begin with a song.

Ask for students to volunteer to read the poem or sing the song that was created during the former lesson.

Discuss

Ask:

- How do people affect each other in regards to happiness?
- What do people say that makes you happy?
- What do you like to hear?
- What don't you like to hear?
- What kinds of words naturally are said by people who are happy?
- What values are at the root of the words you like to hear?
- What would the world be like if everyone were kind?
- What would the world be like if everyone were happy?

Write the following Reflection Points on the board:

- ♦ Give happiness and take happiness.
- ♦ Kind and constructive words create a happier world.
- ♦ Happiness follows giving happiness, sorrow follows giving sorrow.

Then, ask:

- What kinds of words are like thorns?
- Are there any sentences you think cause such harm you would you like them to vanish from the human vocabulary?
- What kinds of words would you like to hear from your friends?
- If a person gave you a compliment, but you did not feel they meant it, how would you feel?
- When a person makes one appreciative comment and you feel they really mean it, how do you feel?
- Is it important to be genuine? Why?
- What would you like to hear from your parents?
- If you were a parent, what would you tell your child?

Activity

Invite the students to get together in small groups and write a list entitled, "The Words I Want to Hear." Different groups may decide to address their list to different populations: parents, friends, teachers, producers, CEOs, etc.

Ask each group to pick their favorite saying, put it on a long piece of paper artistically and put it on the wall.

Close with a relaxation/focusing exercise.

Homework: Give happiness through your words to two people today, tomorrow, and the day after tomorrow.

HAPPINESS LESSON 4

Talking to Myself

Begin with a song.

Feedback: Ask the students to report back on their giving words of happiness homework from Happiness Lesson 3.

Lesson Content

Write the Reflection Point on the board:

♦ When there is love and peace inside, happiness automatically grows.

Build Concept: "Talking to Myself" is an acknowledgment of the process that occurs within every individual. We all talk to ourselves with a silent voice. This is called self-talk or inner dialogue. In this unit on Happiness, this is an important aspect to think about, as self-talk can be positive or negative, encouraging or discouraging. There are immediate consequences on our physical and emotional energy when we are positive or negative with ourselves.

Discuss: "In the last lesson, we talked about happiness and giving happiness to others. Today, let's talk about the things we say to ourselves."

Ask:

• What kinds of things can we say to the self to create happiness inside?

• What did you say to yourself when you did your homework of giving happiness through words to others?

• What happens to your emotional energy when you speak kindly to yourself?

• What happens when you give yourself a "hard time"? (When someone is very critical with his or herself.)

• What happens to your feelings when you say, "I'll never be able to do it?" or "I'll never make it."

• Are the feelings different when you say, "This is a bit scary, but I'll do my best?"

• What do you say to yourself when you make a mistake?

Say, "Notice your tone of voice when you speak to yourself. What do you say to yourself when you're afraid that you'll fail at something? What is the emotional effect when one calls the self "Stupid"? It's wonderful when people feel bad when they make a mistake because it simply means they want to do it right. But, we have a lot more energy to do the right thing when we say to the self: "Okay, I made a mistake. I'm human. I can learn from mistakes. What can I do next time so I do not repeat the mistake?" Discuss.

Then draw three columns on the board, putting the following headers at the top of the column: Situation; Discouraging; and Encouraging/ Empowering. Ask them to make three similar columns on a piece of paper. Fill out the columns with the content from the questions below.

Situation	Discouraging	Encouraging/Empowering

Ask:

- Does anyone ever have difficulty starting on an assignment? (Write "assignment needs to be done" under the column titled "Situation.")
- What are examples of thoughts students say to themselves that are discouraging in this situation? (Write two of the replies under the column titled "Discouraging.")
- What can you say to encourage yourself when it is difficult to get started on an assignment? (Write a few of the replies under the column titled "Empowering.")
- Let's do a disappointing situation. Please give me an example. What are discouraging things people say to themselves? (Continue to fill in the columns as described.)
- What can you say to yourself that is encouraging in this situation?
- What differences do you notice in the tone of voice that you use to yourself when you say things that are critical or discouraging versus encouraging?

Activity

Step 1. Instruct the class to divide in half or in small groups. Ask the students to continue to generate situations that are challenging, and fill in the remaining columns with discouraging and encouraging or empowering thoughts.

Step 2. Invite each group to share some examples of discouraging thoughts and the empowering thoughts that can replace them.

Close with a relaxation/focusing exercise.

HAPPINESS LESSON 5

Advice to Myself and Research on Happiness

Begin with a song.

Feedback: Ask the students if any of them have experimented with replacing discouraging thoughts with empowering thoughts. Allow those who wish to share to do so, actively listening and validating as appropriate.

Write the following Reflection Points on the board:

- ◆ Having good wishes for everyone gives happiness inside.

♦ Happiness of mind is a state of peace in which there is no upheaval or violence.

♦ When there is a feeling of hope and purpose, there is happiness.

Five-Minute Activity

Invite the students to write a note to themselves, giving themselves advice about how they would like to talk to themselves.

Lesson Content

One of the main things you can do to be happy is to change discouraging and negative thoughts to positive and empowering thoughts. What are other things? Let's look at some research on happiness.

What is the Science of Happiness? By Berkeley Wellness
From a scientist's point of view, what is happiness?
Source: https://www.berkeleywellness.com/healthy-mind/mind-body/article/what-science-happiness

Researchers think of happiness as having satisfaction and meaning in your life. It's the propensity to feel positive emotions, the capacity to recover from negative emotions quickly, and holding a sense of purpose. Happiness is not having a lot of privilege or money. It's not constant pleasure. It's a broader thing: Our ability to connect with others, to have meaningful relationships, to have a community. Time and again — across decades of research and across all studies — people who say they're happy have strong connections with community and with other people.

Money doesn't matter? Really?!
Studies show that money increases happiness when it takes people from a place where there are real threats — poverty — to a place that is reliably safe. After that, money doesn't matter much.

Research on happiness began to increase in the early 1980s and took a leap in 2000 with the positive psychology movement. Martin Steligman, Director of the Positive Psychology Center and the leader of the positive psychology movement, notes "happy people are more productive at work, learn more in school, get promoted more, are more creative and are liked more." They also have better relationships and are healthier. Happiness is strongly linked to having strong social connections and contributing to something good that is bigger than yourself. This branch of psychology focuses on what helps people be mentally healthy rather than on pathology.

More of our happiness is under our conscious control than was previously thought. In her research on happiness, Sonja Lyubomirsky and her colleagues studied identical twins along with other research and concluded happiness is 50 percent genetic, 10 percent circumstantial and 40 percent intentional, that is, under our control.

Source: https://www.berkeleywellness.com/healthy-mind/mind-body/article/what-science-happiness

She (Lyubomirsky) attributes 40 percent — nearly half the variance — to our daily life experiences. The people you see, the activities you do, how you see your world each day. Now, not all researchers agree with her model. But if it is right, then we have the capacity to change our own happiness. We can adopt a new perspective on other people that's less fearful or competitive. We can engage in some sort of self-awareness practice like gratitude or prayer.

While many people think if they won the lottery, got a new car, a new house or a promotion they would be much happier, studies show this is not the case. People adapt to their new circumstances with time and return to the same level of happiness. Getting out of a toxic relationship, a difficult job situation, or another situation which feels confining may increase happiness for a while, but to maintain that level people need to control how they think and act.

Sonja Lyubomirsky studied twelve strategies that measurably increase happiness levels. (Not in order.) In *The How of Happiness: A Scientific Approach to Getting the Life You Want*, she details these strategies. To name all twelve: 1. nurture relationships, 2. do activities that truly engage you, 3. count your blessings, 4. avoid over-thinking and social comparison 5. savor life's joys, 6. practice kindness, 7. cultivate optimism, 8. take care of your body, 9. develop coping strategies, 10. forgive, 11. practice spirituality and 12. commit to your goals.

Discuss/Share

Invite their reactions to the information presented and allow them to discuss.

Comment: In the research, please note the importance it gives to nurturing relationships and strong social connections as a way of happiness. This can mean having one, two or three good friends . . . in real time. There is actual research linking a lot of time on social media to depression in teens and young adults.

Ask:

- We have heard that social comparison is a happiness robber. Do you think that is true?
- What might be thoughts of social comparison people might have when they see some postings on social media?
- What are other thoughts people can have that are not happy thoughts when they see some postings on social media?
- If you didn't care what other people thought of you, would you be happier?
- John Wooden shared the following statement with his university basketball players in an effort to get them not to worry about what others said about them: "Never worry about your reputation, only worry about your character." What does that mean?
- Let's take a couple of the thoughts of social comparison that you have shared. Can you come up with an empowering thought instead that also lets you not worry or over-think?

Activity

Step 1. Ask the students to write down the 12 strategies Researcher Sonja Lyubomirsky noted that increase happiness levels, leaving space below each item. Ask them to individually reflect on each item and think of ways they are doing that or ideas to do that. They may wish to give themselves a rating of 1 to 10 on each item.

Step 2. Ask the students to write down 20 count-your-blessings statements, that is, things for which they are grateful.

Step 3. Invite students to form groups of three and discuss their thoughts, feelings and ideas about strategies 1, 2 and 3: nurture relationships, do activities that truly engage you and count your blessings.

Close with a relaxation/focusing exercise.

HAPPINESS LESSON 6

Fun and Savoring Joy

Begin with a song that creates a feeling of happiness.

Feedback: Ask the students if they can share examples of replacing discouraging thoughts with empowering thoughts. Allow those who wish to share to do so, actively listening and validating as appropriate.

Activity

Step 1. Share that they have touched on four things in the list of 12 from the research on strategies that create happiness: 1. nurturing relationships, 2. doing activities that truly engage them, 3. counting your blessings, and 4. avoiding over-thinking and social comparison. Invite them to share either though journaling individually or in groups of three their process in regards to those four things.

Step 2. Share that today you would like them to think about one of the other happiness strategies: savor life's joys. Invite them to play a game, do a circle dance or a line dance, or do something else together than takes five to ten minutes but is fun.

Step 3. Ask:

- Do you think it is important to play or have a bit of fun sometimes? (Yes. Unlike most of the answers this one does have a "right" answer!)

Step 4. *Reflection:* Play some relaxation music and ask them to reflect on the following:

❖ Please think of three or four times in your life when you were "savoring life's joys." . . . . Perhaps you were with family . . . perhaps you were with friends. . . . Perhaps you were in nature and simply being in the present moment . . . a time when you were really enjoying yourself. . . . Please write those down.

❖ Please reflect on moments with others that create joy.

❖ Please reflect on what kinds of things you do alone that creates joy.

❖ Please reflect on what helps you be in a space where you can enjoy yourself and others.

Step 5. Share some of your reflections for a few minutes in groups of three.

Close with a relaxation/focusing exercise.

HAPPINESS LESSON 7
Including and Excluding

Begin with a song.

Discuss/Share

Ask:

- Quite often groups of students will form cliques. Why do you think these form?
- What are sensible reasons for having groups of friends? What are good things about cliques?
- In schools, sometimes members of one group will shun members of other groups. How do you think people feel when they are left out?

- Do you ever get left out? How do people feel when that happens?

Comment: The educator may wish to share on this subject as appropriate to the culture and circumstances. The educator may wish to share some stories she or he knows — about teens or young adults who have been rejected by others and committed suicide, or about others who have become violent and killed others in retaliation for rejection.

> ➤ Discuss any of their concerns regarding rejection, suicide or teens killing other teens.

Inform: We have talked about five of the happiness strategies. Another one is to practice kindness.

Ask:

- How would practicing kindness help with the concerns we have been discussing?
- Would practicing kindness eliminate the concerns we have been discussing?
- How could we put kindness into practical action? What would that look like?
- What would people need to stop doing?
- What would be needed instead?
- How can we be inclusive rather than exclusive?
- What can you do when you see that someone has been left out?
- Great. Are there a few volunteers to role play that for us?
- Great. Any more ideas on what else would help?
- Are there a few volunteers to role play that for us?

Activity

Paint or draw a picture of the colors of happiness or kindness, contrasting that with the colors of rejection. Or, make a collage of imagines of happiness or happiness and sorrow.

Close with a relaxation/focusing exercise.

HAPPINESS LESSON 8
Feelings of Sadness

Note to Educator: This lesson can be done if there is an atmosphere of respect and trust among the students, and the educator is comfortable actively listening and dealing with issues of sadness.

Begin with a song.

Ask:

- What is the opposite of happiness? (Sadness, depression and sorrow are often answers given.)
- What creates these feelings? (Acknowledge their responses, actively listening and validating as appropriate.)
- Can someone please give an example of something you feel sad about?
- What quality or anti-quality and value or anti-value is happening when this occurs?

Individual Activity

➢ Make a list of things you feel sad about in one column.
➢ Note down by each item, in a second column, the qualities or anti-qualities and values or anti-values that you associate with that item. (Such as rejection, loss, feeling not valued, disrespect, discrimination, etc.)
➢ Make a third column. What quality or value would eliminate this problem?

Discuss

Ask:

- How can we make ourselves feel better when we are sad?
- How can we nurture the self? What types of things help?
- What kinds of things can you think to increase the feeling of happiness?
- Can we change the way we view things; look at things another way?

Comment: We have discussed six of the strategies for happiness. Another was to cultivate optimism. Ask:

- Pessimism, the opposite of optimism, is a downer. It's thinking, I'm no good anyway, why try. People aren't going to like me anyway, why try. Can anyone think of any other pessimistic statements?
- What is optimism?
- Why would looking at life as a glass half full instead of half empty help?
- Can anyone give an example of that?
- Would some of your empowering statements fit this category? Which pessimistic statements have you been able to turn into empowering statements?
- Some people have a negative view of the world and are pessimistic. Others can see the negative in the world but also believe in the human capacity for good and their own power to make a difference. They can usually maintain an optimistic

view. An example of this is climate change. Are you in the optimistic camp that will work for positive change?

- What other examples of optimism can you think of?

Comment: Another strategy for happiness is to take care of your body. When you are feeling sad or low, it is especially important to take care of your body. Eating healthy, getting enough sleep and exercise help to manage our emotions and recover from feeling sad or low. Part of eating healthy is to not have too much sugar. Sugar, especially refined white sugar or high fructose corn syrup, is a vitamin B robber and has been found to destabilize the emotions.

- Any questions about this?
- What else have you found helps you stay healthy?

Comment: It's a delicate balance sometimes. It is so important to lovingly accept the self and all of our feelings and emotions . . . but it is also important to use our wise nurturing voice to keep ourselves safe.

- How else can we keep the self safe from sad things?

Provide a safe space for the young adults to discuss their ideas. Actively listen and validate as appropriate, and challenge them to find a way to change any negative, bitter or pessimistic thoughts to more empowering ones.

Activity

Write a poem, draw a picture or a cartoon about optimism and pessimism, or create colorful optimistic statements to put around your space.

Invite those who wish to share to do so.

Close with a relaxation/focusing exercise.

HAPPINESS LESSON 9

Creating Happiness or Sorrow at Home

Begin with a song.

Mind Mapping a Discussion

As you facilitate a discussion with the students with the questions below, mind map or ask for a couple of volunteers to mind map the outcome of the discussion. Please put Giving Happiness on one side of the board and Giving Sorrow on the other side. Make lists of things below different categories, on each side of the board, such as To Myself, To My Sisters and Brothers, To My Parents, My Sisters and Brothers to Me, My Parents to Me.

Ask:

- What things do you do at home that create happiness?
- What do other people in your home do that creates happiness?
- What do you do that creates sorrow that you would like to stop doing?
- What would help you stop that? What other behavior can you try instead?
- How many of you have older brothers and sisters? What kinds of things did you like to do with them when you were little?
- Do you think your younger brothers and sisters would like to do that with you?
- How can we contribute to other peoples' happiness while maintaining our own?
- What do others do that creates sorrow?
- How do you feel when that happens?
- What can you do to keep yourself safe?
- Does anyone else have any suggestions that have been successful in a similar situation?

Activity

Step 1. Divide the group in small groups to discuss the above. Ask them to think about ways to give happiness while maintaining their own happiness.

Step 2. If it seems appropriate for your group's situation and culture, invite them to discuss situations in which people are giving sorrow. Ask them to generate respectful statements in an "I feel _____ when _____," format with a suggestion for a more helpful behavior in an effort to improve a situation. For example: "I feel more pressured and anxious when you talk to me like that when I am already doing my homework. It would help if you would just smile at me and say, 'I know you can do it.'"

Step 3. Ask each group to role play one situation. They can choose ways to give happiness or ways to generate happiness and stop sorrow.

Step 4. *Comment:* We have looked at eight of the strategies for happiness. You are developing and have been developing coping strategies in many of the Living Values Education lessons, and you just did a great job again. Another strategy for happiness is to forgive.

Ask:

- Has anyone experienced resentment toward others?

Inform: There is a saying that resentment is like poison, you drink it and think it is going to hurt someone else. Resentment hurts the person feeling it, as we feel bad. Resentment acts like a barrier with another person, interfering or blocking positive feelings toward each other. Perhaps sometimes you don't want to have a positive relationship again, but sometimes you would like to not feel resentment. One way to do that is to work on forgiving them.

Ask:

- When you want to forgive someone, what kinds of things do you normally do?
- Would you like to try a forgiveness exercise?
- If the answer is yes: Start by thinking of a person you have a little resentment towards. Not a lot of resentment, but just a little.

Forgiveness Exercise

"Sit comfortably and let your body relax... As you breathe slowly, let your mind be still and calm.... Starting at your feet, let yourself relax ... relax your legs . . . stomach ... shoulders, neck ... face. . the eyes ... and forehead.... Let yourself be surrounded by the light of peace.... Let your mind be serene and calm ... breathe deeply ... concentrate on stillness.... Be peace. Let yourself be surrounded by the light of love. Now, say to yourself ... I am a loving powerful person.... I forgive me.... I forgive him or her.... From now on there will only be respect between us. ... I am a kind amazing person.... I forgive me.... I forgive him or her.... From now on there will only be caring and respect between us.... Repeat this to yourself in your own words.... Such as, I am a beautiful soul.... I forgive me.... I forgive her.... From now on there will only be respect between us.... Repeat these four phrases to yourself in your own words, using the name of the person you would like to forgive. (Pause for one full minute.) Now, breathe in the light of peace . . . let go of any tension ... and slowly bring your attention back to this room.

Inform: If this feels okay for you, experiment with it once a day or a week and let me know if you feel better in a week. For some people it takes a week, and for others it takes longer.

Homework: Invite them to do three or four good deeds at home without telling anyone.

Note to Educator: If you note during this lesson that some of the young adults seem to have a very difficult home life, you may wish to speak to them privately to advise them about available resources.

Close with a relaxation/focusing exercise.

HAPPINESS LESSON 10 — Optional Drug Awareness
Drugs and Alcohol Speak

Begin with a song.

Discuss/Share

Generate a discussion based on the questions below. You might want to ask some of the questions a few times, so that a variety of responses can be given. Actively listen to their stories. You may wish to mind map the effects of each drug they mention and the downward spiral. Ask "*The effects of being hooked*" questions for each drug they mention that is being sold or used in the neighborhood.

Ask:

- It is said that sometimes people take alcohol or drugs as a way to stop their pain or unhappiness, in an effort to be happy and not feel what is troubling them. Do you think this is true?
- Have you known of people who started taking drugs for this reason?
- What other reasons are there for people to take drugs?
- Can anyone think of any other reasons people take drugs?
- What drugs are sold in this area?
- What are the effects of _____ (the drug they used and/or alcohol) when someone first takes it?

The effects of being hooked questions:

- What are the effects once someone is addicted? (Show the relationship on the mind map by drawing an arrow from one effect to the next, drawing it downward.)
- What can happen after that? (For example, stealing money in order to be able to buy the drug. Show the relationship on the mind map by drawing an arrow from one effect to the next, drawing it downward.)
- What are the consequences of that? (Again, show the relationship, drawing an arrow.)
- What else can happen to someone's body when they're on _____?
- What are other dangers of taking _____? (For example, HIV infection.)
- Would anyone like to share something else about drugs?

Activity

Step 1. Together, summarize the harmful things that happen to youth and adults that take drugs and alcohol.

Step 2. Invite students to form small groups of five or six to make posters about the negative effects of one drug or alcohol and present them to the rest of the class. Perhaps between the groups they can explore all the drugs that are sold locally on the streets. Ask them to put their advice on the poster in the form of a slogan.

Step 3. Ask the groups to present their poster with a small skit/sketch, with one person representing a drug that can talk. What would the drug say? Others in the group can respond to what the drug says, play the role of drug dealers, victims, etc. Lead the applause.

Close with the Garden of Respect exercise or another relaxation/focusing exercise of their choice.

HAPPINESS LESSON 11 – Optional Drug Awareness
Mind Mapping the Effects of Drug and Alcohol Abuse

Note to Educator: While this lesson is appropriate for teens and young adults in many societies, it may be inappropriate in some societies. The educators using these materials will need to decide if it is relevant to your particular situation and culture.

Aim and Objectives: The aim of this lesson is to allow young adults to explore the effects of taking drugs and look at healthier alternatives to achieve their goals. The objectives are to become aware of:

1. the various emotions they are trying to experience through the intake of drugs;
2. how drugs may give a temporary experience but set up maladaptive behaviors that interfere with attainment of those emotions/goals in the long term;
3. the negative side effects physically; and
4. healthier alternative methods to experience the sought for emotions and experiences.

Begin with a song.

Process

Step 1. Ask students to list the various drugs they are aware of in the local community. Write the names in a column on the board.

Step 2. Ask the students about the different emotional experiences of each drug, and list those in an adjacent column.

Step 3. In another adjacent column, list by each drug the related side effects. Ask the students about physical and negative emotional experiences. If they are not aware of all the negative effects, inform them, and list those also.

Step 4. List the emotions the individual is seeking to experience in the fourth column.

Step 5. Ask the students about healthier alternative methods of achieving those experiences and also list these. Ask questions, such as:

- What is true happiness?
- Are you really confident if the feeling of confidence is only there when a drug is taken?
- With an addiction you are not free, you are depending on a chemical to make you feel happy for a short time. Does happiness include freedom from compulsion?
- What can you do instead to feel happy?

Example:

Drug	Experience	Side Effects	Seeking to Experience	Alternative Method
Alcohol	happiness confidence carefree	expensive loss of control violence/anger unconsciousness effects health negatively	happiness freedom respect	
Cannabis	relaxed/calm peaceful understanding feeling free sociable	tiredness eating lots of sweets loss of memory loss of motivation negative effect on brain development if laced can lead to psychosis	peaceful unity harmony	
LSD	visual experience knowledge distorted perception	bad experience destroys brain cells	knowledge	
Speed	energy alive	heart palpitations lack of appetite	enthusiasm power	

– Contributed by Steve Eardley and Marie Ange Samuel

Activity

Mind map the effects of drug and alcohol abuse with the young adults. They can include as few branches or as many as they wish: the self, family, relationships, health, business, education and/or society. Ask them to put down all the things they have heard about and experienced regarding the effects of drug use. They may wish to make drawings, illustrating some of the effects.

Note to Educator: Accept whatever they produce. It is fine if they note initial positive effects. The negative will far outweigh the positive.

Creative Expression

Divide the class into small groups and invite them to create a poem or song about their findings. When they are finished, each group can present their creation. If there is not time for all of them to present, allow them to share at the beginning of the next lesson.

End with the Taking Care of Me Relaxation/Focusing Exercise.

Close with a relaxation/focusing exercise.

HAPPINESS LESSON 12 — Optional Drug Awareness
Drug Dealers May Seem Nice at First

Begin with a song.

Discuss/Share

Inform: Drug dealers have no regard for others. If they did, they wouldn't be dealing drugs. In some countries, once vulnerable young people are hooked on drugs, they use them as mules or slave labor.

Ask:

- Drug dealers use all kinds of ways to get people hooked on drugs. Sometimes they even use children to sell drugs, once they have them hooked. What have you seen in our area?

- How else do people get others to take drugs in our area?

Note to Educator: Please add further information about some of the problems young people are having in your area or country with drugs and alcohol abuse, or common ways drug dealers entice others into trying drugs.

Ask:

- Do you think the drug dealers care if drugs ruin your life?

- Do they care about you? (No.)

- What do drug sellers care about? (Money.)

- What other tricks do they use to get people to take drugs?
- Why do you think they want you to use drugs?
- Usually adults take drugs when they feel bad and don't know how to stop feeling bad. Can you think of things they could do instead?
- Sometimes young people take drugs because they feel upset. They get desperate when things are bad or sad and so they try to feel better with drugs. Are there other times that you think young people feel like taking drugs?

Comment: Sometimes prescription drugs or alcohol are available at home and people get started on substance abuse through that.

- What can you do to feel better when you feel sad or upset? (Help them generate alternatives. Ask others for their ideas. If they do not mention it, you might wish to include such ideas as thinking of the Peace Star or asking a friend for help. If their reasons include physical needs, help them find some sensible solutions.)
- What you do think drug sellers need to learn? What would you like to tell them?

Activities

Step 1. Divide the students into groups of five to seven to create dramas/skits about drug dealers and their interactions with young people or children. Some of the dealers may be their own age.

Step 2. Invite them to present their drama. If they need more time, allow them to present it during the next lesson.

Step 3. If appropriate to your situation, create the opportunity for some of the skits to be shown to other young people or to the community. If this is to be done, you might wish to take time during another lesson to create props, practice and advertise the event with posters made by the students. Encourage their "voice" against drug dealers and harmful drugs.

End with the Respect Star exercise or another relaxation/focusing exercise of their choice.

HAPPINESS LESSON 13
Drinking, Driving, Blame and Communication Skills

Begin with a song.

Share a Story

Read the short story or ask the students to read "Blame" on line by Kathy Gale. A true story about a family that blamed frequently, and another family that never blamed, is driven home to a college student whose friend is accidently killed. The Joy of Reading Project kindly gave their permission to post this story on the international LVE site, www.livingvalues.net. You will find it under For Schools / Young Adults / Download Free Stories And/or read the short story or ask the students to read "Crying's Okay" on line by Kirk Hill, also from The Joy of Reading Project.

Or, read another story or two on drinking and driving, or discus incidents in your local area of which the students are aware.

Discuss/Share

Invite the young adults to discuss their responses to the stories and debate the questions that follow.

Ask:

- Is drinking a method to achieve happiness? Why or why not?
- What is the relationship of blame in relationships and its relationship to happiness?
- How can you communicate positively rather than blame?

Activity

Step 1. Instruct the class to form small groups and invite them to discuss: If they were to suggest communication skills for healthy families, what skills and ways of being would they include if you wanted everyone in the family to be happy?

Step 2. Invite each group to present their finding to the entire class. Their presentation may take any form, including role playing a family or a song about blame and its effect on happiness.

Close with a relaxation/focusing exercise.

HAPPINESS LESSON 14
Empowering Sentences

Begin with a song.

Small Group Activity

Step 1. Ask each student to bring out their Empowerment Logs. Ask them to form small groups and discuss some of their most effective Encouraging/Empowering Thoughts with each other.

Step 2. Discuss the following reflection point: When one is content with the self, happiness comes automatically.

Step 3. Invite each group to take a turn standing in front of the class, each individual stating one empowering sentence he or she likes.

Activity

Group Story Game: If time still remains, have a good time making up two stories, one story where everyone gives sorrow, and another story where everyone gives happiness. Do the unhappy story first. Start with the same beginning situation, and go around the room asking each student to add something to the story. Then, make up a story in which everyone gives happiness. Enjoy.

Close with a relaxation/focusing exercise of your choice.

HAPPINESS LESSON 15

Thinking About Purpose

Begin with a song.

Write the following Reflection Points on the board.

♦ When there is a feeling of hope and purpose, there is happiness.

♦ Happiness is earned through pure and selfless attitudes and actions.

♦ When one is content with the self, happiness comes automatically.

Reflection

Inform: We have looked at ten of the strategies for happiness. The last two are practice spirituality and commit to your goals. I leave practice spirituality to you . . . for each of us has our own unique relationship with the divine. In this lesson, however, is an opportunity to look at your purpose and goals. To commit to your goals was the twelfth strategy for happiness.

Play some music and give the students time to reflect and write down their responses as you ask the following questions slowly. They are likely to need two or more minutes for many of the questions.

• What is your purpose?

• Think about the experiences that give you happiness that you wrote about during the first lesson and have thought about during this values unit. What values did you put down?

- Think about the things that are important in your life now, and the values inherent within those.
- What would you like to achieve in your life?
- What are your goals?
- What are the values within those things?
- Can you "be" some of those values while you are achieving other aims (i.e., education, professional)?
- What is worth doing your best for?
- Can you be content inside if you know you are doing your best?

Sharing

Ask them to form small groups of three or four and talk about their purpose and goals, and whatever they would like to share from their reflection.

Activity

Make a colorful drawing in the form of a medallion of their goals and purpose and the values that give them happiness.

Close with a relaxation/focusing exercise of their choice.

HAPPINESS LESSON 16

Character, Development and the Sustainable Development Goals

Begin with a song.

Discuss the Reflection Points:

- ♦ When all resources are focused on socioeconomic infrastructure at the expense of the development of the character, then priorities in life are misrepresented and there is a gradual erosion of happiness.
- ♦ Values help people assess priorities and allow for proactive and preventive measures to take place at opportune moments.
- ♦ Lasting happiness is a state of contentment within.

Activity

Step 1. Invite the students to form the same groups they were with during the previous SDGs lessons. Ask them to explore the Reflection Points. Are these true? Ask them to research an example of this and design a value-based proactive measure that would resolve the problem.

Step 2. Ask them to think of their reflections as they explore the effect of happiness on the SDGs. If everyone in the world were able to be in their natural nature of giving, that is, in a state that creates real happiness, how would the SDGs be affected? Do any more SDGs need to be added?

Step 3. Ask them to write specific ways holding the value of happiness would affect the SDGs on which their group is focused and write those on orange Leaves.

Step 4. Invite them to share their example from Step 1 and their Happiness Leaves with the entire group.

Step 5. Invite the groups to attach their orange Happiness Leaves to the class artistic presentation of the SDGs.

Close with a relaxation/focusing exercise.

HAPPINESS LESSON 17
Ten Principles of Happiness

Begin with a song.

Activity

Step 1. Invite the students to work individually and generate their own principles of happiness.

An example: **Ten Principles of Happiness**

       Pursue your dreams.

       Be generous of heart, give happiness.

       Be kind.

       Laugh — with others, and at yourself.

       Allow yourself some relaxing time.

       Think deeply about what matters to you.

       Lovingly accept yourself.

       Accept others.

       Believe in yourself.

       Enjoy the present.

Step 2. Invite them to form small groups and share their ten principles of happiness.

Step 3. Put on some happy music and ask them to dance/move acting out their ten principles silently as they enjoy being happy.

Step 4. If there is time, simply enjoy by sharing some of the songs or poems they have most enjoyed during this unit, or play a happy game.

Close with a relaxation/focusing exercise.

Happiness Activities in Subject Areas

Language/Literature

Write a Reflection Point on the board every day. Ask students to write an essay on one or more of the points. On another day they could write a personal story, illustrating one of the Reflection Points.

Select reading materials that depict happiness and examine what creates happiness in the works studied. You may want to choose folk tales, old legends, books that powerfully illustrate moments of happiness or sorrow, or works of philosophers of ancient cultures — or use your own favorite childhood stories about happiness.

Enjoy reading stories to young children.

Write a reflective personal essay on when you are content with yourself. Or, if you are not, write a letter of advice to yourself about how to be more content.

Write a story on The Secrets of Happiness. Perhaps students can illustrate the story.

Needs and Wants

Step 1. Each student is to create a list of 12 things that give him or her happiness in life.

Step 2. As a class, discuss the difference between needs and wants.

Step 3. The students can discuss their choices in groups of three or four. Reduce the list to six items, then three items.

Step 4. The students can then write a letter of appreciation to the people connected with those items.

— Contributed by Ruth Liddle

Jewels of Happiness Game

Educator Preparation / Materials Needed: Each group of two to four players will need one or two dice, "jewels" (colored counters or buttons), one marker piece for each player, materials to make one game board and 24 cards.

Introduction: Happiness is a priceless treasure. You can't buy it, but you can acquire it and accumulate it. In this game the aim is to collect as many "jewels" of happiness as you can.

Activity: Students can make the game boards and cards. Each game board has five rows intersecting five columns making a total of 25 spaces. Each game needs 24 cards, each being the same size or smaller as one square on the board. Twelve cards are the "no jewel" cards and twelve have "jewels" at the top of the card, indicated by *κ* ♥ *or α*. Samples of jewel cards are below, or students can make their own.

Jewel Cards

κ ♥ You help someone without being asked to.	*κ ♥ You make a list of all the people you are thankful to.*	*κ You make a list of all the possessions you are lucky to own.*	*κ ♥ ♥ You play with your little brother.*	*κ ♥ You make a new friend.*
κ ♥ α You write a letter to someone to tell them how special they are.	*κ ♥ α You give your parents a small gift as a token of your appreciation.*	*κ ♥ You make a special birthday gift for someone.*	*♥ You share your favorite snack with your friends.*	*κ You cheer yourself up with a happy song.*
κ You share a happy memory with someone.	*κ ♥ You tell your grandmother one reason why you love her.*	*♥ You thank your neighbor for her thoughtful-ness, even though the gift is not your taste.*	*κ ♥ You visualize your family smiling and laughing together.*	*♥ α You send a loving thought to an unhappy person.*
κ ♥ α You smile and say hello to everyone on the way to school.	*κ You tidy your room without being asked.*	*κ ♥ You prepare a special meal for your family.*	*κ ♥ You give one of your parents a day off by doing some of their chores.*	*♥ You smile and step back when someone cuts into the line in front of you.*

κ ♥ α You send thoughts of peace and happiness to everyone in the world.	κ ♥ You make effort to be friendly to someone you have had difficulty with.	♥ You say yes to your friend's suggestion to do homework together.	♥ α You tell your teacher one thing you like about the way she or he teaches.	κ ♥ α You visit a beautiful place and tell yourself how lucky you are.
♥ You let go of your idea for the group because you know others have good ideas, too.	κ α You give someone else a chance to shine.	κ ♥ α You do everything with love.	κ ♥ α You look forward to the future, seeing problems as opportunities to learn.	κ ♥ α You think "What will happen as a result?" before you take action.
κ ♥ α Your friends are arguing. You don't take sides, but continue to be friends with all.	κ ♥ You spend five minutes a day sending peaceful thoughts into the world.	♥ α You read about the life of someone who makes a positive contribution to the world.	♥ You think, "Do I really need this?" before you buy something.	κ You volunteer to help someone do something useful.

No Jewel Cards

You give up hope that you will ever get better at something.	You think it is impossible for your friend to change.	You think about all the ways you are better than your friends.	Your face changes when someone does something you dislike.	You think you'll never be successful as everyone else.
You remind people of the mistakes they have made.	You think of the past more than the present.	You always image the worst things that could happen.	You avoid going on family outings.	You sulk when your teacher asks you to do something.
You ignore someone who tries to join your group.	You laugh at someone's new haircut.	You make up a bad rumor about someone.	You say something mean about someone you like because someone popular does not like her.	You do not correct someone when they have wrong information about someone else.

How to Play: Players place their marker pieces on the center jewel square. The 24 small cards are shuffled and placed face down to cover the remaining squares on the board (12 jewel cards and 12 no jewel cards). Players shake the dice to decide who plays first. The first player shakes and moves her marker piece horizontally or vertically the number of spaces indicated. She turns over the card on that square. If it is a jewel card, she reads the card and takes the number of "jewels" indicated (0, 1, 2 or 3.) Players take turns to shake and move. The winner is the person with the most jewels when the last card has been turned over.

Other uses for Jewel Cards:

❖ As discussion starters. Have you ever felt like this? Which of these three situations would bring the most happiness to you? To your mother? To your friend?

❖ As a topic for journal responses — as a class or individually.

❖ To encourage students to create their own cards based on their life experience.

❖ As a prewriting activity.

❖ A follow-up task could include creating a conversation, skit or scene from a play for two or more characters based on their situation.

❖ Create your own happiness game with an illustrated board and box. Produce an advertisement for TV, radio, the Internet, or a popular magazine to promote your game.

— Contributed by Ruth Liddle

History/Social Studies

Ask students to think about the last two Happiness Reflection Points and support or contradict the statements with examples from history.

Look for examples of countries that strive to meet the basic human rights and needs of their people. Contrast the incidence of civil war and social unrest in these countries versus countries that provide for the needs of only a minority of its populace.

Science

What scientific inventions have contributed to the happiness of humankind? Are there inventions that have created sadness?

Discuss: Is the purpose of science to make humankind happier? Why or why not? (If no, ask: What would that be the purpose of science in a better world?)

Discuss ways in which science could contribute to the happiness of humankind.

Art

Draw happiness.

Play happy music and ask the students to paint the feeling of being happy.

Study the Reflection Points and create slogans of happiness. Use these slogans in the creation of posters or pictures. Discuss where you feel each of these should be placed. For example, these could decorate different agencies, hospitals, or children's centers. Consider placing them at different locations.

Discuss the following Reflection Point: Good wishes for everyone gives happiness inside. Ask students to consciously practice having good wishes for themselves, each other, each other's work, and even the teacher for that day. Discuss this exercise the next day and ask them to continue having good wishes for the rest of the week.

Look at pictures and photographs of people in a moment of happiness. Draw your own face with an expression of happiness. Look in the mirror as you draw.

Work in two's and make a happy drawing of each other.
— *Contributed by Eleanor Viegas*

Make an abstract painting of your happy feelings. Make the colors and shapes dance on the paper. Look at pictures by Paul Klee, Chagall, Kandinsky and regional artists of your culture. Inform the students that part of the task is just experiencing happy feelings as they draw and expressing these with colors.
— *Contributed by Eleanor Viegas*

Paint two actions of happiness in the middle of a picture. Extend out the colors of the consequences of those actions.

Drama

Students can create and present a puppet show on happiness to younger students, or they can enact a script or story taking up the contrast of happiness and sorrow.

Music

Enjoy and play happy music celebrating life throughout the ages. Experience how some music automatically uplifts us. Find a piece of music that everyone agrees creates the feeling of happiness. Ask, "How does that occur? What are differences in music itself that make it sound happy or sad?"

Discuss what increases the happiness within the music class. Experiment with asking for suggestions from the young adults, and giving more positive feedback. What is the result?

Home Economics

Discuss the following Reflection Point:
- ◆ Kind and constructive words create a happier world.

Ask students to think of a week-long project that relates to that point. Have them brainstorm ideas, then each can decide what he or she wants to commit to. Ideas could include: keeping track of their verbal comments during class, creating a list from comments said at home, or doing this in regard to comments they say outside.

Make a practical or decorative object for home that will remind students of their own beauty inside and help them stay content.

Physical Education/Dance

At the start of the period, play a game that everyone loves — with the teacher joining in!

Dance a dance of happiness.

Play a game or do something that creates lots of laughter.

OPTIONAL UNIT: SUBSTANCE ABUSE

Drug and Alcohol Abuse Lessons for Frequent Users

As we all know, substance abuse ravages the lives of many people, young and old. If the group of young adults you are working with has a problem with substance abuse, you may wish to do the lessons in this unit. They are taken from *Living Values Activities for Drug Rehabilitation*. This program has been highly successful in Vietnam where it is used in many private and government rehabilitation clinics. The Ministry of Labor reported in March of 2008 that LVE's program for drug rehabilitation was the most successful program in government drug rehabilitation clinics.

It is **essential** to complete the peace, respect and love values units before doing these lessons, as they build the understanding, attitudes and skills necessary to complete the lessons successfully. The skills and understanding built during the peace, respect and love values units allow the participants to co-create with you a safe accepting atmosphere in which they can be honest.

As the facilitator you will need excellent active listening and validating skills in order to carry out these lessons successfully. A caring, matter of fact, firm and yet supportive nonjudgmental attitude is vital in facilitating these lessons. Shaming and blaming are not part of Living Values Education. If at all possible, please take part in an LVE Educator Workshop.

Note to Educator: **Please begin with Optional Drug Awareness Lessons 10, 11 and 12 in the Happiness Unit prior to doing the following lessons.**

SUBSTANCE ABUSE LESSON 1 — Optional Drug Use and Abuse Lesson
A Relationship with the Wrong Partner

Begin with a song.

Ask the young people how they are and how the last few days have been. Listen. Ask them if they would like to share any of their thoughts or reactions to the last session together.

Activity

Say, "Today, our lesson is on looking at what happens due to drug use and abuse."

Mind Map: Form small groups of five or six and invite the young adults to mind map the effects of drug abuse and/or alcohol versus being in recovery, that is, being dry/sober. In the mind map they are to include the branches of self, family, relationships, business and society. Ask them to put down all the things they have heard about and experienced regarding the effects of drug use and abuse. Provide large pieces of flip-chart paper. They may wish to make drawings, illustrating some of the effects. Allow them 30 minutes to do this.

Note to Facilitator: Accept whatever they produce. It is fine if they note initial positive effects. The negative will far outweigh the positive.

Lesson Content

Inform: Developing an addiction can be compared to different stages in a love relationship — with the wrong partner! As we go through each stage, we get more involved — but this partner of drugs has no mercy. Its hold on us gets stronger and stronger and we become powerless over our lives as this 'partner' takes control.[9]

Say, "When some people get their first high on drugs think those highs will last forever."

Ask:

- Was that true for you?

Stage 1. Infatuation — Experimental Use

You and your drug meet through curiosity or peer pressure. You have positive early experiences, you feel euphoric, calmed, soothed, relaxed, and more comfortable socially. You have increased self-confidence, energy and power.

Ask:

- Did you experience this?

Stage 2. Honeymoon — Recreational Use

Drugs are helping you to cope with bad feelings, memories and/or stress. You're in love with the drug and think this friend will be there forever. The drug begins to leave an imprint in your brain; the brain is changed biochemically.

Stage 3. Betrayal — Misuse

---

[9] This concept is borrowed from Alcoholics Anonymous.

Because you're using the drug more, the negative after-effects start becoming more of a problem. What you saw during the honeymoon is not what you are experiencing now. The high doesn't feel as good. Problems start mounting up.

Ask:

- Did you experience this? Would anyone like to share?

Comment: When drug use is first started, the first experiences are the best drug highs of your life. In the first experience there is usually a 'high' of intense pleasure; the brain has released a large amount of dopamine. Dopamine is the name of the neurotransmitter associated with the pleasure center in the brain.

Some people continue to use in an attempt to recapture or re-experience the first high. But the experience is downhill after that. What happens is that with repeated drug use there is a gradual depletion of dopamine; even with more of the drug less dopamine is released. With nothing in the dopamine 'bank account,' there is not enough dopamine to feel a 'normal' amount of pleasure; users are more vulnerable to negative feelings. They often feel anxious, agitated and/or depressed. The drug is then craved; they use just to try to feel "normal" again. These users do not enjoy the regular activities of life they used to enjoy as the dopamine levels are so depleted."

Ask:

- Did you experience this? Would anyone like to share?
- Once you started to be addicted to the drug, what activities did you no longer enjoy — that you used to enjoy?

One of the many reasons why it is difficult to stay clean and sober is that it usually takes six to nine months for the brain to recover from the dopamine depletion. So, for six to nine months after you stop using, not only do people in recovery not enjoy many normal activities they used to enjoy, but you may also feel depressed, tired and uninterested in anything. The good news is that the brain can regenerate a supply of dopamine. Recovery involves sobriety, rest, healthy food, and moderate exercise in order for our brain to have time to replenish the normal levels of dopamine. However, if you use again, the brain will need another six to nine months to recover again."

Ask:

- Those of you who have been addicted to a substance, after you were clean and sober, how long did it take you to enjoy those same activities?
- Are you enjoying them to the same extent that you did earlier?
- What activities are you enjoying now?

Inform: One of the good things about the relaxation/focusing exercises, is that they help the brain to develop dopamine again. So, if you are not enjoying regular activities, do some of the relaxation/focusing exercises — and it will help you to enjoy other things again.

Stage 4. On the Rocks (The Relationship is Falling Apart) — Abuse

In an attempt to recapture the honeymoon, you increase drug use. You begin to lose control of your use. You feel guilty, remorseful, and self-esteem is lowered. You compromise your values.

Ask:

- Did you experience this? Would anyone like to share?

Stage 5. Trapped — Dependence

You need to use the drug to feel normal. You use to alleviate withdrawal symptoms. You feel desperate, become more obsessed, use compulsively, and do things you never would have imagined doing before. All areas of your life deteriorate.

Discus/Share

Say, "While some of you have suffered from your addiction, it seems to be part of human nature to sometimes want to brag and tell stories about how high one got and how exciting one was. It is hard to renounce this. As human beings every one of us has a need to feel special; everyone wants to feel respected and loved."

Ask:

- If you continually create the attraction for that wrong partner . . . what will the consequences be?
- Why do you want to talk about your past adventures with the wrong partner?
- What do you want from the other person? (Admiration and the feeling of camaraderie are two possible answers.)
- What else can you talk about that will allow you to get that?
- What other things interest you?
- What would you like to learn about?
- What would you like to do with your life?
- If someone is bragging about their drug experiences, how can you protect yourself from building that attraction again?
- What can you say in a respectful or peaceful way that could turn the conversation away from interest in that wrong partner?

Artistic Expression

Ask each group to create a poem or song about their findings. When they are finished, each group can present a few thoughts and their poem or song. If there is not time for all of them to present, allow them to share at the beginning of the next lesson.

End with the Dealing with Pain with Courage and Kindness Exercise.

SUBSTANCE ABUSE LESSON 2 — Optional Drug Use and Abuse Lesson
The Downward Spiral of Using

Begin with a song.

Ask the young people how they are and how the last few days have been. Listen. Ask them if they would like to share any of their thoughts or reactions to the last session together.

Lesson Content

Inform: Today, let's take a closer look at addiction and the downward spiral of drug use.

Ask:

• Who can tell me what addiction means?

Thank you. The dictionary defines addiction as: a chronic neglect of the self in favor of something or someone else.

When someone becomes addicted to alcohol or drugs there is a predictable downward spiral. The following five stages can help us understand the progression of drug use.

Ask:

• When you are first addicted, do you realize it?

Please share the following information:

Stage 1. Denial Belief Systems

Addicts usually deny that they are addicted as they think addicts are <u>other people</u> who use 24 hours a day, 7 days a week. They might say:

"I don't use 24/7, so I'm not an addict." Or:

"I can control my use, so I'm not an addict."

"I can stop any time, so I'm not an addict."

"God made it, so it has to be good for you!"

They ignore the concerns and worries of friends and family about their drug use and deny that many of their problems are due to drug use.

Ask:

- Did any of you have these thoughts?
- Were there other thoughts that helped you deny that you were addicted?
- What helped you realize you were addicted?

Stage 2. Regular Use of Drug of Choice

Addicts have an obsession with their drug of choice. That is, their thoughts are most often on drugs. They:

frequently think about the next high and plan ways to get high;

get excited and anxious in anticipation of the next high;

get frustrated or panicky if someone or something gets in the way of their drug use;

spend most of their time, energy and attention thinking about drugs; and

protect the supply of the drug, often at great emotional or personal cost.

Addicts become compulsive about their drug use. They usually:

feel driven to use in spite of what will happen;

make one or more unsuccessful attempts to stop using; and

even with a sincere desire to stop, drug use starts up again.

Ask:

- Would anyone like to share some of your experiences about this?

Stage 3. Tolerance and Withdrawals

As regular use of the drug continues:

there is an increase in the amount of use with NO increase in the desired effect;

there is an increase in use to maintain the same effect;

there is less pleasure from the drug than there was in the beginning;

symptoms of withdrawal begin;

the drug turns against the user, causing negative effects, but the drug use continues; and one or more areas of life are negatively affected. This can include:

    a. relationships

    b. work/school/housework

    c. finances

    d. psychological health

    e. physical health

f. judgment and behavior

    g. self-esteem/values

    h. social/recreational activities

    ➤ Invite them to share their experiences in relation to the points above. Ask the participants how many areas of their life were negatively affected by drug use.

Stage 4. Continued Use Despite Consequences

The addict continues to use despite physical, emotional and mental effects.

Physical Effects: Ask participants to list the physical effects of their drug of choice. For example, for alcohol this would be: headaches, ulcers, brain damage, heart problems, inability to have sex, decreased sperm count, abnormal sperm cells, emphysema, cirrhosis of the liver and pancreatitis. Pregnant women are at risk for causing fetal alcohol syndrome.

With intravenous drug use, there is an increased incidence of HIV/AIDS and hepatitis B and C. The physical effects of heroin use can include: fatal overdose, collapsed veins, infection of the heart lining and valves, abscesses, cellulites, and liver disease. Pulmonary complications, including various types of pneumonia, may result from the poor health condition of the abuser, as well as from heroin's depressing effects on respiration (NIDA).

Emotional and Mental Effects: obsessive thoughts, irrational thinking, addictive lifestyle behavior and thoughts, feelings covered up, tense, anxious, sad, upset, irritable, depressed, guilt, shame, dishonesty, feelings of helplessness, confusion, lack of motivation/drive, loss of self-respect, social isolation, fears, and intolerance. Ask participants if they would like to add to the list.

Relationship Consequences: loss of communication, unhealthy dependencies, arguing and fighting, infidelity, neglecting children and family, neglecting family responsibilities and loss of trust and respect. Job problems increase with absenteeism, job inefficiency and interpersonal conflicts.

Stage 5. Loss of Control

At this stage, the addict begins to use the drug in larger amounts, over longer periods of time than intended; once high, doesn't walk away until the supply is gone; even though he or she may not be using daily, binges last longer; spends lots of time getting the drug, using the drug and recovering from the effects; the drug is controlling the person rather than the person controlling the drug.

— Five Stages contributed by Linda Slauson

Activity Options

Option One: Supply participants with art materials and allow them to draw their own downward spiral in groups of four. They may wish to add their own details and elaborate on the effects through their artwork.

Option Two: The groups could do a skit or song. Invite them to share afterwards.

End with the Respect Star Exercise or another Relaxation/Focusing Exercise of their choice.

SUBSTANCE ABUSE LESSON 3 — Optional Drug Use and Abuse Lesson
How do you feel about what happened?

Begin with a song.

Ask the young people how they are. Listen. Ask them if they would like to share any of their thoughts or reactions to the last session together. Ask if anyone would like to share a discouraging thought that they changed into an empowering thought.

Discussion Activity

Step 1. Please put up the following chart on the board.

1. What was happening in your life before you started using drugs?	2. What attracted you to drugs? What did you think you would get from drugs?	3. What did you get as a result of using drugs?	4. Negative or painful things that happened as a result of using drugs.	5. How did you feel about what happened?

Step 2. Inform them that each person will have seven minutes in which to share their story by talking about the topic in all five columns.

Point out columns four and five.

Regarding column four, say: "Today, you may share something painful or negative that happened as a result of using drugs."

Regarding column five, say: "Please tell us how you felt about the experience you shared."

Step 3. Ask them to form groups of three, asking them to form different groups than before. Remind them of the importance of actively listening to others with compassion and respect. Each person in the group is to take a turn sharing his or her answers to the five questions and has seven minutes to share. The other two in the group are both to listen. (The facilitator should call time when each seven-minute segment is over.)   Each

Talker may share with the two people in the group what was appreciated about the way they listened.

Step 4. After everyone has shared in their small groups, ask for a volunteer from each group to share. Write some of their responses in columns four and five.

Step 5. Ask for volunteers to summarize the content in each column, pointing out the most common responses. Thank everyone for sharing.

Do the following relaxation/focusing exercise.

The Leaf of My Lesson Relaxation/Focusing Exercise

"Let your body be relaxed and still. . . . Take in a deep breath, breathing in peace. . . . As you breathe out, let the tension go out the bottoms of your feet. . . . Breathe in peace . . . breathe out any tension through the bottoms of your feet. . . . As you breathe in peace, let the light of peace relax your whole body . . . letting your legs fill with light . . . letting your abdomen and chest fill with light. . . . With each breath, relax more, and let the light of peace gradually come into your back . . . and arms . . . your shoulders and neck . . . and your face. . . . Imagine your place of peace and yourself in that place of peace. . . . It might be by a river with the water flowing gently by. . . . It might be in a forest . . . with rays of light filtering through the leaves of the trees. . . . Imagine yourself relaxing in the place of peace you create in your mind. . . . Feel the core of peace within you. . . . Let the peace of your place of peace surround you. . . . When you are quiet inside . . . still . . . you can feel this peace. . . . As you enjoy the beautiful place of peace you have imagined, let a large leaf float into your hand. . . . As you look at the leaf, you see that a lesson you have learned from your painful experience because of drugs is written on its surface. . . . Look at the words on the leaf. . . . (Pause for at least one full minute.) Experience the beauty of the lesson you have learned. . . . If there is any pain inside . . . acknowledge it and accept it. . . . Let the peace inside you surround the pain . . . What does the leaf say to the pain? . . . (Pause for a minute.) Would the pain like to answer the leaf? . . . What does it say? . . . What value does it think will make you gentle and strong? . . . All that you want to be? . . . What you naturally are? . . . (Pause for half a minute.) Fill yourself with the feeling of that value. . . . Give the love of the light of peace to the pain. . . . Let the peace of your place of peace surround you. . . . Let the leaf of your lesson grow more beautiful as you experience the importance of what you have learned. . . . Allow it to stay as it is or change form. . . . Let the beauty of that become written on your heart. . . . This is something you know is important. . . . Now deepen your peace . . . become still . . . become stable . . . experience the peace at your core. . . . Gradually bring your attention back to this room."

Close by asking the group to stand in a circle. Ask each person to share one sentence about what they learned from the experience today.

SUBSTANCE ABUSE LESSON 4 — Optional Drug Use and Abuse Lesson
My List of Negative or Destructive Behaviors When Using

Begin with a song.

Ask the young people how they are. Listen. Ask them if they would like to share any of their thoughts or reactions to the last session together. Ask if anyone would like to share a discouraging thought that they changed into an empowering thought.

Lesson Content

➢ Please put up the chart from the last lesson.

➢ Point out things on the chart, comparing information within columns and between columns, for example:

In column one: Note if there are contrasts. For example, "Some of you were good students before using drugs, some of you were not."

Ask:

• Is there anything you all had in common?" (There may or may not be.)

• How did you feel before you started using drugs — overall? (Accept all answers.)

In column two: Note the different things they wanted from drugs.

In column three:

Ask:

• Did you get what you wanted?

• What do you think might have helped you get more of what you wanted?

• What values would have helped at that point in time?

• Are you developing those values now?

In column four: Summarize some of the content. For example, it might be appropriate to say, "As with others who became addicted to drugs, your life started to fall apart and you experienced a lot of pain and sorrow. When people are addicted, their mind is not their own. Many people do things they wish they had not done, once they are clean and sober again."

Ask:

- Have some of you experienced that?

Contrast column one and four. For example, "Some of you were good students prior to drugs; after drugs you quit studying." "Some of you had good relationships with your parents before drugs; after drugs those relationships were damaged."

In column five: Note the different emotions they have shared.

Ask:

- Are there any emotions that some of you experienced that were the same before and after drugs? (Shame, embarrassment, anger, feeling rejected, feeling like a failure, hurt, etc.)

Note to Facilitator: Refer to the "Under the Anger" diagram below. The drawing above the word "ANGER" represents flames. The +'s represent each person's positive core values and qualities.

Anger

Hurt, Fear, Shame or feeling Unsafe
Everyone wants to be valued, respected or loved.

+ +

+ + + +

+ +

Inform: In an earlier lesson, we talked about the feelings under anger. When we get angry, there is hurt or fear or embarrassment or feeling unsafe underneath and often unmet needs. So, anger is a secondary emotion. The hurt, fear, shame or feeling unsafe come first when people do not feel valued, respected, or loved.

Ask:

- Do you think everyone wants to be loved, valued and respected? (If their response is no, please ask them why and explore it.)

Inform: When babies don't get love, they die. As we grow, if we do not receive love and respect, we often feel hurt, afraid or embarrassed and feel ashamed. When people are mean, parents are abusive, or peers are rejecting, we can carry inner scars for years. Sometimes people even feel that they are no good.

> Point to the + signs. "Even though some of you may sometimes feel that you are no good, each and every one of you cares about values and has positive qualities.

Inform: Usually, people are doing the best they can. Let's look at column one again. There are two main reasons why people get trapped in drugs:

One: They want to belong, to feel valued, respected and/or loved.

This can take the form of wanting the approval of friends. It can also take the form of experimenting with drugs in order to experience the self as loving or wise (the hoped-for spiritual high) or to feel wild and exciting and doing what the 'popular group' does.

Two: Others are trapped because they don't know how to deal with the pain they are already experiencing in life. They want to feel loved and valued, but don't. They are using drugs to try to feel better, to get rid of the pain."

Note to Facilitator: Clarify any examples if they have questions about this. For example, they may say that they take drugs for excitement. First, accept their answers, but then look deeper. What is under the excitement? Is it an attempt to appear exciting to your peers? Is that a quest for approval, a desire to feel valued by them? Or underneath the need for excitement is there the desire to feel important, to be seen as someone unique and valuable? Or, is it an effort to escape from the pain of feeling boring, non-unique and without value?

Inform: We all want to be loved, valued and respected and it can be painful when we don't feel that. You can learn to never be trapped by drugs again. Your life can get better again. Part of learning to be free of drugs is having the courage to understand yourself and your emotions."

Note to Facilitator: Speak to the ease or quickness of becoming addicted to the substance(s) the young people were using or abusing. There are many misconceptions, for example, people believed for years that cocaine was not addictive. The example for heroin is given below. There is no need to give this example if heroin is not being used in your area.

Heroin example: Say, "People like to think they are immortal — that perhaps addiction happens to others, but it will not happen to them. Heroin is especially dangerous — just a few doses can create physiological addiction and being powerless over drugs. Some people think that if they snort it or smoke it, they will not get addicted;

this is simply not true. Once physically addicted, the drug is in control. Heroin has no mercy. Addiction affects the chemicals in your brain and willpower disappears. The only way to maintain recovery, is to not use."

Activity

Say, "To really deeply think about this, to help you think about whether you want to take drugs again, I want each one of you to make a list of <u>all</u> the negative or destructive behaviors that you did while addicted. This may be very hard for some of you to do, but it will be worth it. Being honest with yourself and others is essential for recovery."

Hand out two sheets of paper to each person. (Copy the grid from the appendix or have them make their own grid.) Explain what they are to do in each column, giving the examples below.

Negative or destructive behavior.	Who was affected?	Loss for him/her/them.	Loss for me.	My feeling about it now.
Stealing money.	My mother.	No money for food for the holiday. . .	My parents were very unhappy with me. They were very angry.	Shame. Depressed.
Stealing money.	My friend, N.	Less money for school. Loss of trust in me.	Loss of my best friend.	I feel sad and stupid inside that I lost my best friend.
Sold drugs.	I got others hooked.	They started not going to school and failing in school, too.	I failed in school and got arrested for selling.	It was stupid to use drugs. I'm angry with me and the person who got me hooked.

Circle around while the participants are working individually, giving help if requested. Give respect to each and every one as you do this.

Ask them to finish the list before the next lesson. In addition, they are to do the following homework.

Homework: Hand out the Homework Sheet for Lesson 31, "My Personal Lessons." This can be found in the appendix. They are to use the list that they started today to summarize the negative or destructive behaviors. For each behavior on this sheet, they are to think about the anti-value they experienced that caused sorrow, then the lesson in it for them, and the values that will give them strength. Ask them to bring it to the next class.

Example:

Negative or destructive behavior.	The anti-value that causes sorrow.	My personal lesson.	The values that will give me strength.
Stealing	Dishonesty. Lack of respect for my family and friends.	I love my family and friends. I want loving and respectful relationships in my life. Drugs kill my love and our relationship.	Integrity Love Respect

Do the following relaxation/focusing exercise.

Dealing with Pain with Courage and Gentleness Exercise

"Let your body be relaxed and still. . . . Take in a deep breath, breathing in peace. . . . As you breathe out, let the tension go out the bottoms of your feet. . . . Breathe in peace . . . breathe out any tension through the bottoms of your feet. . . . As you breathe in peace, let the light of peace relax your whole body . . . letting your legs fill with light . . . letting your abdomen and chest fill with light. . . . With each breath, relax more, and let the light of peace gradually come into your back . . . and arms . . . your shoulders and neck . . . and your face. . . . You have had courage to share something that is painful. . . . Sometimes we hold the pain of what we have experienced in part of our body . . . sometimes it can be like an ache in our chest . . . sometimes in our throat. . . . Stay relaxed and still inside. . . detach from the pain . . . but see it. . . . Imagine the ache where you experience your pain to have a color. . . . Let the pain fill up with that color of light in that one small place. . . . Relax . . . be still . . . breathe in peace. . . . Let your tension go out the bottoms of your feet. . . . Breathe in the light of peace . . . let the tension go out the bottoms of your feet. . . . You are a courageous person. . . . You are a person who knows the importance of peace . . . and respect. . . . Let the light of peace accept the ache. . . . Let the light of peace surround your ache. . . . Let the light of peace soften the edges of the ache . . . let the light of peace become powerful inside. . . Let the light of peace soften the intensity of the color of the pain. . . . Accept the pain . . . it is painful, but as you begin to accept it, it will no longer be frightening. . . . Once you learn what it has to say, it will gradually begin to fade. . . . It has only come to help you see what is important in life. . . . Be gentle with the pain . . . and give it the love of your light of peace. . . . When the pain is not pushed away it becomes smaller. . . . What does it want you to know? . . . See the color of the pain . . . let it begin to lessen. . . . See the light of peace again. . . let it become powerful once more. . . . Breathe in peace. . . let the tension go out the bottoms of your feet. . . . Ask the pain to go away for now. . . . Tell it that you will allow it to come again and in time it will soften . . . and bloom into understanding . . . as you are learning to heal yourself. . . . You are learning how to be peace and give peace. . . . You are learning how to be respect and give respect. . . . You are learning how to be gentle with your pain so that you can help others heal their pain. . . . You are courageous. . . . Breathe in peace . . . let go of tension. . . . Breathe in peace . . . let any tension go out the bottoms of your feet. . . . Be in stillness. . . . Now bring your awareness back to this room."

End with a song or by standing in a circle and inviting each person to say one word about how they are feeling.

SUBSTANCE ABUSE LESSON 5 — Optional Drug Use and Abuse Lesson
My Personal Lessons and the Values that Will Give Me Strength

Begin with a song.

Ask the young people how they are. Listen. Ask them if they would like to share any of their thoughts or reactions to the last session together. Ask if anyone would like to share a discouraging thought that they changed into an empowering thought.

Activity

Step 1. Divide them into groups of three. Each person is to have eight minutes to share a couple experiences from their list of negative behaviors while addicted, and the related anti-values, personal lessons and values they feel are important as a result of those experiences. Remind them to listen with caring, respect and compassion. Ask them to tell their listeners what they appreciated about their listening afterwards.

Step 2. Invite them to write a poem or song about their experiences or feelings. Alternatively, they may wish to create a poem or song with a message to others or create a skit/sketch. Allow them to share if there is time.

Close with The Leaf of My Lesson Relaxation/Focusing Exercise.

SUBSTANCE ABUSE LESSON 6 — Optional Drug Use and Abuse Lesson
Relapse Prevention — Triggers

Begin with a song.

Ask the young people how they are. Listen. Ask them if they would like to share any of their thoughts or reactions to the last session together. Ask if anyone would like to share a discouraging thought that they changed into an empowering thought.

Lesson Content

Say, "You have created a caring, respectful, creative space (or name the atmosphere that they have created)." Ask the following question, allowing all those who wish to answer to do so.

- How do you feel you have grown? What have you learned during our lessons?

Say, "Great. Your growth will help you stay clean — stay off drugs. Sometimes that is not going to be easy as your body may sometimes want the drugs.

Inform: In the next few lessons, you will be asked to explore the triggers that might make you want to take drugs again. By triggers I mean little things that happen that make you want to take drugs. It can be a smell, seeing someone else take drugs, or feeling bad when someone is disrespectful to you. Drugs affect the brain. It is not that you are weak to feel attracted to drugs. Once the body has had them — and has been addicted — then the brain reacts differently than it did before, and the cravings can be powerful. So, in order be able to live a life of values — and to have serenity and good relationships in your life — you will need:

- ❖ Knowledge about your triggers
- ❖ The ability to recognize and deal with your emotions
- ❖ Help from true friends
- ❖ Empowering thoughts, and
- ❖ Determination to stay off drugs

Let's look at triggers. There are many different types. Today let's look at physical triggers that elicit memories. For example, at your home you may be surrounded by memories of times when you were using drugs: you may be in the same bedroom, use the same toilet, and walk past where you used to buy drugs. Perhaps you will smell the drug or see someone using. All of these can be triggers to have you remember the highs of _____ (name the drug to which they were addicted) and the feelings you experienced when you used. These memories can serve as triggers to tempt you to use again. These types of triggers stimulate desire — desire for something outside of us to make us happy — the drug."

Ask the following questions, writing down their responses on the board. Allow time for many to respond to the questions.

- What are your physical triggers that might create a desire for drugs?
- What things can you do that will help you deal with these triggers?

"Great. Thank you.

Inform: There is a saying used in Alcoholics Anonymous, HALT. H stands for hungry, A for anger, L for lonely and T for tired. Halt means stop. The meaning is to stop and be careful, take care of yourself when you are hungry, angry, lonely or tired. When we are experiencing these things, we are much more vulnerable to letting a trigger sidetrack us down the road of drugs."

Activity

Step 1. Divide the class in groups of five or six. Ask them to discuss the triggers that concern them, that they feel will still attract them. Each group is to select three main triggers and make a large poster, with the triggers and the things that they think will help them overcome the attraction. What values will help the most in these situations?

Step 2. Invite each group to present their poster to the entire group when finished. (Keep the posters for the next lesson.)

End with a relaxation/focusing exercise of their choice.

SUBSTANCE ABUSE LESSON 7 — Optional Drug Use and Abuse Lesson
Skits/Sketches about Physical Triggers

Begin with a song.

Ask the young people how they are. Listen. Ask them if they would like to share any of their thoughts or reactions to the last session together. Ask if anyone would like to share a discouraging thought that they changed into an empowering thought.

Activity

Step 1. Ask the groups that were together during the last lesson to get together again. Ask each group to create a skit/sketch about some of the triggers they discussed previously. Each is to demonstrate the disempowering thoughts that lead to responding to the trigger. Then replay the scene; this time demonstrate empowering thoughts the person can use and healthy options they can take.

Step 2. Invite the groups to share their dramas.

End with a relaxation/focusing exercise of their choice.

SUBSTANCE ABUSE LESSON 8— Optional Drug Use and Abuse Lesson
A True Friend Listens and Supports

Begin with a song.
Ask them how they are. Discuss the positives and problem-solve any difficulties.

Discuss/Share

Inform: Today, I will be asking you to be in groups of three. All of you will have a chance to talk about your triggers and practice being a True Friend, that is, being supportive of the Talker.

Ask:

- How would you like a friend to respond to you when you are talking about things that are troubling to you? (Give several people a chance to respond.)
- Great. Any more ideas?
- What don't you want someone to do when you are talking about things that trouble you?
- Anything else?

Lesson Content

There are many ways to be a True Friend when a friend is talking about something he or she is concerned about. I like that you thought of _____.
(Name some of the ideas they shared a minute ago.)

- ❖ **Actively listen**
- ❖ **Validate**
- ❖ **Reassure** the Talker by sharing your similar experiences — let the Talker know, that he or she is not an object of scorn — on the path of recovery we all have difficult experiences at times.
- ❖ **Encourage or give hope** to the Talker, saying you know it is difficult, but just relax and continue on, staying clean one day at a time. Perhaps let them know the qualities you see in him or her.
- ❖ Help the Talker **Explore Options**. Ask open-ended questions, such as:
  - What do you think might help you in this situation?
  - What thoughts make you feel weaker when you see/smell this trigger?
  - What thoughts make you feel more full of your values at this time?

❖ **Support the Talker.** A True Friend may support in a variety of ways. Many times, it will be by listening and encouraging as noted above. It may also be by giving company, going with the person to apply for a job, or eating a meal together.

Sometimes it may be supportive to be honest about the trouble they might be inviting by engaging in behaviors that are self-deceptive. If the True Friend feels it is important to be honest about their perceptions when the other person is doing something to make them more vulnerable to drugs, they may want to share their concerns with "I" messages. For example, "I am concerned as I notice you are going with your cousins that originally got you into drugs." Or, "I am concerned as I see you not applying for jobs when you have good qualifications. Would you like to share with me what's going on?" Or, "I am concerned as you say you are feeling happy, but you are complaining and nervous, always looking around as if you are afraid of something. What's going on?"

True Friend Activity

Ask participants to break into groups of three. One is to be the Talker, one the True Friend and one the Observer. Each person in the group is to have ten minutes of interaction with the True Friend. Then the Observer can share what was seen for a few minutes. Then rotate roles so that each person gets to play each part.

The talker is to share what physical triggers he or she is concerned about facing. Suggest that the Talker share:

❖ the triggers they are concerned about, and
❖ how they might feel in the situation.

The True Friend is to actively listen and validate as appropriate while the Talker is talking. **After** the Talker seems to be calm and have finished sharing his or her feelings, the True Friend may do one or more of the options discussed during the Lesson Content segment.

Discuss/Share

Ask:

- What was your experience talking with a "true friend"?
- What helped, what did not help?
- Is there anything else a true friend could do that would help?
- Are there other kinds of support you think you would like to give as a "true friend" or that you would like to receive?

- What do others think? Would that be okay? Why or why not?
- What guidelines would you suggest for true friends?

Closing

Do a relaxation/focusing exercise of their choice.

Ask them to sit or stand in a circle and share one word that reflects how they feel.

SUBSTANCE ABUSE LESSON 9 — Optional Drug Use and Abuse Lesson
Relapse Prevention — Reasons, Lies, Excuses, and Temptation

Begin with a song.

Ask them how they are. Discuss the positives and problem-solve any difficulties.

Discuss/Share

There is a saying, "Until you run out of reasons, lies and excuses to yourself, you will use again." (Anonymous)

Ask:

- What are lies we can tell ourselves regarding drinking and drugs? (For example: Just one little drink/snort/line won't hurt.)
- What other lies do you think people might tell themselves?
- What does the wise part of yourself understand about the lies you might attempt to tell yourself?

Share: An example of an excuse is "I didn't want to be the only one at the party not having a drink in my hand." The person might continue, "How did I know drinking would make me want to use again?" Drinking or using a new drug can easily create a desire for your old favorite drug — and once a substance is in your system your brain works differently. Your coping skills usually disappear."

Ask:

- What excuses might you create to use again?
- What does the wise part of yourself understand now about those excuses?

Share: Sometimes people in recovery create reasons in their mind about using again — so that they feel justified. They will say things like, "My parents or my girlfriend caused this . . ."

Ask:

- What is wrong with this sentence?

Share: No one can **cause** you to take drugs. You may not like what they did, you may not like a situation, but you are the only one responsible for you — and your own emotions and actions. No one can cause you to relapse. And, the good news is, you cannot cause anyone else to relapse.

Ask:

- Do you have any questions about this? (Discuss as needed.)
- What reasons have you seen people create to use drugs again?
- What reasons might you be tempted to create?
- What does the wise part of yourself understand now about those reasons?

Activity

Step 1. Ask the participants to write five of their best reasons, lies or excuses, and have their wise self to respond.

Step 2. When they are finished writing, invite them to break into groups of three to share.

Step 3. *Inform:* Sometimes when people are tempted to try drugs again, they imagine a wonderful scene in their mind about how great they will feel and what terrific things will happen."

Ask:

- Do any of you ever do that?
- What do you imagine?
- Is that reality?

Step 4. When you are tempted to try drugs again and imagine wonderful scenes and feelings, one thing you can do is:

- Counter that illusion **immediately** with images in your mind of the awful things that happened to you while you were addicted to drugs. Think of those scenes in a detached way for just a few seconds to build your determination not to take that one hit or one drink.
- Then think one of your favorite empowering thoughts in relation to staying clean.
- Then remember several encouraging, positive scenes that are important for you.

Step 5. Let's experiment for a few minutes now. Play some relaxation music and speak the following commentary slowly.

Imagining Going Beyond Temptation Commentary

"Please relax and imagine in your mind a scene in which you are tempted to take drugs. . . . Perhaps it is a physical trigger, such as smelling the drug or seeing someone else high . . . or perhaps it is a certain person that offers you the drug. . . . What does your mind imagine? Stop those images of getting high. . . . Let the mind freeze. . . . Bring in peace . . . detach. Now play a few quick scenes . . . of awful things that happened when you were addicted . . . or as a result of being addicted. . . . See those imagines in a detached way. . . . Now think of why you are committed to staying clean. . . . Say to yourself one of your favorite empowering thoughts . . . let your determination build. . . . Say your empowering thought to yourself again . . . let your determination build. . . . Now think of three especially positive moments when you were clean . . . perhaps talking to a friend . . . enjoying the musical evenings or dramas . . . or doing your compassion experiment. . . . Think of three scenes that were especially fulfilling for you. . . . As you think of the first scene go over the details of that in your mind . . . what things looked like . . . the sounds of the music or words that were spoken . . . your feelings. . . . Allow yourself to enjoy that scene. . . . What value were you experiencing at that time? . . . Bring the experience of that value into your mind. . . . Now bring a second positive scene that was meaningful for you in your mind . . . and experience that. . . . (Pause for one and a half minutes.) What value were you experiencing or demonstrating at that time? . . . Now bring a third positive scene into your mind and remember that fully. . . . (Pause for one and a half minutes.) Now think of what you are building in your life . . . how you will be able to help others be free. . . . What is your favorite value? . . . Bring the experience of that value into your mind and let the feeling of that value fill every cell of your body. . . . (Pause for 30 seconds.) Breathe in that value . . . be still within. . . . Now gradually bring your attention back to this room."

Step 6. Ask:

- Would anyone like to share their experience?
- Were you able to reduce or eliminate the feeling of being tempted?

Inform: Another option is to do the same thing in your mind, but not to imagine the awful things that happened while you were addicted. However, usually imagining the awful things will help you counter the illusion of the wonderful things you want to believe that drugs bring. The commentary we did was long and slow. Ideally, you want to get to a point where you feel tempted, and can go immediately into a positive experience of your values . . . and remember several wonderful things that were value highs.

You might try thinking of your values, how you are helping others, or think of positive, fulfilling scenes with people that are or have been important in your life. It is important to do this for several minutes in order to build your emotional energy and determination. Waiting several minutes also helps the brain not act on the automatic drug wiring in the brain. If you wait for 15 minutes, you are rewiring your brain to a non-drug response.

Homework: Ask them to do this commentary every day until the next lesson. Their objective is to shorten the time of feeling tempted and increase the intensity of their values experience.

SUBSTANCE ABUSE LESSON 10— Optional Drug Use and Abuse Lesson
Relapse Prevention — My Friends Who Use

Begin with a song.

Hold circle time. Ask how writing in their journals is going. Would anyone like to share a discouraging thought that they changed into an empowering thought?

Discuss

Present the situation for discussion: "Sometimes you will be surrounded by or encounter your drinking or drug-addicted friends. They keep inviting you to just join them 'once.'"

Ask:

- How would you feel in such a situation?
- What would be the most tempting situation for you?
- What would be another difficult situation for you?
- At what times might it be a good idea to explain to your friends your new understanding about drugs and how you are working without drugs to have a happier life?
- When would it not be a good idea to explain? (For example, when they are already high.)
- Would it have helped you to have a friend explain?
- What other things could you do to manage this situation?
- What value(s) could you use in this situation to help you manage this situation?
- How would you feel when you use the value?

Activity

Ask the participants to develop skits/sketches. As before, they may choose their situation and act out both negative and positive possibilities for the situation. They may put extra people in their dramas if they wish.

Each group is to present their role-play/skit to the entire group. The participants may identify the values used.

End with a relaxation/focusing exercise of their choice.

SUBSTANCE ABUSE LESSON 11 — Optional Drug Use and Abuse Lesson
Relapse Prevention — Going Beyond Excuses and Temptation

Begin with a song.

Ask them how they are. Discuss the positives and problem-solve any difficulties.

Discuss/Share

Say, "It can be difficult to deal with friends that are still using drugs."

Ask:

- What did you identify with in the dramas?
- What skills are you feeling more comfortable with?
- What skills do you think you need to develop further?
- When is it best to avoid these situations?
- Is it best to avoid them as much as you can?
- Does part of you not want to avoid these situations?
- What can you think to yourself to help you stay clean?

Activity

Step 1. Ask the participants to divide into groups of four. Everyone is to have the opportunity to role-play themselves in a situation about which they are concerned. They may ask the other people in the small group to role-play their friends. One person should be the observer. Allow each person 5 minutes. Let the person playing himself or herself have the option of stopping the role-play, saying "Erase that. Replay," so that he or she can practice doing it the way they wish.

Step 2. Gather the entire group together and ask them to share their experiences. What was easier this time?

End with a relaxation/focusing exercise of their choice.

HAPPINESS LESSON 12 — Optional Drug Use and Abuse Lesson
Relapse Prevention — Descending Spirals

Begin with a song.

Ask them how they are. Discuss the positives and problem-solve any difficulties.

Discuss/Share

Share what you are comfortable with, such as: I hope you will keep what you have learned from these lessons active in your life, and become a True Friend to people in need. Sharing with others is always important — for when our hearts are big, we are happy.

You were asked to review your journal of discouraging thoughts and empowering thoughts this last week. Today the activity is to make yourself a poster of a spiral. You will be making two posters, one of a descending spiral and another of an ascending spiral.

These posters are items for your Kit. The purpose of the Kit is to help you remember your special qualities, the special friends you have, and help you enjoy living the values. You may want to call it your Living My Values Kit, Self-Respect Kit, Survival Kit — whatever you would like. It is sometimes helpful to have a few special things that help you at times when you might feel a little down, or discouraged or vulnerable. Hopefully, it will help you stay empowered — and help you not fall into the powerlessness and misery of being under the influence of drugs again. Some of the things you have made already might be items that you would want in your Kit.

Today, you are asked to make a descending spiral. On this poster, you can put your most discouraging thoughts, feelings and actions. As you know, thoughts lead to feelings, and feelings can lead to actions. You are being asked to put down your discouraging thoughts and the most miserable of your feelings and actions while you were addicted to drugs — as a reminder of what happened then. Illustrate it to remind you of past negative events. Sometimes it is difficult to stay off drugs. At those moments of desire, it helps some people to remember the most awful experiences on drugs.

During the next lesson, you will be asked to make a poster of an ascending spiral. On that, you are to put the empowering thoughts that are most important to you, the ones you really believe in, those that help you experience your natural values and qualities. You are being given separate pieces of poster paper, as most people benefit by only looking at the positive — and knowing that they are creating a life of happiness and freedom. You may want to have that one visible in your room. However, the negative poster will be there if you need it."

Ask:

* Any thoughts or questions?

Activity

Supply art supplies and poster paper. They may wish to draw out their spiral on a regular piece of paper before making it on the poster paper.

Allow them to briefly show their poster, along with one sentence: "I want to stay off drugs because _____."

End with a relaxation/focusing exercise of their choice.

SUBSTANCE ABUSE LESSON 13 — Optional Drug Use and Abuse Lesson
Relapse Prevention — Ascending Spirals

Begin with a song.

Ask them how they are. Discuss the positives and problem-solve any difficulties.

Activity

Supply art supplies and poster paper. They may wish to draw their ascending spiral on a regular piece of paper before making it on the poster paper. Ask them to include their values — as the seeds of their empowering thoughts — as well as the positive feelings and actions.

Allow them to briefly share their posters, along with one of their most empowering thoughts.

End with a relaxation/focusing exercise of their choice.

RESPONSIBIITY

UNIT EIGHT: RESPONSIBILITY

Responsibility Lessons

Responsibility is a value important for society, and for the wellbeing, productivity and happiness of the individual. It allows young people to build good habits and relationships, and grow toward their potential. In this values unit, responsibility is looked at from different angles, from the serious to the ridiculous, in an attempt to engage students in seeing the relevance and benefit of this value for the self, others and the world — and how they can make a positive difference.

Please feel free to add to the list of Reflections Points your favorite sayings from different cultures, legends or admired individuals.

The values planning team may wish to choose one subject area, daily, to play a song. Select songs you feel the students will relate to; ones that are appropriate for their age. You may want the students to bring in songs that evoke the desire to fulfill a responsibility, such as "Circle of Life" by Elton John. Perhaps play the song, "Conviction of the Heart," by Kenny Loggins. Some students enjoy learning traditional songs.

Occasionally include a Relaxation/Focusing Exercise during values time.

Responsibility Reflection Points

- ♦ Responsibility is doing your share.
- ♦ Responsibility is accepting what is required and carrying out the task to the best of your ability.
- ♦ A responsible person fulfills the assigned duty by staying true to the aim. Duties are carried out with integrity and a sense of purpose.
- ♦ If we want peace, we have the responsibility to be peaceful.
- ♦ If we want a clean world, we have the responsibility to care for nature.
- ♦ When one is responsible, there is the contentment of having made a contribution.

- As a responsible person, I have something worthwhile to offer — and so do others.
- A responsible person knows how to be fair, seeing that each gets a share.
- With rights there are responsibilities.
- Responsibility is not only something that obliges us, but is also something that allows us to achieve what we wish.
- Each person can perceive her or his own world and look for the balance of rights and responsibilities.
- "The test of our progress is not whether we add to the abundance of those who have much; it is whether we provide enough for those who have too little." — *Franklin D. Roosevelt*
- Global responsibility requires respect for all human beings.
- Responsibility is using our resources to generate positive change.

RESPONSIBILITY LESSON 1
Trust Walk

Play a song as the students enter. Introduce the unit on the value of responsibility by asking the students what responsibility means. Accept all responses.

Activity

Say, "Today, we will play with responsibility by having a trust walk." To do a trust walk, half the class wears blindfolds. One partner is responsible for carefully leading his or her blindfolded partner around, guiding physically as well as offering verbal information to manage uneven areas and to help the partner feel safe and comfortable. Do this for 10 minutes, then reverse roles.   — *Contributed by Pilar Quera Colomina*

Discuss/Share

Afterwards, give a few minutes for each pair to share their feelings with each other as the one trusting and the one responsible during the trust walk.

Ask the entire group:
- How did you feel when you felt your partner was responsible?
- How would you have felt if your partner were not responsible?
- Is there anything you would like everyone in the world to be responsible for? What might that be?

Ask each person to come up with a definition of responsibility and write it at the top of a page as the first entry of each one's Personal Responsibility Journal.

Group Story Game: Say, "Let's do the group story game. Each person can say one, two or three sentences — no more — and then the next person continues the story. In this group story, I want you to make up something about a person or an entire community of people who are not responsible." Ask one of the students to start. Allow them to continue to go around until everyone who wishes to do so has contributed to the story.

Then say, "The character (or the community) is now sleeping."

Ask:

- What would you like to tell the character/people of the community? Please softly tell them what you think they need to know about responsibility.
- What other advice would you like to share so they get to know what they need to know?

"Well done! Now let's know that they heard you all . . . and let's continue with the story! (One in which the people heard the message and are responsive to it, that is, are responsible.) Lead the applause when they are done.

Close with a song or a relaxation/focusing exercise of their choice.

RESPONSIBILITY LESSON 2
Mind Mapping Responsibility and Irresponsibility

Begin with a song.
Discuss the Reflection Points.

- Responsibility is doing your share.
- Responsibility is accepting what is required and carrying out the task to the best of your ability.
- As a responsible person, I have something worthwhile to offer — so do others.

Mind Mapping Activity

"Today, let's explore the amazing differences between responsibility and irresponsibility through mind mapping."

Mind Map: Begin by drawing a large circle on the white board, putting Responsibility on the right side and Irresponsibility on the left side. Start with a branch for Self on the Responsibility side of the circle, asking them what happens when there is Responsibility in the Self and writing in brief their responses. Then ask them what happens when there is a lack of responsibility in the Self. The students are to supply all the answers. Also do separate branches for Families, Friends, Education, Business, Society and International Relationships on both responsibility and irresponsibility. Perhaps they would like to add caring for the environment.

Creative Activity

Divide the students into groups of six to eight. Ask each group to create a song or poem about responsibility or responsibility versus irresponsibility. It could be a rap song. Allow them to perform their creation for the group.

RESPONSIBILITY LESSON 3
I Believe In . . .

Begin with a song.

Discuss/Share

Ask:

- What do you believe in?
- Do you believe in peace?
- Do you believe in caring for the environment?
- Using the value of responsibility, what does it mean if we really believe in these things?
- What kinds of actions does someone do who cares for the environment? (Make a list on the board as they call out answers.)

Take another item that several young adults say they believe in and ask:

- If you believe in this, what type of behavior supports that belief? What would you do?
- Does responsibility mean that your beliefs and actions are consistent?
- What else does it mean?

Write the following Reflection Points on the board. Ask what they think about the points. "Are they true?" Discuss them in light of the previous questions.

- ◆ Responsibility means that you try your best to do what you believe in.
- ◆ If we want peace, we have the responsibility to be peaceful.
- ◆ If we want a clean world, we have the responsibility to care for nature.
- ◆ With rights there are responsibilities.

♦ As a responsible person, I have something worthwhile to offer — and so do others.

Share concept: If we believe in certain principles or values, then what we do or how we act should support our beliefs and values. For instance, if someone believes in caring for the environment, but then pollutes a stream and wastes water, then that person is not walking their talk.

Activity

Step 1. Play some relaxing music and instruct the young adults to write their responses as you slowly ask the following questions. Allow them sufficient time to reflect and write.

- What else do you believe in?
- Do you believe in loyalty?
- Do you believe in being a good friend?
- Do you believe in being a good student?
- Do you believe in loving families?
- What rights and contributing actions (responsibilities) go with each "I believe . . ." statement you have made?

Step 2. Invite students to form small groups and share some of the things they believe in.

Step 3. Invite each individual to choose three of their most important "I believe in . . ." statements. Ask them to follow each sentence starting with "I believe in . . .", with a sentence starting with, "I want the right to . . .", and then, "My responsibilities are . . ."

Step 4. Ask students to stand in a circle to share one of their "I believe in . . ." statements.

Close with a relaxation/focusing exercise.

Homework: Ask the young adults if they would like to select one or more actions in support of their "I believe in . . ." statements to do daily while doing this values unit on responsibility. Ask them to note those actions in their Personal Responsibility Journal, any consequences of doing that action, and how they felt.

RESPONSIBILITY LESSON 4
People Who Made a Difference

Educator Preparation: Select a short story, essay or article about a person who has made a positive difference for your country, heritage, or the region through personal commitment and responsibility. Or, ask a few students to bring in their favorite reading about this topic.

Begin with a song.

Write the following Reflection Points on the board:

♦ Responsibility is not only something that obliges us, but is also something that allows us to achieve what we wish.

♦ Responsibility is using our resources to generate positive change.

Activity

Step 1. Provide paper and colored pencils or crayons and ask the young adults to artistically write and decorate one of their "I believe in . . ." statements while several students and/or the teacher reads orally from their favorite passages about a person who has made a positive difference through their personal commitment.

Step 2. Discuss any reactions to the readings. Ask about the second Reflection Point on the board in relation to a person featured in the readings: "What were this person's resources?" Perhaps that person's only resources were his or her personal energy of commitment, the ability to speak persuasively, or . . .?

Step 3. Put all the decorated statements on the bulletin board or wall, slightly overlapping them.

Close with a relaxation/focusing exercise.

RESPONSIBILITY LESSON 5

Responsibilities in the Home

Begin with a song.

Discuss/Share

Please write the Reflection Points on the board.

♦ Responsibility is doing your share.

♦ Responsibility is accepting what is required and carrying out the task to the best of your ability.

♦ When one is responsible, there is the contentment of having made a contribution.

♦ With rights there are responsibilities.

Please use the following questions to generate a discussion. Please actively listen and validate as appropriate.

- How did you learn about responsibility as a child?
- Do you consider yourself responsible now?
- Sometimes people are responsible in some areas, and not others. In what areas are you responsible?
- How would you teach your children responsibility?
- What responsibilities do parents have?
- Some parents do not teach their children to be responsible. For example, they do not give them chores to do and do not allow them to take the consequences for their actions. Such children often end up feeling "entitled", that is, that the world should serve them and they shouldn't have to work hard or do their share. One of the consequences of being raised in this way is they are not grateful for what they have or what others do for them. Another is that they do not develop many of the living skills needed for life. Have you ever met someone who feels "entitled"? What are the pros and cons of being raised in such a way?
- If you choose to be a parent, what kind of parent will you be when you are an adult? What responsibilities will be important to you?
- What advantages will your children have if you teach them to be responsible?
- What happens when parents do not fulfill their responsibilities?
- How do you feel when other people do not do what they say they will do?
- What responsibilities do sons or daughters have?
- What happens when children do not fulfill their responsibilities?
- What are your responsibilities at home?
- What feelings do you have sometimes that interfere with you wanting to be responsible?
- How do you show your parents you are responsible?
- What contributions do you make to your family?
- What contributions do you feel proud of?

Reflective Activity

- Sometimes people don't feel like being responsible. Perhaps they are tired, they are overwhelmed with too much to do, or angry at someone and resent doing something for him or her, or they are out of balance and aren't getting enough fun time or time to themselves. When we are happy and in balance and relationships are good, it is easy and fun to be responsible. Please reflect and then write down ways to help you take care of yourself and stay in balance. (Give them several minutes.)

- If there is something that you want to be responsible about, what kinds of statements do you say to yourself or could you say to yourself that help you do the action you need to do to be responsible? Please write those down. (Give them two or three minutes.)

- Please reflect for a moment about your home life. Is there a responsibility you would like to take up? It may be something simple, such as playing or spending time with a younger sibling every day, or it may be a commitment to help with one or two meals a week, or a commitment to be more green at home. . . . Think about what your family needs . . . and imagine what that would look like and feel like . . . and what will change as a result. (Give them two minutes to reflect.)

Activity

Step 1. Divide the class into small groups of three or four. Ask them to share some of their thoughts during the reflective exercise, that is, how to care for themselves and stay in balance, what empowering thoughts help them be responsible and an activity they would like to be responsible for.

Step 2. Invite them to individually write an appreciative poem or note to someone in their life that has helped them be responsible.

Close with the Flowers of Respect Relaxation Exercise.

RESPONSIBILITY LESSON 6

A Class Project, Being Responsible

Note to Educator: Your class may already be involved with an ongoing Caring for the Earth and Her Oceans project. If so, that's wonderful. Please continue and simply tie in bits of information from the lessons in the unit that are relevant and appropriate as you continue with the environmental project, and positively affirm their efforts to take responsibility. If you are not engaged in an ongoing project, you may wish to continue with this lesson.

Begin with a song.

Discuss/Share

Ask:

- One definition of responsibility is doing our share. What would happen if everyone in the world decided to work together to end the climate change crisis? Do you think we would be able to do it?

Possible comment: If there are naysayers, tell them that it is possible. For example: "It is has been said that if everyone were to adopt a vegetarian diet, we would be able to end the climate change crisis within two years. It is possible to do, it is just about enough people developing the will to do it, and then having the power to be responsible and carry out the necessary action."

Ask:

- Shall we take up a class project? What would you like to do?

Note to Educator: If you and the students are considering an environmental project, you may wish to look at the Simplicity and Caring for the Earth and Her Oceans Lesson 13 for some ideas. If they are already doing an environmental project, perhaps look at it in terms of taking up a short-term project that requires all being responsible.

Or, in accordance with your situation, you may wish to invite them to organize a meal together or plan and carry through on a flower or vegetable garden. Or, each student could take up a responsibility at school. Perhaps some of them could be conflict resolution mediators or some would like to tutor. Ask the students about tasks they would like to be responsible for. Be open to talking about their experiences and helping them generate solutions to any problems.

Activity

Once the students have decided what they would like to do, invite them to list materials needed and the tasks that need to be done. Suggest that teams accept responsibility for different tasks.

Close with a relaxation/focusing exercise.

RESPONSIBILITY LESSON 7

Responsibility to the Self

Begin with a song.

Discuss/Share

Write the following Reflection Point on the board:

♦ Each person can perceive her or his own world and look for the balance of rights and responsibilities.

Discuss Homework Results: Ask students about their homework of doing one or more responsible actions each day.

Ask:

- How do you feel when you fulfill your responsibilities?
- What have you enjoyed?
- Has anything been difficult?
- How do you feel and what are the consequences when you do not fulfill your responsibilities?
- How are you encouraging yourself?
- What responsibilities do we have to ourselves?
- How do we balance caring for others and caring for the self?
- Is part of taking care of the self being responsible?
- In the midst of being responsible to others, what things can you do to take care of you?

Activity

Step 1. In small groups, discuss the times when it is difficult to be responsible, and the emotion underneath.

Step 2. Invite them to generate things they can think or do to help them feel better in a healthy way.

Step 3. Ask them to present their findings in a skit or a song to the entire group.

Close with a relaxation/focusing exercise.

RESPONSIBILITY LESSON 8
Responsibility as a Student

Begin with a song.

Discuss

- What responsibilities do you have as students?
- What responsibilities do teachers have?
- Imagine a school where none of the teachers carried out any of their responsibilities. What would happen?

- How do you feel when you fulfill your responsibilities as a student?
- How do you feel, and what are the consequences when you do not fulfill your responsibilities?
- What are your long-term goals?
- What are your short-term goals?
- Is there a hardest time of the year for you to want to fulfill your student responsibilities? When?
- What thoughts help you stay focused and responsible?
- What helps you be freer from stress?

Activity Options

After doing one of the following options, continue with their responsibility project.

Option One:

Step 1. Ask students to choose one subject in which they would like to improve. On a scale of 1 to 10, 10 being the highest mark — how do they rate themselves?

Step 2. Instruct the students to think about something they can do to improve in that subject to get nearer their goal. The students can form pairs to talk this over. Their new behaviors should be specific, practical, and easily observable. In this way, students can see when they are making progress toward their goal.

Step 3. Ask the students to write down three concrete things they can do.

Step 4. In three days, ask students in each pair to review their progress, and encourage each other to continue working toward their goal.

Option Two:

Step 1. Invite students to form small groups of four to five and discuss methods to keep up their motivation during stressful times at school. They may wish to include a variety of methods, such as empowering thoughts, one- or two-minute exercise breaks during class such as stretching, brain gym or jumping, or short relaxation/focusing exercises. Or, they may wish to suggest?

Step 2. Ask each group to prepare something to share with the entire class.

Step 3. Ask the class if they would like to try some of these options as a group. For example, would they like to do exercise for one minute after 20 minutes of sitting? Which of the empowering thoughts would they like as encouraging slogans on the wall?

Close with a relaxation/focusing exercise.

RESPONSIBILITY LESSON 9

Dealing with Guilt Constructively

Begin with a song.

Discuss/Share

Inform: Some people are very sensitive and others are not sensitive at all, they appear hardened or mean.

Ask:

- Which one would you rather be and why?
- Which one do you think feels more guilt?
- What are the advantages of being sensitive to yourself and others?
- What are the disadvantages of being sensitive to yourself and others?
- What are the advantages of being not sensitive to yourself and others?
- What are the disadvantages of being hardened or mean?
- Which would you rather have as your best friend, a sensitive person or a hardened mean person?
- So, is it good to feel guilt sometimes?
- Do all of you sometimes feel guilty about something you did or did not do? (If the answer is yes, say: "Congratulations. That means you are all good people!)

Inform: Guilt is very important when you do something wrong, for five seconds ... or until you realize what you would rather have done instead.

Feeling sad, ashamed or guilty about a mistake you have made is natural. It simply means you regret what happened and would have liked to have done something different. Sometimes we also feel bad when we are irresponsible, that is, about not doing something we know in our heart was important to do. It might have been something like not visiting a relative when they were ill or not sticking up for a friend or an animal when they were bullied.

Ask the following question and discuss, actively listening and validating as appropriate.

- How do you feel when you do not do something you thought you should do?
- What kinds of things do you feel a little bad about if you don't do?
- What kinds of things do you feel very bad about?

Inform: We all make mistakes sometimes. We are all human. But feeling guilty or sad for a long time takes away our energy.

337

A constructive thing to do instead is:

1. Lovingly accept yourself and your emotions.
2. Think about what you wish you would have done.
3. Identify the value or quality you need for that.
4. Imagine that quality and feel it in your mind.
5. Talk kindly to yourself. Know that the next time that circumstance occurs, you will have the power to do what you want to do.

Activity

Write the five steps on the board. Ask the students to write a personal essay in their Personal Responsibility Journal, applying those five steps to a situation they would like to change.

After doing the above, continue with their responsibility project.

Close with a relaxation/focusing exercise.

RESPONSIBILITY LESSON 10

Responsibility Builds Trust

Begin with a song.

Discuss

- How do you feel when people do not do what they say they will do, that is, act irresponsibly?
- How do you feel when your friend gossips about you or lets you down?
- How do you feel when your friend is trustworthy?
- How does responsibility build trust?
- What can we say to friends when they are irresponsible or let us down?

Activity

Step 1. Ask the students to form groups of five. Each student in the group is to generate two situations in which he or she feels someone has let him or her down or has been irresponsible in some way.

Step 2. They are to role play those situations, coming up with two solutions for each problem. Suggest they begin communicating with an "I" message, that is, "I feel _____ when _____." Another definition for responsibility is the ability to respond. Ask them to express their feelings, explain and encourage rather than blasting with anger the other person playing the irresponsible role. Use communication skills learned during the Peace, Respect and Happiness Values Units.

Step 3. After each role play, discuss the consequences of their actions, that is, the consequences of doing nothing or of communicating well.

Step 4. Ask if there are real problems they are currently confronting and invite them to create Situation Cards and discuss and role play them as part of generating positive, appropriate solutions.

Close with a relaxation/focusing exercise.

RESPONSIBILITY LESSON 11
Global Responsibility

Begin with a song.

Discuss the following Reflection Points:

♦ Global responsibility requires respect toward all human beings.

♦ A responsible person knows how to be fair, seeing that each gets a share.

♦ Responsibility is using our resources to generate a positive change.

♦ A responsible person fulfills the assigned duty by staying true to the aim. Duties are carried out with integrity and a sense of purpose.

Ask, actively listening and affirming as appropriate:

• If you could tell every person in the world that he or she had to be responsible, in what ways would you want people to be responsible?

• Would those changes bring about the changes you think would benefit the world?

• What is our global responsibility?

• What changes do you think would benefit our community/school?

• What would you like everyone to be responsible for?

• What would you want them to do?

• What would you want them not to do?

• As a person, what responsibilities do you have to others? To society?

• What is our societal responsibility?

• What is our moral responsibility?

Activity

Ask students to form small groups and write responsibility guidelines for each person in the world — the Global Citizen.

If there is additional time, continue with the class responsibility project or do the next lesson.

Close with a relaxation/focusing exercise.

RESPONSIBILITY LESSON 12
Rights of the Global Citizen

Begin with a song.

Activity

Step 1. Form the same small groups as in the previous lesson. Each group is to discuss what they feel the rights of a global citizen should be — that is, the rights of every person in the world. Write these Rights of a Global Citizen on a poster.

Step 2. Next, each small group is to examine their Responsibility Guidelines for the Global Citizen and compare it with their list of Rights. Do these support each other? Do any of the responsibilities need to be changed so that each person could have the rights? Make a poster of these responsibility guidelines.

Step 3. Invite each group to share their poster. They may wish to give a voice to the rights, as a group or as members of different cultural groups.

Step 4. Put up their posters.

Close with a relaxation/focusing exercise.

RESPONSIBILITY LESSON 13
Working for a Better World

Ask the students to share their reactions to the posters.

Note to Educator: Some young adults may be cynical, feeling it would never be possible to achieve on our planet all the rights and responsibilities they recommended on their posters. Cynicism is the result of disappointment at not having the world the way we know it can be. Acknowledge their feelings and concerns. Then point out that human beings make a difference. Humans created the type of world we have now, and the youth of today will create the world of tomorrow. They are taking an important step in that process by understanding what type of world they want and the rights and responsibilities it entails.

Begin with a song.

Activity

Look for examples in the real world of people achieving those rights, and of others behaving responsibly. Many people are working for a better world. For example, free and fair elections are now taking place in many more countries, apartheid has ended, strong efforts to work for protecting and caring for our planet are happening in some countries of the world, and literacy is increasing in many countries. What are effective people, programs or policies that are creating positive change? Perhaps look at the twelve examples of best practices from the United Nations Global Conference on Habitat for Humanity or ways in which the poorest of the poor are helped through United Nations Development Programs and non-governmental organizations (NGOs). Are there NGOs in your area working to improve education, health or human rights of people?

Discuss the Reflection Point:

♦ A responsible person fulfills the assigned duty by staying true to the aim. Duties are carried out with integrity and a sense of purpose.

Plan: Ask the class to think of their posters, and select one small achievable project for which they could take responsibility. It may be a project that each one could do individually, such as treating each person they meet with dignity. Or, it could be a project where they provide a service to children in the neighborhood, or . . . ? Ask the students about tasks they would like to be responsible for. Be open to talking about their experiences and helping them generate solutions to any problems.

Close with a relaxation/focusing exercise.

RESPONSIBILITY LESSON 14

Responsibility Is Integrity — and Sustainable Development Goals

Begin with a song.

Introduce the topic: "It seems that much of what has gone amiss in history is people having selfish aims based on greed or an arrogant desire for power. We discussed some examples of this when we examined the value of honesty. Let's build upon the idea."

Reflect on the points:

♦ There is enough for man's need, but not enough for man's greed.

♦ A responsible person fulfills the assigned duty by staying true to the aim. Duties are carried out with integrity and a sense of purpose.

Ask:

- Can you think of any more examples?
- If you were in charge of our country's money, what would be your aim?
- What do you think the responsibility of a country leader should be, serving the people of the country and the planet or enriching his own pocket?
- If someone urges you to cheat on your job by taking some money, and that person tells you it's only a little bit of money, what would be your responsibility?
- Is cheating being true to your values?

Activity

Step 1. Invite the students to form the same groups they were with during the previous SDGs lessons. Ask them to explore the effect of responsibility on the SDGs. If everyone in the world were able to be responsible with integrity how would the SDGs be affected? Do any more SDGs need to be added?

Step 3. Ask them to write specific ways holding the value of responsibility would affect the SDGs on which their group is focused and write those on white Leaves.

Step 4. Invite them to share their Responsibility Leaves with the entire group.

Step 5. Invite the groups to attach their white Responsibility Leaves to the class artistic presentation of the SDGs.

Step 6. Look at your artistic creation of the SDGs and how many leaves are attached to the SDGs. How many SDGs are affected if these eight values were lived?

Step 7. Congratulate the students on their efforts.

Close with a relaxation/focusing exercise.

RESPONSIBILITY LESSON 15
An Image or Skit

Begin with a song.

Activity

Ask the students to create an image of what they believe in. Below the image, each one is to write four new ways they have become responsible.

Alternative Activity: Divide the students into groups of 8 to 10 and ask them to create a skit demonstrating irresponsibility and/or responsibility. It can be a comedy or a drama. Perhaps they can use as props some of the slogans or posters created during this values unit.

Responsibility Activities in Subject Areas

Language/Literature

Add to the Reflection Points using wisdom from your own culture, quotes, and your own slogans.

Study folk tales about responsibility. You may have favorites or know of others of different cultures.

Read stories about people who have made sacrifices in order to be morally or personally responsible and thereby saved the lives of many.

History/Social Studies

Explore responsibility through the regular curriculum, for example, learning about the different governing roles, public service, the functioning of associations, or the content of the Convention on the Rights of the Child.

— Contributed by Pilar Quera Colomina and Sabine Levy

Government Architects

Ask students to design two types of government. In both governments, there are Prime Ministers, and the citizens are peaceful and responsible. 1) Design one government where ministers operate on the laws of accumulating power. 2) Design another government where there is a balance of law and love and absolute respect for the human rights of all.

Discuss:

- How do the two societies differ?
- What are the benefits of each society, both to the citizens and to the world at large?
- Which government is more responsible in terms of caring for its citizens?
- What are the responsibilities of the citizens in a better world for all?

Science

Read a current work or United Nations report or agreement on ecological responsibility.

Preventable Mishaps

There have been many scientific mishaps because a number of individuals did not take responsibility and stay true to the aim. Think of industrial accidents that have taken place or airplane accidents in which people died because of technical faults. Another example: Because some lab technicians did not take proper care with tests, some people have thought they had a disease when they did not; others have thought they were healthy when they needed immediate treatment.

Consider the following additional Reflection Point and discuss in context of the above:

- ◆ A responsible person perseveres, not stubbornly with a blind focus, but with the motivation of fulfilling the assigned duty by staying true to the aim. When the role is played accurately, there is efficiency and effectiveness which result in satisfaction and contentment at having made a significant contribution.
- Can you think of other scientific mishaps because of one person's lack of responsibility?

Speaking Out

- What type of scientist would you like to be?
- What would help you do that?
- What would you like to say to the scientists of the world?

Economics

A Responsible Business

Consider the following Reflection Point:

- ◆ A responsible person fulfills the assigned duty by staying true to the aim. Duties are carried out with integrity and a sense of purpose.

Ask:

- If you were in charge of a business or corporation, what would your aims be?
- What is our global responsibility?
- What is our societal responsibility?
- What is our moral responsibility?

Ethics of Responsible Businesses

Investigate the message of high-level seminars for businesses that work to encourage businesses to build a better world.

Art

Discuss responsibility, using Reflection Points of your choice. Discuss how responsibility plays a role in the context of art. Ask students to make an art project of their perceived responsibilities. It could be a poster, a charcoal drawing, or something symbolic to them.

Create a project. Perhaps students would like to exhibit their work at a local shopping center. List various responsibilities to do with that endeavor. Ask for volunteers for the different tasks.

Music

Discuss:
♦ Responsibility is playing our role to the best of our ability.

Ask:
- What happens when we do this in a band or an orchestra?
- What happens to the band when someone does not act responsibly? For example, not learning a piece of music or not showing up on time for rehearsals or the performance.
- How would you feel as a member of the band or orchestra?
- What happens when we do not act responsibly as a student?
- As a parent?
- As a gardener?
- As an accountant?
- How do we feel inside when we take responsibility in our roles? What is the benefit?
- What attitude helps you enjoy being responsible?

Play some of the songs of your country or other countries which are evoking social change.

Home Economics

Say: "Today, let's have fun with responsibility. As humans we are very lucky — we can create things — we do create our world. In responsibility, there is doing our share of a task. So, what would you like to create? (Offer possible options in your setting.) Shall we start with a meal? Shall we start with a vegetable garden? Shall we decorate the class? Shall we . . . ? Ask students to choose, then ask them to list materials needed and the tasks that need to be done. Have teams accept responsibility for different tasks. For example, if you decide to make a Mexican or a Moroccan meal (because that is the cultural unit you are studying), one small group can work on decorations, another group on obtaining ingredients, etc.

Physical Education/Dance

Since students and cultures are different, the teacher can best assess areas in which responsibility needs to be addressed. Engage the students in a discussion about responsibilities and sports activities.

Ask:

- Do you have a responsibility to the self? To the team?
- Why is each role equally important in a team?
- How can you best fulfill your responsibilities?
- What are the obstacles to fulfilling your responsibilities?
- What can you do to help overcome any obstacles?

Dance/Movement

Dance irresponsibility changing to responsibility.

APPENDIX

Item 1: All Values

How to Mind Map

A Mind Map is a powerful graphic technique that engages both sides of the brain. It can be used in many different ways — to outline stories, plan talks, organize details for functions, or to create and develop thoughts about a topic. It is simple to use. Using the values words is an excellent way to begin to learn "mind mapping" and understand the effects of values and anti-values.

Mind Mapping

1. Take a blank piece of paper this size or larger and place it horizontally, or use a whiteboard with a large group.
2. Start in the center with a Central Image that personally represents the topic about which you are writing/thinking. You can put the value of focus inside one side of a circle, and the name of the anti-value on the other side. Images can be added to the circle later, representing the overall outcome of the group's input.
3. The Main Themes around the Central Image are like the chapter headings of a book. Print the words and place them on lines of the same length. The central lines can be curved and organic, i.e., like branches of a tree to the trunk. For example, when exploring values you might always want to use Self, Family and Our organization/school. However, feel free to explore other areas such as Society, Business, Health, Environment and World.
4. Start to add a Second level of thought for one of the branches. Allow the students to supply all the answers and acknowledge them as you write their responses. These words are linked to the main branch that triggered them. The lines connect and are thinner.

5. Add a Third or Fourth level of data, as response continue. Use images as much as you wish. If students are doing a mind map individually, they may "hop about" the Mind Map as the links and associations occur to them.

6. Add Dimension to your Mind Maps if you wish. Box and add depth around the word or image, use different colors and styles, and if you like, add arrows to show connections.

7. Have fun making each Mind Map beautiful, artistic, colorful, and imaginative.

Item 2: Peace

Conflict Resolution Steps

Introduce yourself and ask them to introduce themselves.

Ask both students: Do you want help?

If both answer "yes", proceed. If one says "no", tell them both to go to the office.

To Student One:	To Student Two:
Please tell us what happened.	Please repeat what he or she said.
To Student Two:	To Student One:
Please tell us what happened.	Please repeat what s/he said.
To Student One:	To Student Two:
How did you feel when that happened?	Please repeat what s/he said.
To Student Two:	To Student One:
How did you feel when that happened?	Please repeat what s/he said.
To Student One:	To Student Two:
What would you like to stop?	Please repeat what s/he said.
To Student Two:	To Student One:
What would you like to stop?	Please repeat what s/he said.
To Student One:	To Student Two:
What would you like him/her to do instead?	Please repeat what s/he said.
To Student Two:	To Student One:
What would you like him/her to do instead?	Please repeat what s/he said.
To Student One:	To Student Two:
Can you do that?	Can you do that?

To both: Can you make a firm commitment to do what you've both agreed to? If they both say "yes", compliment their good listening and willingness to work on a solution.

If one of them says "no," ask each student to think of something he or she would like the two to do that would solve the problem. Ask them to think of ideas until they both agree they have a good solution and can commit to trying to carry it through.

Item 3: Simplicity and
Caring for the Earth and Her Oceans

The Globe Is Already Above 1°C, on Its Way to 1.5°C
Article by Climate Central, Published 9 October 2018

The Paris Climate Change Agreement set a goal of "holding the increase in the global average temperature to well below 2°C (3.6°F) above pre-industrial levels and pursuing efforts to limit the temperature increase to 1.5°C (2.7°F)." In that agreement, world leaders asked the IPCC, the preeminent climate science body, "to provide a Special Report in 2018 on the impacts of global warming of 1.5°C above pre-industrial levels and related global greenhouse gas emission pathways." After being formally approved by all the UN country representatives, that special report was released this week.

Human activities have already warmed the planet about 1°C (1.8°F) since the pre-industrial era, defined by the IPCC as the latter half of the 19th century. At the current rate of warming, Earth would reach the 1.5°C threshold between 2030 and 2052. Limiting warming to 1.5°C is not easy and requires drastic changes to our energy, transportation, food, and building systems. Net CO_2 emissions need to drop 45 percent from their 2010 levels by 2030, and reach net-zero by 2050 (meaning that any remaining CO_2 emissions would need to be offset by removing carbon dioxide from the atmosphere).

Meeting this goal involves a large jump in renewables for the global energy supply, providing 70-85 percent of electricity use by 2050. Moreover, because CO_2 remains in the atmosphere for centuries, we have already committed to future warming with our historical emissions. As a result, even with drastic emissions cuts, meeting this 1.5°C goal likely means a brief exceedance, or overshoot, of the 1.5°C threshold before returning to that level for the longer term and requires some removal of CO_2 from the atmosphere — either via reforestation, soil carbon sequestration, or technological advancements enabling direct capture of carbon from the atmosphere.

Even limiting warming to 1.5°C comes with higher risks from extreme heat, drought, and heavy precipitation. This harms agriculture, food and water supplies, human health, and the oceans. Optimum agricultural belts will shift, water supplies will be at additional risk, and disease-carrying insects will move into new areas. Additionally, an extra half-degree Celsius (about 1°F) from 1.5°C to 2°C would magnify impacts:

- Doubling the number of people affected by water scarcity
- Doubling the losses of corn yields in the tropics

- Increasing by 10 times the frequency of ice-free summers in the Arctic Ocean
- Losing 30 percent more coral reefs (meaning a total of 99 percent of coral reefs will disappear)
- Losing an additional 50 percent of global fisheries
- Adding 10 million people to those affected by sea level rise

With current technologies in place, drastic changes still make the goal of limiting warming to 1.5°C possible, but the window is rapidly closing to meet that goal.

Source: https://www.climatecentral.org/gallery/graphics/the-globe-is-already-above-1c

Item 4: Simplicity and
Caring for the Earth and Her Oceans

UN Report: Nature's Dangerous Decline 'Unprecedented';
Species Extinction Rates 'Accelerating'

This first half of the article on the UN website gives specific results of the Global Assessment Report produced by the Intergovernmental Science-Policy Platform on Biodiversity and Ecosystem Services. It is supplied here for students without internet access.

Source: https://www.un.org/sustainabledevelopment/blog/2019/05/nature-decline-unprecedented-report/ (Accessed May 2019.)

PARIS, 6 May – Nature is declining globally at rates unprecedented in human history – and the rate of species extinctions is accelerating, with grave impacts on people around the world now likely, warns a landmark new report from the Intergovernmental Science-Policy Platform on Biodiversity and Ecosystem Services (IPBES), the summary of which was approved at the 7th session of the IPBES Plenary, meeting last week (29 April – 4 May) in Paris.

"The overwhelming evidence of the IPBES Global Assessment, from a wide range of different fields of knowledge, presents an ominous picture," said IPBES Chair, Sir Robert Watson. "The health of ecosystems on which we and all other species depend is deteriorating more rapidly than ever. We are eroding the very foundations of our economies, livelihoods, food security, health and quality of life worldwide."

"The Report also tells us that it is not too late to make a difference, but only if we start now at every level from local to global," he said. "Through 'transformative change', nature can still be conserved, restored and used sustainably – this is also key to meeting most other global goals. By transformative change, we mean a fundamental, system-wide reorganization across technological, economic and social factors, including paradigms, goals and values."

"The member States of IPBES Plenary have now acknowledged that, by its very nature, transformative change can expect opposition from those with interests vested in the status quo, but also that such opposition can be overcome for the broader public good," Watson said.

The IPBES Global Assessment Report on Biodiversity and Ecosystem Services is the most comprehensive ever completed. It is the first intergovernmental Report of its kind and builds on the landmark Millennium Ecosystem Assessment of 2005, introducing innovative ways of evaluating evidence.

Compiled by 145 expert authors from 50 countries over the past three years, with inputs from another 310 contributing authors, the Report assesses changes over the past five decades, providing a comprehensive picture of the relationship between economic development pathways and their impacts on nature. It also offers a range of possible scenarios for the coming decades.

Based on the systematic review of about 15,000 scientific and government sources, the Report also draws (for the first time ever at this scale) on indigenous and local knowledge, particularly addressing issues relevant to Indigenous Peoples and Local Communities.

"Biodiversity and nature's contributions to people are our common heritage and humanity's most important life-supporting 'safety net'. But our safety net is stretched almost to breaking point," said Prof. Sandra Díaz (Argentina), who co-chaired the Assessment with Prof. Josef Settele (Germany) and Prof. Eduardo S. Brondízio (Brazil and USA).

"The diversity within species, between species and of ecosystems, as well as many fundamental contributions we derive from nature, are declining fast, although we still have the means to ensure a sustainable future for people and the planet."

The Report finds that around 1 million animal and plant species are now threatened with extinction, many within decades, more than ever before in human history.

The average abundance of native species in most major land-based habitats has fallen by at least 20%, mostly since 1900. More than 40% of amphibian species, almost 33% of reef-forming corals and more than a third of all marine mammals are threatened. The picture is less clear for insect species, but available evidence supports a tentative estimate of 10% being threatened. At least 680 vertebrate species had been driven to extinction since the 16th century and more than 9% of all domesticated breeds of mammals used for food and agriculture had become extinct by 2016, with at least 1,000 more breeds still threatened.

"Ecosystems, species, wild populations, local varieties and breeds of domesticated plants and animals are shrinking, deteriorating or vanishing. The essential, interconnected web of life on Earth is getting smaller and increasingly frayed," said Prof. Settele. "This loss is a direct result of human activity and constitutes a direct threat to human well-being in all regions of the world."

To increase the policy-relevance of the Report, the assessment's authors have ranked, for the first time at this scale and based on a thorough analysis of the available evidence, the five direct drivers of change in nature with the largest relative global impacts so far. These culprits are, in descending order: (1) changes in land and sea use; (2) direct exploitation of organisms; (3) climate change; (4) pollution and (5) invasive alien species.

The Report notes that, since 1980, greenhouse gas emissions have doubled, raising average global temperatures by at least 0.7 degrees Celsius – with climate change already impacting nature from the level of ecosystems to that of genetics – impacts expected to increase over the coming decades, in some cases surpassing the impact of land and sea use change and other drivers.

Despite progress to conserve nature and implement policies, the Report also finds that global goals for conserving and sustainably using nature and achieving sustainability cannot be met by current trajectories, and goals for 2030 and beyond may only be achieved through transformative changes across economic, social, political and technological factors. With good progress on components of only four of the 20 Aichi Biodiversity Targets, it is likely that most will be missed by the 2020 deadline. Current negative trends in biodiversity and ecosystems will undermine progress towards 80% (35 out of 44) of the assessed targets of the Sustainable Development Goals, related to poverty, hunger, health, water, cities, climate, oceans and land (SDGs 1, 2, 3, 6, 11, 13, 14 and 15). Loss of biodiversity is therefore shown to be not only an environmental issue, but also a developmental, economic, security, social and moral issue as well.

"To better understand and, more importantly, to address the main causes of damage to biodiversity and nature's contributions to people, we need to understand the history and global interconnection of complex demographic and economic indirect drivers of change, as well as the social values that underpin them," said Prof. Brondízio. "Key indirect drivers include increased population and per capita consumption; technological innovation, which in some cases has lowered and in other cases increased the damage to nature; and, critically, issues of governance and accountability. A pattern that emerges is one of global interconnectivity and 'telecoupling' – with resource extraction and production often occurring in one part of the world to satisfy the needs of distant consumers in other regions."

Other notable findings of the Report include:
- Three-quarters of the land-based environment and about 66% of the marine environment have been significantly altered by human actions. On average these trends have been less severe or avoided in areas held or managed by Indigenous Peoples and Local Communities.
- More than a third of the world's land surface and nearly 75% of freshwater resources are now devoted to crop or livestock production.
- The value of agricultural crop production has increased by about 300% since 1970, raw timber harvest has risen by 45% and approximately 60 billion tons of

renewable and nonrenewable resources are now extracted globally every year – having nearly doubled since 1980.

- Land degradation has reduced the productivity of 23% of the global land surface, up to US$577 billion in annual global crops are at risk from pollinator loss and 100-300 million people are at increased risk of floods and hurricanes because of loss of coastal habitats and protection.

- In 2015, 33% of marine fish stocks were being harvested at unsustainable levels; 60% were maximally sustainably fished, with just 7% harvested at levels lower than what can be sustainably fished.

- Urban areas have more than doubled since 1992.

- Plastic pollution has increased tenfold since 1980, 300-400 million tons of heavy metals, solvents, toxic sludge and other wastes from industrial facilities are dumped annually into the world's waters, and fertilizers entering coastal ecosystems have produced more than 400 ocean 'dead zones', totalling more than 245,000 km2 (591-595) – a combined area greater than that of the United Kingdom.

- Negative trends in nature will continue to 2050 and beyond in all of the policy scenarios explored in the Report, except those that include transformative change – due to the projected impacts of increasing land-use change, exploitation of organisms and climate change, although with significant differences between regions.

The Report also presents a wide range of illustrative actions for sustainability and pathways for achieving them across and between sectors such as agriculture, forestry, marine systems, freshwater systems, urban areas, energy, finance and many others. It highlights the importance of, among others, adopting integrated management and cross-sectoral approaches that take into account the trade-offs of food and energy production, infrastructure, freshwater and coastal management, and biodiversity conservation.

Also identified as a key element of more sustainable future policies is the evolution of global financial and economic systems to build a global sustainable economy, steering away from the current limited paradigm of economic growth.

"IPBES presents the authoritative science, knowledge and the policy options to decision-makers for their consideration," said IPBES Executive Secretary, Dr. Anne Larigauderie. "We thank the hundreds of experts, from around the world, who have volunteered their time and knowledge to help address the loss of species, ecosystems and genetic diversity – a truly global and generational threat to human well-being."

Further Information on Key Issues from the Report

Scale of Loss of Nature

- Gains from societal and policy responses, while important, have not stopped massive losses.

- Since 1970, trends in agricultural production, fish harvest, bioenergy production and harvest of materials have increased, in response to population growth, rising demand and technological development, this has come at a steep price, which has been unequally distributed within and across countries. Many other key indicators of nature's contributions to people however, such as soil organic carbon and pollinator diversity, have declined, indicating that gains in material contributions are often not sustainable.

- The pace of agricultural expansion into intact ecosystems has varied from country to country. Losses of intact ecosystems have occurred primarily in the tropics, home to the highest levels of biodiversity on the planet. For example, 100 million hectares of tropical forest were lost from 1980 to 2000, resulting mainly from cattle ranching in Latin America (about 42 million hectares) and plantations in South-East Asia (about 7.5 million hectares, of which 80% is for palm oil, used mostly in food, cosmetics, cleaning products and fuel) among others.

- Since 1970 the global human population has more than doubled (from 3.7 to 7.6 billion), rising unevenly across countries and regions; and per capita gross domestic product is four times higher – with ever-more distant consumers shifting the environmental burden of consumption and production across regions.

- The average abundance of native species in most major land-based habitats has fallen by at least 20%, mostly since 1900.

- The numbers of invasive alien species per country have risen by about 70% since 1970, across the 21 countries with detailed records.

- The distributions of almost half (47%) of land-based flightless mammals, for example, and almost a quarter of threatened birds, may already have been negatively affected by climate change.

Indigenous Peoples, Local Communities and Nature

- At least a quarter of the global land area is traditionally owned, managed, used or occupied by Indigenous Peoples. These areas include approximately 35% of the area that is formally protected, and approximately 35% of all remaining terrestrial areas with very low human intervention.

- Nature managed by Indigenous Peoples and Local Communities is under increasing pressure but is generally declining less rapidly than in other lands –

although 72% of local indicators developed and used by Indigenous Peoples and Local Communities show the deterioration of nature that underpins local livelihoods.

- The areas of the world projected to experience significant negative effects from global changes in climate, biodiversity, ecosystem functions and nature's contributions to people are also areas in which large concentrations of Indigenous Peoples and many of the world's poorest communities reside.

- Regional and global scenarios currently lack and would benefit from an explicit consideration of the views, perspectives and rights of Indigenous Peoples and Local Communities, their knowledge and understanding of large regions and ecosystems, and their desired future development pathways. Recognition of the knowledge, innovations and practices, institutions and values of Indigenous Peoples and Local Communities and their inclusion and participation in environmental governance often enhances their quality of life, as well as nature conservation, restoration and sustainable use. Their positive contributions to sustainability can be facilitated through national recognition of land tenure, access and resource rights in accordance with national legislation, the application of free, prior and informed consent, and improved collaboration, fair and equitable sharing of benefits arising from the use, and co-management arrangements with local communities.

Global Targets and Policy Scenarios

- Past and ongoing rapid declines in biodiversity, ecosystem functions and many of nature's contributions to people mean that most international societal and environmental goals, such as those embodied in the Aichi Biodiversity Targets and the 2030 Agenda for Sustainable Development will not be achieved based on current trajectories.

- The authors of the Report examined six policy scenarios – very different 'baskets' of clustered policy options and approaches, including 'Regional Competition', 'Business as Usual' and 'Global Sustainability' – projecting the likely impacts on biodiversity and nature's contributions to people of these pathways by 2050. They concluded that, except in scenarios that include transformative change, the negative trends in nature, ecosystem functions and in many of nature's contributions to people will continue to 2050 and beyond due to the projected impacts of increasing land and sea use change, exploitation of organisms and climate change.

Policy Tools, Options and Exemplary Practices

- Policy actions and societal initiatives are helping to raise awareness about the impact of consumption on nature, protecting local environments, promoting sustainable local economies and restoring degraded areas. Together with initiatives at various levels these have contributed to expanding and strengthening the current network of ecologically representative and well-connected protected area networks and other effective area-based conservation measures, the protection of watersheds and incentives and sanctions to reduce pollution.

- The Report presents an illustrative list of possible actions and pathways for achieving them across locations, systems and scales, which will be most likely to support sustainability. Taking an integrated approach:

- In *agriculture*, the Report emphasizes, among others: promoting good agricultural and agroecological practices; multifunctional landscape planning (which simultaneously provides food security, livelihood opportunities, maintenance of species and ecological functions) and cross-sectoral integrated management. It also points to the importance of deeper engagement of all actors throughout the food system (including producers, the public sector, civil society and consumers) and more integrated landscape and watershed management; conservation of the diversity of genes, varieties, cultivars, breeds, landraces and species; as well as approaches that empower consumers and producers through market transparency, improved distribution and localization (that revitalizes local economies), reformed supply chains and reduced food waste.

- In *marine systems*, the Report highlights, among others: ecosystem-based approaches to fisheries management; spatial planning; effective quotas; marine protected areas; protecting and managing key marine biodiversity areas; reducing run- off pollution into oceans and working closely with producers and consumers.

- In *freshwater systems*, policy options and actions include, among others: more inclusive water governance for collaborative water management and greater equity; better integration of water resource management and landscape planning across scales; promoting practices to reduce soil erosion, sedimentation and pollution run-off; increasing water storage; promoting investment in water projects with clear sustainability criteria; as well as addressing the fragmentation of many freshwater policies.

- In *urban areas*, the Report highlights, among others: promotion of nature-based solutions; increasing access to urban services and a healthy urban environment for low-income communities; improving access to green spaces; sustainable production and consumption and ecological connectivity within urban spaces, particularly with native species.

- Across all examples, the Report recognises the importance of including different value systems and diverse interests and worldviews in formulating policies and actions. This includes the full and effective participation of Indigenous Peoples and Local Communities in governance, the reform and development of incentive structures and ensuring that biodiversity considerations are prioritised across all key sector planning.

- "We have already seen the first stirrings of actions and initiatives for transformative change, such as innovative policies by many countries, local authorities and businesses, but especially by young people worldwide," said Sir Robert Watson. "From the young global shapers behind the #VoiceforthePlanet movement, to school strikes for climate, there is a groundswell of understanding that urgent action is needed if we are to secure anything approaching a sustainable future. The IPBES Global Assessment Report offers the best available expert evidence to help inform these decisions, policies and actions – and provides the scientific basis for the biodiversity framework and new decadal targets for biodiversity, to be decided in late 2020 in China, under the auspices of the UN Convention on Biological Diversity."

Item 5: Simplicity and
Caring for the Earth and Her Oceans

What We Can Do Daily List

Note from the author: The below is not a definitive list. It simply contains ideas of practical things to do daily, some of which may have not been generated during the lessons. Send in any ideas not on the list to content@livingvalues.net and we'll add it to the next edition of the book! Thank you for helping our beautiful Earth and Her Oceans … and all of us!

Decrease fossil fuel energy use and conserve water

❖ Turn off the lights when leaving the room for more than a few minutes.

❖ Turn off the television, and put computers and gadgets on sleep mode/off when not in use.

❖ When it's cold, wear a sweater and socks before turning on the heat.

❖ When it's hot, don't set the temperature very low on the AC unit.

❖ Turn off the water when brushing your teeth.

❖ Short showers use less water than baths.

❖ Water outdoor plants early or late in the day to minimize evaporation.

❖ Cooler water releases less pollutants into the water when washing clothes.

❖ Use a clothes rack instead of a dryer when possible.

❖ If possible, use sustainable energy sources such as solar power.

❖ Walk or bicycle when practical.

❖ Consider an eco-friendly or zero emissions vehicle.

❖ Consider doing a few errands at once rather than making more trips in the car.

❖ Carpool.

Food – Avoid plastic, go organic and reduce or eliminate meat and dairy consumption

❖ Use and reuse glass or durable plastic bottles daily instead of single-use plastic bottles for carrying water.

❖ Pack food in reusable containers when going out; use paper instead of plastic bags.

❖ Buy vegetables and other food products with the least packaging possible.

❖ Buy organic food products, if possible.

❖ Being vegan dramatically reduces your carbon footprint. Consider reducing or eliminating meat and dairy consumption.

❖ Grow some of your food, if possible. Use organic fertilizers only.

❖ Buy locally grown organic food when possible.

❖ Never use or accept plastic straws.

❖ Carry your own reusable cup for use at places that usually serve paper, plastic or Styrofoam cups.

❖ If you must use disposable plates, use paper plates, never plastic or Styrofoam.

❖ Use metal or wooden utensils instead of single-use plastic forks and spoons.

❖ Use a cloth napkin instead of paper napkins. If you wish to reduce washing, perhaps each person can have their own cloth napkin with a different color or pattern and wash them once a week.

❖ If possible, compost food scraps or use resin compostable garbage bags instead of plastic.

At School

❖ Set up recycling bins.

❖ Use paper on both sides.

❖ Pick up trash from the grounds.

❖ Plant trees.

❖ Compost.

❖ Create an organic garden.

General

❖ Bring your own reusable bags to stores rather than accepting plastic bags.

❖ Buy fewer clothes and fewer things.

❖ Buy clothes with natural fibers, rather than with plastic fibers, when possible.

❖ Reuse, repurpose, recycle, refill.

Household Products

❖ Use planet-friendly detergents and cleaning products.

❖ Use hygiene products without harmful chemicals.

❖ Use cooler water when washing clothes as it releases less plastic fibers into the water system.

❖ Rather than use aerosol sprays that emit hydrofluorocarbons, use sprays with a manual pump.

Use Renewable Energy Sources

❖ Promote and use renewable energy sources, such as solar and wind.

Promote Healthy Land and Sea Use and Sustainable Practices with those in your connection — people, schools, restaurants, businesses, city councils, legislators. . . .

❖ Talk to managers or owners of stores and restaurants about eco-friendly practices when you see non-friendly practices.

Item 6: All Values

Relaxation / Focusing Exercises

Physical Relaxation Exercise

Sit comfortably . . . be aware of how you are feeling . . . and relax. . . . As you begin to relax your muscles, take in a deep breath . . . and let your body feel heavy. . . . As you breathe out, focus your attention on your feet. . . . Tighten all your muscles for a moment . . . and then relax them . . . let them stay relaxed. . . . Now become aware of your legs, letting them be heavy . . . tightening the muscles . . . and then relaxing them. . . . Breathe in slowly . . . and as you exhale, let any tension melt away. . . . Now tighten your hands for a moment . . . and then relax. . . . Be aware of your breathing, and take in a deep breath. . . . As you breathe out, let any tension melt away. . . . Breathe in deeply again . . . let the air out slowly . . . and let go of any tension. . . . Now tighten the muscles in the back and the shoulders . . . and then relax them. . . . Move your shoulders up . . . and relax as you move them down. . . . Tighten the muscles in your hands and arms . . . and then relax them. . . . Gently move the neck . . . first to one side, then to the other . . . relax the muscles . . . . Now tighten the muscles of the face . . . the jaw . . . and then relax the face and the jaw. . . . Let the feeling of wellbeing flow through the body. . . . Focus again on your breathing, breathing in deeply . . . and then letting go of any tension. . . . I am relaxed . . . I am peace . . . I am ready to be at my best.

— Contributed by Guillermo Simó Kadletz

Peace Relaxation Exercise

Let the body be relaxed and still. Let go of thoughts about the world outside, and slow down within. Be in the present, focusing on this moment in time. . . . Breathe in deeply . . . and let go of any tension through the bottoms of your feet. . . . Breathe in deeply again . . . and let go of any tension through the bottoms of your feet. . . . Breathe in deeply . . . and let the mind be still. Slowly absorb waves of peace. . . . Imagine being outdoors on a clear day — in a beautiful setting. . . . You may imagine being by the ocean, or in a meadow. . . . As you picture the beauty of nature in front of you, absorb waves of peace. . . . Let the self feel totally safe and relaxed. . . . Let the self feel beyond time. . . . You are full of natural tranquility. . . . You are naturally peaceful. . . . Think of your natural qualities . . . be present . . . and lovingly accept the self. . . . Surround the self with love . . . surround the self with peace. . . . When I am at peace, I am able to access my creativity and strengths . . . I am able to be part of creating a peaceful world. . . . I bring my attention back to the room . . . peaceful . . . peaceful . . . focused . . . alert.

Peaceful Star Relaxation Exercise

One way to be peaceful is to be silent inside. Take a deep breath . . . and let yourself be surrounded by peace. . . . Be aware of any tension . . . and let it begin to release as you breathe out.... Take in a deep breath of peace . . . and slowly breathe out, letting go of any tension. . . . For a few moments, think of the stars in the sky and imagine yourself to be as still as a star in the distance. They are so beautiful in the sky . . . so quiet and peaceful. . . . Let the body be still. . . . Relax your toes and legs . . . relax your chest and stomach . . . and your shoulders. . . . Relax your arms . . . and your face. . . . Be aware of your breathing . . . and allow the feeling of peace to come into your mind. . . . Let a soft light of peace surround you. . . . Be surrounded by peace . . . stillness . . . be peace. . . . You, the tiny star, are naturally peaceful. . . . Relax into the light of peace. . . . Let the self be still and peaceful . . . You are focused . . . concentrated . . . peaceful . . . content . . . a star of peace.

Garden of Respect Relaxation Exercise

Sit comfortably and let your body relax. . . As you breathe slowly, let your mind be still and calm. . . . Starting at your feet, let yourself relax . . . relax your legs . . . stomach . . . shoulders, neck . . . face . . . the eyes . . . and forehead. . . . Let your mind be serene and calm . . . breathe deeply . . . concentrate on stillness. . . In your mind picture a flower . . . enjoy its fragrance . . . observe its color . . . enjoy its beauty. . . . Each person is like a flower . . . each one of us is unique . . . yet we have many things in common. . . . Picture a garden around you with many varieties of flowers . . . all of them beautiful . . . each flower with its color . . . each flower with its fragrance. . . giving the best of themselves. . . . Some are tall with pointed petals, some have rounded petals, some are big and others little . . . some have soft colors . . . others have bright colors . . . some attract the eye because of their simplicity. . . . Each one of us is like a flower . . . enjoy the uniqueness of each one. . . . Each adds beauty to the garden . . . all are important. . . . Together they form the garden. . . . Each flower has respect for itself. . . . When one respects the self it is then easy to respect others. . . . Each one is valuable and unique . . . with respect the qualities of others are seen. . . . Perceive what is good in each one . . . each has a unique role. . . each is important. . . . Let this image fade in your mind, and turn your attention to this room again.

I Am A Mountain Relaxation Exercise

Allow yourself to relax and be aware of how you are feeling. . . . Take in a deep breathe . . . and release it, letting go of any tension. . . . Take in a deep breathe . . . and let the body relax. . . . Now visualize yourself as a mountain. . . . If you were a mountain what would that mountain look like? . . . . Would it be a large mountain? . . . Would it have lots of trees and foliage? . . . Would it have a granite cliff on one side? . . . . As you visualize yourself as a mountain . . . ground in your self-respect. . . . Think of two or three of your qualities or values. . . . You are stable . . . you are strong . . . you are powerful . . . . Breathe in and feel yourself to be like a mountain, stable, strong . . . connected to the beautiful Earth. . . . Sometimes in nature there are winds or rain or storms. . . . The rains are just rain, the wind is just wind . . . they do not affect the mountain. . . . Sometimes people are negative . . . they are like rain or wind when they are not happy with who they are at that moment . . . and don't know how to stay in their self-respect. . . . If there is sometimes a person who is like rain or a wind . . . ground more deeply into your self-respect. . . . Visualize the self as a mountain, stable and strong. . . . You are beautiful. . . . The rain and wind will not last forever . . . . Observe the rain . . . observe the wind . . . feel your quiet yet awesome strength. . . . As the rain stops, enjoy the warmth of the sun. . . . In the sunlight, across the valley, perhaps there are other mountains . . . family or friends. . . . Breathe in deeply . . . and relax. . . . I am a mountain. . . . I am connected . . . to me . . . to the Earth . . . to other beautiful mountains. . . . I ground in my self-respect . . . Breathe out and relax more. . . . Now . . . slowly bring your attention back to the room . . . feeling relaxed . . . and centered.

Star of Respect Relaxation Exercise

Think of the stars . . . imagine the self in the silence the stars seem to radiate. They are so beautiful in the sky, they sparkle and shine . . . quiet and peaceful. . . . Be very still. . . . Relax your toes and legs. . . . Relax your stomach . . . and your shoulders. . . . Relax your arms . . . and your face. . . . Feel safe . . . and allow peace to surround you . . . . Inside you are like a star . . . peace is at your core. . . . You are capable . . . you are who you are. . . . Each person brings special qualities to the world . . . you are valuable. . . . Enjoy the feeling of respect inside. . . You are stars of respect . . . let yourself be quiet and peaceful inside. . . . Focus. . . . You are concentrated . . . full of respect . . . content. . . . Slowly bring your attention back to the room . . . feeling relaxed . . . focused . . . and ready to be at your best.

Lovingly Accepting the Self Relaxation/Focusing Exercise

Let the body be relaxed and still. Let go of thoughts about the world outside, and slow down within. . . . Allow yourself to be in the present, focusing on this moment in time. . . . Let the mind be still, and slowly absorb waves of peace. . . . Imagine being outdoors in a world where everyone is kind and caring. . . . Imagine a garden or a meadow . . . or an ocean or river . . . whatever you wish. . . . And in the picture of your mind imagine a world where everyone knows they are love . . . and are loved . . . and are capable. . . . Breathe in slowly and relax. . . . Let a light of love surround you. . . . Each child comes into the world with love and beauty. . . . Sometimes people around us forget to remind us of our love and beauty because they are stressed . . . or busy . . . or mean . . . or have too many burdens. . . . Or maybe they just don't have enough love inside themselves to let others know they are gorgeous and worthy of love. . . . I may not like what others do, but for now I let that go . . . and I go into the truth that I have love at my core. . . . (Please pause for at least ten seconds.) Allow yourself to breathe in love. . . . Allow yourself to know that you are good . . . you are worthy of love. . . . Lovingly accept the self . . . your positive qualities . . . and even your negative emotions. . . . Accept yourself exactly as you are. . . . Breathe in that loving acceptance of the self. . . . Each person comes into the world to bring a special gift of his or her qualities . . . and his or her talents. . . . Be still . . . quiet within . . . focused . . . and enjoy feeling full of love and peace. . . . As you begin to bring your attention back to this place . . . allow yourself to feel loving acceptance of yourself. . . . Please wiggle your toes and move your shoulders . . . and bring your attention fully back to this place, fresh and alert.

Dissolving Stress with Love Relaxation/Focusing Exercise

Be aware of your surroundings . . . be mindful of your emotions . . . and take in a deep breath of the light of love. . . . As you exhale, let any tension go out the bottoms of your feet. . . . Breathe in the light of love . . . breathe out any tension through the bottoms of your feet. . . . As you breathe in the light of love, let your muscles relax. . . . Sometimes we experience stress or tension or anxiety. . . . Be aware of where you hold that in your body. . . . Now breathe in the light of love . . . relaxing that area . . . and lovingly accept your emotions. . . . Perhaps that area has a dull gray light. . . . Accept that gray light and know that sometimes fear makes us doubt our ability or our worth. . . . Let the light of love begin to surround that area of gray . . . and begin to dissolve the edges. . . . I am good . . . I am worthy of love . . . I am worthy of respect . . . all will be well. . . . I acknowledge my goodness . . . and the vulnerability of myself . . . and all others. . . . Each of us desires peace . . . and love . . . and sometimes we are not sensitive to our own needs . . . or the needs of others. . . . The light of love surrounds all of me . . .

and this area of gray . . . and that area of gray becomes smaller. . . . I lovingly accept my stress and my beauty. . . . I now let the light of strength mix with the light of love. . . . I am capable to facing my challenge. . . . I have the strength to stay in the present and enjoy doing one thing at a time. . . . I am loving, I am strong, I am powerful . . . I am light. . . . Breathe in . . . and now gradually bring your attention back to this space, feeling light and refreshed.

Sending Love Relaxation Exercise

Allow yourself to be aware of how you are feeling at this present moment. Be aware of your breath and any tension in your muscles. Let yourself be surrounded by the light of peace. Breathe in the light of peace and relax. . . . Breathe out any tension. . . . Breathe in the light of peace and let that peace sink into your muscles. . . . You are a peaceful and powerful light . . . full of love. . . . Be a star of peace for a few minutes and send love to people all over the world. . . . Let the self be full of loving energy. . . . We can all send love and peace any time we want. . . . Concentrate on increasing the experience of the light of love . . . let the self relax more. . . . As you relax, that love will automatically extend to people all over the world. . . . Let the body relax more. . . . Take in more love. . . . You are focused . . . you are contributing to a better world. . . . Let the mind be still . . . . Now, move your shoulders, wiggle your toes and bring your awareness back to your surroundings.

Taking Care of Me Relaxation/Focusing Exercise

Let the body be relaxed and still. Slow down within. . . . Breathe in deeply . . . and as you exhale, begin to relax. . . . Be aware of how you are feeling. . . . Breathe in deeply. . . and relax as you exhale. . . . Are your arms tight or your chest? . . . . Is there a feeling of sadness or hurt inside? . . . Allow yourself to feel where you are holding emotion in your body . . . perhaps in your throat . . . perhaps in your chest . . . perhaps in your stomach . . . perhaps in your gut. . . . Breathe in deeply . . . and exhale slowly. . . . Lovingly accept your emotions. . . . Be in the present . . . and lovingly accept how you feel. . . . Pay attention to that feeling . . . accept it with love . . . and it will quiet down a little. . . . Surround your sadness or hurt with the light of love. . . . Visualize the light of love surrounding that pain . . . and feel that love. . . . Breathe in . . . and relax as you breathe out. . . . Let the mind be still . . . and absorb the light of love. . . . Perhaps that area of pain is getting smaller as you absorb the light of love. . . . Feel that light of love. . . . You are lovable and capable. . . . Breathe in slowly and relax. . . . Know you are lovable and capable. . . . Allow yourself to breathe in love. . . . Think for a moment of what quality or value would help you now. . . . Imagine that quality or value taking the form of a jewel and let that jewel appear in front of you. . . . It may be a jewel of love . . . or courage . . . compassion for yourself . . . or others . . . patience . . . or fearlessness. . . . You are a beautiful jewel. . . . You have the courage to be kind to yourself . . . and to live your truth. . . . Be still . . . quiet within . . . focused . . . absorb the light of love and peace. . . . Gradually begin to bring your attention back to this place . . . Wiggle your toes and move your legs . . . and bring your attention fully back to this place.

Sending Peace to the Earth Relaxation/Focusing Exercise

Sit comfortably and let yourself be still inside. . . . Be aware of how your body is feeling. . . . Relax the body and breathe in the light of peace. . . . Let the light of peace surround you . . . . Breathe out any tension . . . and breathe in the light of peace. . . . Breathe out any tension . . . and breathe in the light of peace. . . . Invite the peace to relax your muscles more. . . . This peace is quiet and safe . . . it reminds me that I value peace. . . . Let yourself be very still and think . . . I am me . . . I am naturally full of peace and love. . . . Let your body relax even more . . . and focus on surrounding yourself with the light of peace. . . . The more you concentrate on peace, the more that peace will naturally go outward to nature . . . to the mountains and streams . . . to the clouds and the ocean . . . to the dolphins and the whales . . . to the birds . . . to the animals large and small. . . . Concentrate on peace and see that peace flowing outward to our planet . . . to the rivers and ocean . . . to the trees and the meadows . . . to the mountains and the sky. . . . I am full of peace. . . . I am one who is acting to help our Earth be healthy again. . . . This will happen in time. . . . Our planet will be well. . . . I picture the light of peace all around the Earth . . . and our beautiful oceans being healthy again . . . our beautiful Earth being healthy again. . . . Feeling relaxed and peaceful . . . begin to be aware of where you are sitting and bring your attention back to this room.

Part of Optional Unit on Substance Abuse
Dealing with Pain with Courage and Gentleness Exercise

Let your body be relaxed and still. . . . Take in a deep breath, breathing in peace. . . . As you breathe out, let the tension go out the bottoms of your feet. . . . Breathe in peace . . . breathe out any tension through the bottoms of your feet. . . . As you breathe in peace, let the light of peace relax your whole body . . . letting your legs fill with light . . . letting your abdomen and chest fill with light. . . . With each breath, relax more, and let the light of peace gradually come into your back . . . and arms . . . your shoulders and neck . . . and your face. . . . You have had courage to share something that is painful. . . . Sometimes we hold the pain of what we have experienced in part of our body . . . sometimes it can be like an ache in our chest . . . sometimes in our throat. . . . Stay relaxed and still inside. . .

detach from the pain . . . but see it. . . . Imagine the ache where you experience your pain to have a color. . . . Let the pain fill up with that color of light in that one small place. . . . Relax . . . be still . . . breathe in peace. . . . Let your tension go out the bottoms of your feet. . . . Breathe in the light of peace . . . let the tension go out the bottoms of your feet. . . . You are a courageous person. . . . You are a person who knows the importance of peace . . . and respect. . . . Let the light of peace accept the ache. . . . Let the light of peace surround your ache. . . . Let the light of peace soften the edges of the ache . . . let the light of peace become powerful inside. . . Let the light of peace soften the intensity of the color of the pain. . . . Accept the pain . . . it is painful, but as you begin to accept it, it will no longer be frightening. . . . Once you learn what it has to say, it will gradually begin to fade. . . . It has only come to help you see what is important in life. . . . Be gentle with the pain . . . and give it the love of your light of peace. . . . When the pain is not pushed away it becomes smaller. . . . What does it want you to know? . . . See the color of the pain . . . let it begin to lessen. . . . See the light of peace again. . . let it become powerful once more. . . . Breathe in peace. . . let the tension go out the bottoms of your feet. . . . Ask the pain to go away for now. . . . Tell it that you will allow it to come again and in time it will soften . . . and bloom into understanding . . . as you are learning to heal yourself. . . . You are learning how to be peace and give peace. . . . You are learning how to be respect and give respect. . . . You are learning how to be gentle with your pain so that you can help others heal their pain. . . . You are courageous. . . . Breathe in peace . . . let go of tension. . . . Breathe in peace . . . let any tension go out the bottoms of your feet. . . . Be in stillness. . . . Now bring your awareness back to this room.

Part of Optional Unit on Substance Abuse
The Leaf of My Lesson Exercise

Let your body be relaxed and still. . . . Take in a deep breath, breathing in peace. . . . As you breathe out, let the tension go out the bottoms of your feet. . . . Breathe in peace . . . breathe out any tension through the bottoms of your feet. . . . As you breathe in peace, let the light of peace relax your whole body . . . letting your legs fill with light . . . letting your abdomen and chest fill with light. . . . With each breath, relax more, and let the light of peace gradually come into your back . . . and arms . . . your shoulders and neck . . . and your face. . . . Imagine your place of peace and yourself in that place of peace. . . . It might be by a river with the water flowing gently by. . . . It might be in a forest . . . with rays of light filtering through the leaves of the trees. . . . Imagine yourself relaxing in the place of peace you create in your mind. . . . Feel the core of peace within you. . . . Let the peace of your place of peace surround you. . . . When you are quiet inside . . . still . . . you can feel this peace. . . . As you enjoy the beautiful place of peace you have imagined, let a

369

large leaf float into your hand. . . . As you look at the leaf, you see that a lesson you have learned from your painful experience because of drugs is written on its surface. . . . Look at the words on the leaf. . . . (Pause for at least one full minute.) Experience the beauty of the lesson you have learned. . . . If there is any pain inside . . . acknowledge it and accept it. . . . Let the peace inside you surround the pain . . . What does the leaf say to the pain? . . . (Pause for a minute.) Would the pain like to answer the leaf? . . . What does it say? . . . What value does it think will make you gentle and strong? . . . All that you want to be? . . . What you naturally are? . . . (Pause for half a minute.) Fill yourself with the feeling of that value. . . . Give the love of the light of peace to the pain. . . . Let the peace of your place of peace surround you. . . . Let the leaf of your lesson grow more beautiful as you experience the importance of what you have learned. . . . Allow it to stay as it is or change form. . . . Let the beauty of that become written on your heart. . . . This is something you know is important. . . . Now deepen your peace . . . become still . . . become stable . . . experience the peace at your core. . . . Gradually bring your attention back to this room.

Forgiveness Exercise

Sit comfortably and let your body relax. . . As you breathe slowly, let your mind be still and calm. . . . Starting at your feet, let yourself relax . . . relax your legs . . . stomach . . . shoulders, neck . . . face . . . the eyes . . . and forehead. . . . Let yourself be surrounded by the light of peace. . . . Let your mind be serene and calm . . . breathe deeply . . . concentrate on stillness. . . . Be peace. Let yourself be surrounded by the light of love. Now, say to yourself . . . I am a loving powerful person. . . . I forgive me. . . . I forgive him or her. . . . From now on there will only be respect between us. . . . I am a kind amazing person. . . . I forgive me. . . . I forgive him or her. . . . From now on there will only be caring and respect between us. . . . Repeat this to yourself in your own words. . . . Such as, I am a beautiful soul. . . . I forgive me. . . . I forgive her. . . . From now on there will only be respect between us. . . . Repeat these four phrases to yourself in your own words, using the name of the person you would like to forgive. (Pause for one full minute.) Now, breathe in the light of peace . . . let go of any tension . . . and slowly bring your attention back to this room.

CITED BOOKS, STORIES, WEBSITES AND SONGS

Books

1Bag at a Time. "Plastic Bags in Our Oceans." https://1bagatatime.com/learn/plastic-bags-oceans/ (Accessed April 2019.)

Arias M, Julio, et al. *Living Values: A Tool for Adolescent Development.* 2007. www.livingvalues.net

Berkeley Wellness. "What is the Science of Happiness?" https://www.berkeleywellness.com/healthy-mind/mind-body/article/what-science-happiness (Accessed June 2019.)

Chopra, Deepak. *Ageless Body, Timeless Mind.* New York: Crown Publishing Group, 1994.

Climate Central. "The Globe Is Already Above 1C°." https://www.climatecentral.org/gallery/graphics/the-globe-is-already-above-1c (Accessed April 2019.)

Delors, Jacques, et al. *Learning: The Treasure Within,* Report to UNESCO of the International Commission on Education for the Twenty-first Century. UNESCO Publishing, 1996.

Department of Education, Science and Training, Australian Government. *Values Education Study.* 2003.

Dolphin Research Center. http://www.dolphins.org/marineed_threatstodolphins.php

Gill-Kozul, Carol, Naraine, Gayatri and Strano, Anthony. *Living Values: A Guidebook.* London: Brahma Kumaris, 1995.

Gordon, Thomas. *Parent Effectiveness Training.* New York: Van Rees Press, 1970.

Guterres, António. "The climate strikers should inspire us all to act at the next UN summit." *The Guardian.* 15 March 2019. https://www.un.org/en/climatechange/sg-guardian-op-ed.shtml (Accessed March 2019.)

Gutiérrez, Francisco and Prado, Cruz. *Ecopedagogia e Cidadania Planetária.* Cortez Editora.

Hawkes, Neil. *How to inspire and develop Positive Values in your classroom.* Cambs, U.K.: LDA, 2003.

Intergovernmental Panel on Climate Change. "Global Warming of 1.5 °C"
https://www.ipcc.ch/sr15/ (Accessed April 2019.)

Jampolsky, Gerald. *Love Is Letting Go of Fear.* Millbrae, California: Celestial Arts, 1979.

Lickona, Thomas. *The Return of Character Education.* Educational Leadership 51(3), 1993.

Lovat, Terry and Toomey, Ron. (Ed.) *Values Education and Quality Teaching, The Double Helix Effect.* Riverwood, NSW, Australia: David Barlow Publishing, 2007.

Lumsden, L.S. *Student motivation to learn. ERIC Digest, Number 92.* Eugene, OR: ERIC Clearinghouse on Educational Management, 1994.

Lyubomirsky, Sonia. (2008). *The How of Happiness: A Scientific Approach to Getting the Life You Want.* New York: The Penguin Press.

North, Vanda with Buzan, Tony. *Get Ahead: Mind Map your Way to Success.* Limited Edition Publishing: Buzan Centre Books, Bournemouth, U.K, 1996.

Nunez, Christina. "Climate 101: Deforestation." *National Geographic.* February 2019. https://www.nationalgeographic.com/environment/global-warming/deforestation/ (Accessed April 2019.)

One World One Ocean. http://www.oneworldoneocean.org/pages/why-the-ocean

Otero, H. "The Two Birds." *Parabolas en son de paz.* Madrid: Editorial CCS, 1993.

Pacific Institute. "Bottled Water and Energy Fact Sheet." https://pacinst.org/publication/bottled-water-and-energy-a-fact-sheet/ (Accessed April 2019.)

Pew Trust. "Plastic Pollution Affects Sea Life Throughout the Ocean." https://www.pewtrusts.org/en/research-and-analysis/articles/2018/09/24/plastic-pollution-affects-sea-life-throughout-the-ocean (Accessed April 2019.)

Reigota, Marcos. *O que é educação ambiental.* Google Books, 2017.

Satir, Virginia. *Peoplemaking.* Palo Alto, CA: Science and Behavior Books, Inc, 1972.

Sciencing. "What is the Carbon Footprint of a Plastic Bottle?" https://sciencing.com/carbon-footprint-plastic-bottle-12307187.html (Accessed April 2019.)

Senge, Peter. (Ed.) *Schools that Learn: A Fifth Discipline Fieldbook for Educators, Parents, and Everyone Who Cares About Education.* NY: Doubleday, 2000.

Shea, Kathleen. *Making the Case for Values/Character Education: A Brief Review of the Literature.* 2003. www.livingvalues.net.

Sitarz, Daniel, ed. *Agenda 21.* Boulder, Colorado: EarthPress, 1993.

Stopbullying.gov. A website of the U.S. Department of Health and Human Services. *Bullying Definition.* http://www.stopbullying.gov/what-is-bullying/definition. (Accessed April 2014.)

The Guardian. "What are the main man-made greenhouse gases?"

https://www.theguardian.com/environment/2011/feb/04/man-made-greenhouse-gases (Accessed April 2019.)

The Joy of Reading Project. 2014 – 2019. Gave permission for their stories to be used by LVE and posted for free download at www.livingvalues.net site. Under For Schools / Young Adults / Download Free Stories. The stories in LVEAYA, Book 1 are:

Depoyan, Pam. "I Can't Believe I Did That."

Elias, Kristine. "A Wolf in Sheep's Clothing."

Fenwick, Makaila. "Choices."

Gale, Kathy. "Blame."

Hill, Kirk. "Crying's Okay."

Johnstone, Louise. "Ginger Beer."

Shaffer, Bobbie. "A lesson in ugly."

Tillman, Diane. *Living Green Values for Children and Young Adults.* 2012. This resource and the two series of stories contained within it are available for free-download at www.livingvalues.net as an activity guide for educators and as storybooks for children.

Tillman, Diane. *Living Values Activities for At-Risk Youth.* 2012. *(Restricted-access work:* Special LVE Educator Training required prior to obtaining materials.)

Tillman, Diane. *Living Values Activities for Children Ages 8–14.* Deerfield, FL: HCI, 2000.

Tillman, Diane and Summerfield, Trish. *Living Values Activities for Drug Rehabilitation.* 2005. *(Restricted-access work:* special LVE Educator Training required prior to obtaining materials.)

Tillman, Diane. (2003). *Living Values Activities for Street Children Ages 11–14. (Restricted-access work:* special LVE Educator Training required prior to obtaining materials.)

Tillman, Diane. *Living Values Activities for Young Adults.* Deerfield, FL: HCI, 2000.

Tillman, Diane. *Living Values Activities for Young Offenders.* 2008. *(Restricted-access work:* Special LVE Educator Training required prior to obtaining materials.)

Tillman, Diane. *Living Values Parent Groups: A Facilitator Guide.* Deerfield, FL: HCI, 2000.

Tillman, Diane and Quera Colomina, Pilar. *LVEP Educator Training Guide.* Deerfield, FL: HCI, 2000.

Tillman, Diane G. *Nurturing with Love and Wisdom, Disciplining with Peace and Respect: A mindful guide to parenting.* NC: CSIP, 2014.

Trailes, Henny. Fire in the Jungle. Used with permission from *Visions of a Better World.*

UN Climate Action Summit. https://www.un.org/en/climatechange/ (Accessed April 2019.)

United Nations. Sustainable Development Goals, Knowledge Platform. https://sustainabledevelopment.un.org/ (Accessed May 2019.)

United Nations. *Universal Declaration of Human Rights.* U.N. Publications, New York, USA.

United Nations Climate Change. *UN Climate Change News.* 3 April 2019. https://unfccc.int/news/ renewable-energy-accounts-for-third-of-global-power-capacity-irena (Accessed April 2019.)

United Nations Development Program. *Human Development Report 1992.* New York: Oxford University Press.

_____. *Human Development Report 1993.* New York: Oxford University Press, 1993.

Universal Declaration of Human Rights – An Adaptation for Children. New York: U.N. Publications, 46pp, 1992.

UNESCO. *1995 United Nations Year for Tolerance.* Paris: Office of Public Information, UNESCO, 1995.

Very Well Mind. *Depression Statistics Everyone Should Know.* https://www.verywellmind.com/depression-statistics-everyone-should-know-4159056 (Accessed July 2019.)

Visions of a Better World. A United Nations Peace Messenger Publication. London: Brahma Kumaris, 1993.

West, Larry. *What is the Greenhouse Effect?* May 11, 2018. ThoughtCo. https://www. thoughtco.com/what-is-the-greenhouse-effect-1203853

Songs

Grammer, Red and Kathy. *Teaching Peace.* New York: Smilin' Atcha Music, 1986.

Lennon, John. "Imagine." Parlophone Record Company. 1971.

Loggins, Kenny. "Conviction of the Heart." *Outside: From the Redwoods.* Columbia, 1993.

Nass, Marcia and Max. Songs for Peacemakers. Educational Activities, Inc., 1993. P.O. Box 392, Freeport, NY 11520 USA.

Pebblespash694. "A Song of Peace." www.youtube.com/watch?v=mxidrVmwznU

USA for Africa. "We Are The World." Qwest Record Company.

ACKNOWLEDGMENTS

Educators around the world have contributed activities to Living Values Education since its inception in 1996. Marcia Maria Lins de Medeiros wrote values activities in Brazil when LVE began. She and Paulo Barros have continued to contribute activities and inspire and provide LVE professional development workshops to hundreds of educators. Special appreciation to both of them and Sabine Levy, Ruth Liddle, Natalie Ncube, Pilar Quera Colomina, Trish Summerfield and Eleanor Viegas for their wonderful contributions. These educators who contributed more than one activity are listed on the cover page of the book.

Thank you to all the amazing educators and students around the world who contributed an idea, song, activity or relaxation exercise activity: Fawyi Al-Baqshi, Diana Beaver, Myrna Belgrave, Vicky Calicdan, Amadeo Dieste Castejón, Caroline Druiff, Steve Eardley, Samantha Fraser, Linda Heppenstall, Diana Hsu, Lisa Jennings and her Grade 9 Students, Mick Jones, Kurt Krueger, Roger Miles, Irene Miller, Kristan Mouat, Marcia and Max Nass, Marie Ange Samuel, Guillermo Simó Kadletz, Linda Slauson, Dierich von Horn, and students at West Kidlington School.

Vanda North has been teaching adults and children to Mind Map; one event to create thoughts about a peaceful world was held in a football coliseum! Thanks, Vanda, for teaching me about mind mapping.

Immense thanks to The Joy of Reading Project whose creators gave permission to ALIVE to post their stories on the LVE international website so that people interested in values around the world could avail them free of charge.

I would love to acknowledge the terrific young man who drew the drawings at the beginning of each values unit. He did this for LVE more than 20 years ago and I have lost his name! I am still trying to find it.

Loving appreciation to Diane Holden for her consistent and happy willingness to proofread the LVE books, and to David Warrick Jones for always being ready to help with graphic design and technical support.

Living Values Education continues to thrive because of the dedication, contributions and support of the Association for Living Values Education International Board of

Directors, the ALIVE Associates and Focal Points for LVE, and tens of thousands of LVE educators around the world. Thank you all immensely for your work to create a values-based atmosphere for young people so they can grow toward their potential, for living your values, and for helping create a better world.

I appreciate our LVE family around the globe. Special thanks to Peter Williams, Trish Summerfield, Chris Drake, Raj Miles, Gudrun Howard, Paulo Barros, Taka Gani and Wayan Rustiasa for your continuing commitment and your invaluable cooperation.

Creating LVE is a cooperative event!

*

Thank you to those reading this,
for your love for young adults, and your interest in helping create a better world for all.

About the Author

Diane G. Tillman is the primary author of the award-winning Living Values Education Series of five books, and twelve additional educational resources, including Living Values Education Activities books for street children, children affected by war, young offenders, at-risk youth and young people in need of drug rehabilitation. A Licensed Educational Psychologist and Marriage and Family Therapist, Ms. Tillman worked in a California public school system for 23 years as a School Psychologist. A co-founder of Living Values Education in 1996, she continues to develop content and training materials for the Association for Living Values Education International (ALIVE). In 2018 she began updating and expanding the original LVE Series, published in 2000. Additionally, she has authored a children's book and a parenting guide, "Nurturing with Love and Wisdom, Disciplining with Peace and Respect". In the latter, she illustrates how to bring values into parenting by sharing not only theory but stories about life, her work with children and thousands of parents, and experiences with LVE around the world. A Lead Trainer for ALIVE, Tillman has traveled to more than 30 countries in all regions of the world to conduct training and LVE seminars at conferences and refugee camps, for educators, UNESCO, street-children agencies and Ministries of Education. She is on the Association for Living Values Education International Board of Directors and is the President of LVEP, Inc, the non-profit ALIVE Associate in the U.S.A.